𝔖𝔱𝔞𝔫𝔡𝔞𝔯𝔡 𝔏𝔦𝔟𝔯𝔞𝔯𝔶 𝔈𝔡𝔦𝔱𝔦𝔬𝔫

THE HISTORICAL WRITINGS

OF

JOHN FISKE

ILLUSTRATED WITH MANY PHOTOGRAVURES,

MAPS, CHARTS, FACSIMILES, ETC.

IN TWELVE VOLUMES

VOLUME I

Christopher Columbus

THE DISCOVERY OF AMERICA

WITH SOME ACCOUNT OF ANCIENT AMERICA AND THE SPANISH CONQUEST

BY

JOHN FISKE

IN THREE VOLUMES. VOLUME I

Then I unbar the doors; my paths lead out
The exodus of nations; I disperse
Men to all shores that front the hoary main.
I too have arts and sorceries;
Illusion dwells forever with the wave.
I make some coast alluring, some lone isle
To distant men, who must go there or die

EMERSON

BOSTON AND NEW YORK
HOUGHTON, MIFFLIN AND COMPANY
The Riverside Press, Cambridge

4434

PUBLISHERS' NOTE

THE present edition of the works of John Fiske was planned and in part prepared before his lamented death in July, 1901. It was his wish that it should contain his historical, philosophical, religious, and scientific writings, together with many of his essays, lectures, and addresses. The historical writings, which comprise the first twelve volumes of this edition, present in unbroken sequence the history of this country from its discovery to the adoption of the Constitution of the United States. The only break in the continuity of Mr. Fiske's narrative hitherto has been due to the postponement of his long-cherished plan for telling the story of the relations of the English Colonies in America to the French possessions. This want is now supplied by the publication of his promised book, "New France and New England." Death stayed the historian's hand while he was giving this volume its final preparation for the press. The text is presented precisely as he left it, but the unfinished notes have been completed by one of the most competent of American scholars, Professor Edward G. Bourne of Yale University. The twelve volumes of the historical series are equipped with maps, charts, facsimiles of documents, and other illustrations, and are provided with an accurate general index.

The first four volumes of the miscellaneous writings are occupied with the " Outlines of Cosmic Philosophy." Mr. Fiske repeatedly expressed a desire to issue a new edition of this work, in order to trace the development of his thought upon the great subjects with which it deals. He did not live to carry out this plan. But his friend and fellow-philosopher, Professor Josiah Royce of Harvard University, has supplied for the present edition such annotations as serve to indicate Mr. Fiske's later utterances, in his other writings, upon the themes discussed in the " Cosmic Philosophy."

It will be noted that the ninth volume of the miscellaneous writings presents under a new title, " Studies in Religion," the four remarkable books, " The Destiny of Man," " The Idea of God," " Through Nature to God," and " Life Everlasting." The new title was selected by Mr. Fiske himself, who was especially desirous that these four discussions, already so closely related in significance, should be offered to the public in a single volume. It should be added

PUBLISHERS' NOTE

that the miscellaneous writings, like the historical ones, have been carefully indexed, and that
all possible pains have been taken to insure
throughout the twenty-four volumes a scrupu-
lous fidelity to the author's text.

Boston, 1902.

PREFACE

THE present work is the outcome of two lines of study pursued, with more or less interruption from other studies, for about thirty years. It will be observed that the book has two themes, as different in character as the themes for voice and piano in Schubert's " Frühlingsglaube," and yet so closely related that the one is needful for an adequate comprehension of the other. In order to view in their true perspective the series of events comprised in the Discovery of America, one needs to form a mental picture of that strange world of savagery and barbarism to which civilized Europeans were for the first time introduced in the course of the fifteenth and sixteenth centuries, in their voyages along the African coast, into the Indian and Pacific oceans, and across the Atlantic. Nothing that Europeans discovered during that stirring period was so remarkable as these antique phases of human society, the mere existence of which had scarcely been suspected, and the real character of which it has been left for the present generation to begin to understand. Nowhere was this ancient society so full of instructive lessons as in aboriginal America, which had pursued its own course of development, cut off and isolated from the Old World for probably more than fifty thousand years. The imperishable interest of those episodes in the Discovery of America known as the conquests of Mexico and Peru consists chiefly in the glimpses they afford us of this primitive world. It was not an uninhabited continent that the Spaniards found, and in order to comprehend the course of events it is necessary to know something about those social features that formed a large part of the burden of the letters of Columbus and Vespucius, and excited even more intense and general interest in Europe than the purely geographical questions suggested by the voyages of those great sailors. The descriptions of ancient America, therefore, which form a kind of background to the present work, need no apology.

It was the study of prehistoric Europe and of early Aryan institutions that led me by a natural sequence to the study of aboriginal America. In 1869, after sketching the plan of a book on our Aryan forefathers, I was turned aside for five years by writing " Cosmic Philosophy." During that interval I also wrote " Myths and

Myth-Makers " as a side-work to the projected book on the Aryans, and as soon as the excursion into the field of general philosophy was ended, in 1874, the work on that book was resumed. Fortunately it was not then carried to completion, for it would have been sadly antiquated by this time. The revolution in theory concerning the Aryans has been as remarkable as the revolution in chemical theory which some years ago introduced the New Chemistry. It is becoming eminently probable that the centre of diffusion of Aryan speech was much nearer to Lithuania than to any part of Central Asia, and it has for some time been quite clear that the state of society revealed in Homer and the Vedas is not at all like primitive society, but very far from it. By 1876 I had become convinced that there was no use in going on without widening the field of study. The conclusions of the Aryan school needed to be supplemented, and often seriously modified, by the study of the barbaric world, and it soon became manifest that for the study of barbarism there is no other field that for fruitfulness can be compared with aboriginal America.

This is because the progress of society was much slower in the western hemisphere than in the eastern, and in the days of Columbus and

Cortes it had nowhere "caught up" to the points reached by the Egyptians of the Old Empire or by the builders of Mycenæ and Tiryns. In aboriginal America we therefore find states of society preserved in stages of development similar to those of our ancestral societies in the Old World long ages before Homer and the Vedas. Many of the social phenomena of ancient Europe are also found in aboriginal America, but always in a more primitive condition. The clan, phratry, and tribe among the Iroquois help us in many respects to get back to the original conceptions of the gens, curia, and tribe among the Romans. We can better understand the growth of kingship of the Agamemnon type when we have studied the less developed type in Montezuma. The house-communities of the southern Slavs are full of interest for the student of the early phases of social evolution, but the Mandan round-house and the Zuñi pueblo carry us much deeper into the past. Aboriginal American institutions thus afford one of the richest fields in the world for the application of the comparative method, and the red Indian, viewed in this light, becomes one of the most interesting of men ; for in studying him intelligently, one gets down into the stone age of human thought. No time should be lost in gathering whatever can be learned of his ideas and institutions, before their character has been wholly lost under the influence of white men. Under that influence many Indians have been quite transformed, while others have been as yet but little affected. Some extremely ancient types of society, still preserved on this continent in something like purity, are among the most instructive monuments of the past that can now be found in the world. Such a type is that of the Moquis of northeastern Arizona. I have heard a rumour, which it is to be hoped is ill founded, that there are persons who wish the United States government to interfere with this peaceful and self-respecting people, break up their pueblo life, scatter them in farmsteads, and otherwise compel them, against their own wishes, to change their habits and customs. If such a cruel and stupid thing were ever to be done, we might justly be said to have equalled or surpassed the folly of those Spaniards who used to make bonfires of Mexican hieroglyphics. It is hoped that the present book, in which of course it is impossible to do more than sketch the outlines and indicate the bearings of so vast a subject, will serve to awaken readers to the interest and importance of American archæology for the general study of the evolution of human society.

So much for the first and subsidiary theme. As for my principal theme, the Discovery of America, I was first drawn to it through its close relations with a subject which for some time chiefly occupied my mind, the history of the contact between the Aryan and Semitic worlds, and more particularly between Christians and Mussulmans about the shores of the Mediterranean. It is also interesting as part of the history of science, and furthermore as connected with the beginnings of one of the most momentous events in the career of mankind, the colonization of the barbaric world by Europeans. Moreover, the discovery of America has its full share of the romantic fascination that belongs to most of the work of the Renaissance period. I have sought to exhibit these different aspects of the subject.

The present book is in all its parts written from the original sources of information. The work of modern scholars has of course been freely used, but never without full acknowledgment in text or notes, and seldom without independent verification from the original sources. Acknowledgments are chiefly due to Humboldt, Morgan, Bandelier, Major, Varnhagen, Markham, Helps, and Harrisse. To the last-named scholar I owe an especial debt of gratitude, in common with all who have studied this subject since his arduous researches were begun. Some of the most valuable parts of his work have consisted in the discovery, reproduction, and collation of documents; and to some extent his pages are practically equivalent to the original sources inspected by him in the course of years of search through European archives, public and private. In the present book I must have expressed dissent from his conclusions at least as often as agreement with them, but whether one agrees with him or not, one always finds him helpful and stimulating. Though he has in some sort made himself a Frenchman in the course of his labours, it is pleasant to recall the fact that M. Harrisse is by birth our fellow-countryman; and there are surely few Americans of our time whom students of history have more reason for holding in honour.

I have not seen Mr. Winsor's " Christopher Columbus " in time to make any use of it. Within the last few days, while my final chapter is going to press, I have received the sheets of it, a few days in advance of publication. I do not find in it any references to sources of information which I have not already fully considered, so that our differences of opinion on sundry points may serve to show what diverse conclusions may be drawn from the same data. The most conspicuous difference is that which concerns the personal character of Columbus. Mr. Winsor writes in a spirit of energetic (not to say violent) reaction against the absurdities of Roselly de Lorgues and others who have tried to make a saint of Columbus ; and under the influence of this reaction he offers us a picture of the great navigator that serves to raise a pertinent question. No one can deny that Las Casas was a keen judge of men, or that his standard of right and wrong was quite as lofty as any one has reached in our own time. He had a much more intimate knowledge of Columbus than any modern historian can ever hope to acquire, and he always speaks of him with warm admiration and respect. But how could Las Casas ever have respected the feeble, mean-spirited driveller whose portrait Mr. Winsor asks us to accept as that of the Discoverer of America?

If, however, instead of his biographical estimate of Columbus, we consider Mr. Winsor's contributions toward a correct statement of the difficult geographical questions connected with the subject, we recognize at once the work of an acknowledged master in his chosen field. It is work, too, of the first order of importance. It would be hard to mention a subject on which so many reams of direful nonsense have been written as on the discovery of America; and the prolific source of so much folly has generally been what Mr. Freeman fitly calls "bondage to the modern map." In order to understand what the great mariners of the fifteenth and sixteenth centuries were trying to do, and what people supposed them to have done, one must begin by resolutely banishing the modern map from one's mind. The ancient map must take its place, but this must not be the ridiculous "Orbis Veteribus Notus," to be found in the ordinary classical atlas, *which simply copies the outlines of countries with modern accuracy from the modern map, and then scatters ancient names over them!* Such maps are worse than useless. In dealing with the discovery of America one must steadily keep before one's mind the quaint notions of ancient geographers, especially Ptolemy and Mela, as portrayed upon such maps as are reproduced in the present volume. It was just these distorted and hazy notions that swayed the minds and guided the movements of the great discoverers, and went on reproducing themselves upon newly made maps for a century or more after the time of Columbus. Without constant reference to these old maps one cannot begin to understand the circumstances of the discovery of America.

In no way can one get at the heart of the matter more completely than by threading the labyrinth of causes and effects through which the western hemisphere came slowly and gradually to be known by the name AMERICA. The reader will not fail to observe the pains which I have taken to elucidate this subject, not from any peculiar regard for Americus Vespucius, but because the quintessence of the whole geographical problem of the discovery of the New World is in one way or another involved in the discussion. I can think of no finer instance of the queer complications that can come to surround and mystify an increase of knowledge too great and rapid to be comprehended by a single generation of men.

In the solution of the problem as to the first Vespucius voyage I follow the lead of Varnhagen, but always independently and with the documentary evidence fully in sight. For some years I vainly tried to pursue Humboldt's clues to some intelligible conclusion, and felt inhos-

pitably inclined toward Varnhagen's views as
altogether too plausible ; he seemed to settle
too many difficulties at once. But after becoming convinced of the spuriousness of the Bandini letter (see below, vol. ii. p. 320) ; and ob-
serving how the air at once was cleared in some
directions, it seemed that further work in text-
ual criticism would be well bestowed. I made
a careful study of the diction of the letter from
Vespucius to Soderini in its two principal texts :
1. the Latin version of 1507, the original of
which is in the library of Harvard University,
appended to Waldseemüller's " Cosmographiæ
Introductio " ; 2. the Italian text reproduced
severally by Bandini, Canovai, and Varnhagen,
from the excessively rare original, of which only
five copies are now known to be in existence.
It is this text that Varnhagen regards as the
original from which the Latin version of 1507
was made, through an intermediate French
version now lost. In this opinion Varnhagen
does not stand alone, as Mr. Winsor seems to
think (" Christopher Columbus," p. 540, line
5 from bottom), for Harrisse and Avezac have
expressed themselves plainly to the same effect
(see below, vol. ii. p. 259). A minute study
of this text, with all its quaint interpolations of
Spanish and Portuguese idioms and seafaring

phrases into the Italian groundwork of its diction, long ago convinced me that it never was a *translation* from anything in heaven or earth or the waters under the earth. Nobody would ever have translated a document *into* such an extremely peculiar and individual jargon. It is most assuredly an original text, and its author was either Vespucius or the Old Nick. It was by starting from this text as primitive that Varnhagen started correctly in his interpretation of the statements in the letter, and it was for that reason that he was able to dispose of so many difficulties at one blow. When he showed that the landfall of Vespucius on his first voyage was near Cape Honduras and had nothing whatever to do with the Pearl Coast, he began to follow the right trail, and so the facts which had puzzled everybody began at once to fall into the right places. This is all made clear in the seventh chapter of the present work, where the general argument of Varnhagen is in many points strongly reinforced. The evidence here set forth in connection with the Cantino map is especially significant.

It is interesting on many accounts to see the first voyage of Vespucius thus elucidated, though it had no connection with the application of his name by Waldseemüller to an entirely different region from any that was visited upon that voyage. The real significance of the third voyage of Vespucius, in connection with the naming of America, is now set forth, I believe, for the first time in the light thrown upon the subject by the opinions of Ptolemy and Mela. Neither Humboldt nor Major nor Harrisse nor Varnhagen seems to have had a firm grasp of what was in Waldseemüller's mind when he wrote the passage photographed below in vol. ii. p. 380 of this work. It is only when we keep the Greek and Roman theories in the foreground and unflinchingly bar out that intrusive modern atlas, that we realize what the Freiburg geographer meant and why Ferdinand Columbus was not in the least shocked or surprised.

I have at various times given lectures on the discovery of America and questions connected therewith, more especially at University College, London, in 1879, at the Philosophical Institution in Edinburgh, in 1880, at the Lowell Institute in Boston, in 1890, and in the course of my work as professor in the Washington University at St. Louis; but the present work is in no sense whatever a reproduction of such lectures.

Acknowledgments are due to Mr. Winsor

for his cordial permission to make use of a
number of reproductions of old maps and facsimiles already used by him in the " Narrative
and Critical History of America ; " they are
mentioned in the lists of illustrations. I have
also to thank Dr. Brinton for allowing me to
reproduce a page of old Mexican music, and
the Hakluyt Society for permission to use the
Zeno and Catalan maps and the view of Kakortok church. Dr. Fewkes has very kindly
favoured me with a sight of proof-sheets of
some recent monographs by Bandelier. And
for courteous assistance at various libraries I
have most particularly to thank Mr. Kiernan
of Harvard University, Mr. Appleton Griffin of
the Boston Public Library, and Mr. Uhler of
the Peabody Institute in Baltimore.

CAMBRIDGE, *October* 25, 1891.

CONTENTS

I

CONTENTS

CONTENTS

CONTENTS

CONTENTS

II

PRE-COLUMBIAN VOYAGES

CONTENTS

CONTENTS

CONTENTS

CONTENTS

III

EUROPE AND CATHAY

CONTENTS

CONTENTS

IV

THE SEARCH FOR THE INDIES

Eastward or Portuguese Route

CONTENTS

LIST OF ILLUSTRATIONS

LIST OF ILLUSTRATIONS

THE
DISCOVERY OF AMERICA

I

ANCIENT AMERICA

WHEN the civilized people of Europe first became acquainted with the continents of North and South America, they found them inhabited by a race of men quite unlike any of the races with which they were familiar in the Old World. Between the various tribes of this aboriginal American race, except in the sub-arctic region, there The American aborigines is now seen to be a general physical likeness, such as to constitute an American type of mankind as clearly recognizable as those types which we call Mongolian and Malay, though far less pronounced than such types as the Australian or the negro. The most obvious characteristics possessed in common by the American aborigines are the copper-coloured or rather the cinnamon-coloured complexion, along with the high cheek-bones and small deepset eyes, the straight black hair and absence or scantiness of beard. With regard to stature, length of limbs, massiveness of frame, and shape of skull, considerable divergencies may be noticed among the various American tribes, as indeed is also the case among the members of the white race in Europe, and of other races. With regard to culture the differences have been considerable, although, with two or three apparent but not real exceptions, there was nothing in pre-Columbian America that could properly be called civilization; the general condition of the people ranged all the way from savagery to barbarism of a high type.

Soon after America was proved not to be part of Asia, a puzzling question arose. Whence came these "Indians," and in what manner did they find their way to the western hemisphere? Since the beginning of the present century discoveries in geology have entirely altered our mental attitude towards this question. It was formerly argued upon the two assumptions that the geographical relations of land and water had been always pretty much the same as we now find them, and that all the racial differences among men have arisen since the date of the "Noachian Deluge," which was generally placed somewhere between two and three thousand years before the Christian era. Hence inasmuch as European tradition knows nothing of any such race as the Indians,

Question as to their origin

2

it was supposed that at some time within the historic period they must have moved eastward from Asia into America; and thus "there was felt to be a sort of speculative necessity for discovering points of resemblance between American languages, myths, and social observances and those of the Oriental world. Now the aborigines of this continent were made out to be Kamtchatkans, and now Chinamen, and again they were shown, with quaint erudition, to be remnants of the ten tribes of Israel. Perhaps none of these theories have been exactly disproved, but they have all been superseded and laid on the shelf."[1] The tendency of modern

[1] See my *Excursions of an Evolutionist*, v.   A good succinct account of these various theories, monuments of wasted ingenuity, is given in Short's *North Americans of Antiquity*, chap. iii.   The most elaborate statement of the theory of an Israelite colonization of America is to be found in the ponderous tomes of Lord Kingsborough, *Mexican Antiquities*, London, 1831–48, 9 vols. elephant-folio.   Such a theory was entertained by the author of that curious piece of literary imposture, *The Book of Mormon*.   In this book we are told that, when the tongues were confounded at Babel, the Lord selected a certain Jared, with his family and friends, and instructed them to build eight ships, in which, after a voyage of 344 days, they were brought to America, where they " did build many mighty cities," and " prosper exceedingly." But after some centuries they perished because of their iniquities.   In the reign of Zedekiah, when calamity was impending over Judah, two brothers, Nephi and Laman, under divine guidance led a colony to America.   There, says the veracious

discovery is indeed towards agreement with the time-honoured tradition which makes the Old World, and perhaps Asia, the earliest dwelling-place of mankind. Competition has been far more active in the fauna of the eastern hemisphere than in that of the western, natural selection has accordingly resulted in the evolution of higher forms, and it is there that we find both extinct and surviving species of man's nearest collateral relatives, those tailless half-human apes, the gorilla, chimpanzee, orang, and gibbon. It is altogether probable that the

chronicler, their descendants became great nations, and worked in *iron*, and had stuffs of *silk*, besides keeping plenty of *oxen* and *sheep*. (*Ether*, ix. 18, 19 ; x. 23, 24.) Christ appeared and wrought many wonderful works ; people spake with tongues, and the dead were raised. (3 *Nephi*, xxvi. 14, 15.) But about the close of the fourth century of our era, a terrible war between Lamanites and Nephites ended in the destruction of the latter. Some two million warriors, with their wives and children, having been slaughtered, the prophet Mormon escaped, with his son Moroni, to the "hill Cumorah," hard by the "waters of Ripliancum," or Lake Ontario. (*Ether*, xv. 2, 8, 11.) There they hid the sacred tablets, which remained concealed until they were miraculously discovered and translated by Joseph Smith in 1827. There is, of course, no element of tradition in this story. It is all pure fiction, and of a very clumsy sort, such as might easily be devised by an ignorant man accustomed to the language of the Bible ; and of course it was suggested by the old notion of the Israelitish origin of the red men. The references are to *The Book of Mormon*, Salt Lake City : Deseret News Co., 1885.

4

people whom the Spaniards found in America came by migration from the Old World. But it is by no means probable that their migration occurred within so short a period as five or six thousand years. A series of observations and discoveries kept up for the last half-century seem to show that North America has been continuously inhabited by human beings since the earliest Pleistocene times, if not earlier.

Antiquity of man in America

The first group of these observations and discoveries relate to "middens" or shell-heaps. On the banks of the Damariscotta River in Maine are some of the most remarkable shell-heaps in the world. With an average thickness of six or seven feet, they rise in places to a height of twenty-five feet. They consist almost entirely of huge oyster-shells often ten inches in length and sometimes much longer. The shells belong to a salt-water species. In some places "there is an appearance of stratification covered by an alternation of shells and earth, as if the deposition of shells had been from time to time interrupted, and a vegetable mould had covered the surface." In these heaps have been found fragments of pottery and of the bones of such edible animals as the moose and deer. "At the very foundation of one of the highest heaps," in a situation which must for long ages have been undisturbed, Mr.

Shell-mounds

5

Edward Morse " found the remains of an ancient fireplace, where he exhumed charcoal, bones, and pottery." [1] The significant circumstance is that " at the present time oysters are only found in very small numbers, too small to make it an object to gather them," and so far as memory and tradition can reach, such seems to have been the case. The great size of the heap, coupled with the notable change in the distribution of this mollusk since the heap was abandoned, implies a very considerable lapse of time since the vestiges of human occupation were first left here. Similar conclusions have been drawn from the banks or mounds of shells on the St. John's River in Florida,[2] on the Alabama River, at Grand Lake on the lower Mississippi, and at San Pablo in the bay of San Francisco. Thus at various points from Maine to California, and in connection with one particular kind of memorial, we find records of the presence of man at a period undoubtedly prehistoric, but not necessarily many thousands of years old.

The second group of discoveries carries us back much farther, even into the earlier stages of that widespread glaciation which was the most

[1] *Second Annual Report of the Peabody Museum of American Archæology*, etc., p. 18.

[2] Visited in 1866–74 by Professor Jeffries Wyman, and described in his *Fresh-Water Shell Mounds of the St. John's River*, Cambridge, 1875.

remarkable feature of the Pleistocene period. At the periods of greatest cold " the continent of North America was deeply swathed in ice as far south as the latitude of Phila- The Glacial delphia, while glaciers descended into period North Carolina." [1] The valleys of the Rocky Mountains also supported enormous glaciers, and a similar state of things existed at the same time in Europe. These periods of intense cold were alternated with long interglacial periods during which the climate was warmer than it is to-day. Concerning the antiquity of the Pleistocene age, which was characterized by such extraordinary vicissitudes of heat and cold, there has been, as in all questions relating to geological time, much conflict of opinion. Twenty years ago geologists often argued as if there were an unlimited fund of past time upon which to draw ; but since Sir William Thomson and other physicists emphasized the point that in an antiquity very far from infinite this earth must have been a molten mass, there has been a reaction. In many instances further study has shown that less time was needed in order to effect a given change than had formerly been supposed ; and so there has grown up a tendency to shorten the time assigned to geological periods. Here, as in so many other cases, the truth is doubtless to be sought within the extremes. If we adopt the

[1] *Excursions of an Evolutionist,* i.

magnificent argument of Dr. Croll, which seems to me still to hold its ground against all adverse criticism,[1] and regard the Glacial epoch as coincident with the last period of high eccentricity of the earth's orbit, we obtain a result that is moderate and probable. That astronomical period began about 240,000 years ago and came to an end about 80,000 years ago. During this period the eccentricity was seldom less than .04, and at one time rose to .0569. At the present time the eccentricity is .0168, and nearly 800,000 years will pass before it attains such a point as it reached during the Glacial epoch. For the last 50,000 years the departure of the earth's orbit from a circular form has been exceptionally small.

Now the traces of the existence of men in North America during the Glacial epoch have in recent years been discovered in abundance, as, for example, the palæolithic quartzite imple-

[1] Croll, *Climate and Time in their Geological Relations,* New York, 1875; *Discussions on Climate and Cosmology,* New York, 1886; Archibald Geikie, *Text Book of Geology,* pp. 23–29, 883–909, London, 1882 ; James Geikie, *The Great Ice Age,* pp. 94–136, New York, 1874 ; *Prehistoric Europe,* pp. 558–562, London, 1881; Wallace, *Island Life,* pp. 101–225, New York, 1881. Some objections to Croll's theory may be found in Wright's *Ice Age in North America,* pp. 405–505, 585–595, New York, 1889. I have given a brief account of the theory in my *Excursions of an Evolutionist,* ii.

ments found in the drift near the city of St. Paul, which date from towards the close of the Glacial epoch;[1] the fragment of a human jaw found in the red clay deposited in Minnesota during an earlier part of that epoch;[2] the noble collection of palæoliths found by Dr. C. C. Abbott in the Trenton gravels in New Jersey; and the more recent discoveries of Dr. Metz and Mr. H. T. Cresson.

The year 1873 marks an era in American archæology as memorable as the year 1841 in the investigation of the antiquity of man in Europe. With reference to these problems Dr. Abbott occupies a position similar to that of Boucher de Perthes in the Old World, and the Trenton valley is coming to be classic ground, like the valley of the Somme. In April, 1873, Dr. Abbott published his description of three rude implements which he had found some sixteen feet below the surface of the ground "in the gravels of a bluff overlooking the Delaware River." The implements were in place *Discoveries* in an undisturbed deposit, and could *in the Tren-* not have found their way thither in any *ton gravel* recent time; Dr. Abbott assigned them to the

[1] See Miss F. E. Babbitt, "Vestiges of Glacial Man in Minnesota," in *Proceedings of the American Association*, vol. xxxii., 1883.

[2] See N. H. Winchell, *Annual Report of the State Geologist of Minnesota*, 1877, p. 60.

age of the Glacial drift. This was the beginning of a long series of investigations, in which Dr. Abbott's work was assisted and supplemented by Messrs. Whitney, Carr, Putnam, Shaler, Lewis, Wright, Haynes, Dawkins, and other eminent geologists and archæologists. By 1888 Dr. Abbott had obtained not less than sixty implements from various recorded depths in the gravel, while many others were found at depths not recorded or in the talus of the banks.[1] Three human skulls and other bones, along with the tusk of a mastodon, have been discovered in the same gravel. Careful studies have been made of the conditions under which the gravel-banks were deposited and their probable age; and it is generally agreed that they date from the later portion of the Glacial period, or about the time of the final recession of the ice-sheet from this region. At that time, in its climate and general aspect, New York harbour must have been much like a Greenland fiord of the present day. In 1883 Professor Wright, of Oberlin, after a careful study of the Trenton deposits and their relations to the terrace and gravel deposits to the westward, predicted that similar palæolithic implements would be found in Ohio. Two years afterwards, the prediction was verified by Dr. Metz, who found a true palæolith of black flint at Madison-ville, in the Little Miami valley, eight feet below

[1] Wright's *Ice Age in North America*, p. 516.

the surface. Since then further discoveries have been made in the same neighbourhood by Dr. Metz, and in Jackson County, Indiana, by Mr. H. T. Cresson ; and the existence of man in that part of America towards the close of the Glacial period may be regarded as definitely established. The discoveries of Miss Babbitt and Professor Winchell, in Minnesota, carry the conclusion still farther, and add to the probability of the existence of a human population all the way from the Atlantic coast to the upper Mississippi valley at that remote antiquity.

Discoveries in Ohio, Indiana, and Minnesota ;

A still more remarkable discovery was made by Mr. Cresson in July, 1887, at Claymont, in the north of Delaware. In a deep cut of the Baltimore and Ohio Railroad, in a stratum of Philadelphia red gravel and brick clay, Mr. Cresson obtained an unquestionable palæolith, and a few months afterwards his diligent search was rewarded with another.[1] This formation dates from far back

and in Delaware

[1] The chipped implements discovered by Messrs. Abbott, Metz, and Cresson, and by Miss Babbitt, are all on exhibition at the Peabody Museum in Cambridge, whither it is necessary to go if one would get a comprehensive view of the relics of interglacial man in North America. The collection of implements made by Dr. Abbott includes much more than the palæoliths already referred to. It is one of the most important collections in the world, and is worth a long journey to see. Containing more than 20,000 implements, all found

in the Glacial period. If we accept Dr. Croll's method of reckoning, we can hardly assign to it an antiquity less than 150,000 years.

But according to Professor Josiah Whitney there is reason for supposing that man existed The Cala- in California at a still more remote veras skull period. He holds that the famous skull discovered in 1866, in the gold-bearing gravels of Calaveras County, belongs to the

within a very limited area in New Jersey, " as now arranged, the collection exhibits at one and the same time the sequence of peoples and phases of development in the valley of the Delaware, from palæolithic man, through the intermediate period, to the recent Indians, and the relative numerical proportion of the many forms of their implements, each in its time. . . . It is doubtful whether any similar collection exists from which a student can gather so much information at sight as in this, where the natural pebbles from the gravel begin the series, and the beautifully chipped points of chert, jasper, and quartz terminate it in one direction, and the polished celts and grooved stone axes in the other." There are three principal groups, — first, the interglacial palæoliths, secondly, the argillite points and flakes, and thirdly, the arrow-heads, knives, mortars and pestles, axes and hoes, ornamental stones, etc., of Indians of the recent period. Dr. Abbott's *Primitive Industry*, published in 1881, is a useful manual for studying this collection ; and an account of his discoveries in the glacial gravels is given in *Reports of the Peabody Museum*, vol. ii. pp. 30–48, 225–258 ; see also vol. iii. p. 492. A succinct and judicious account of the whole subject is given by H. W. Haynes, "The Prehistoric Archæology of North America," in Winsor's *Narrative and Critical History*, vol. i. pp. 329–368.

Pliocene age.[1] If this be so, it seems to suggest an antiquity not less than twice as great as that just mentioned. The question as to the antiquity of the Calaveras skull is still hotly disputed among the foremost palæontologists, but as one reads the arguments one cannot help feeling that theoretical difficulties have put the objectors into a somewhat inhospitable attitude towards the evidence so ably presented by Professor Whitney. It has been too hastily assumed that, from the point of view of evolution, the existence of Pliocene man is improbable. Upon general considerations, however, we have strong reason for believing that human beings must have inhabited some portions of the earth throughout the whole duration of the Pliocene period, and it need not surprise us if their remains are presently discovered in more places than one.[2]

[1] J. D. Whitney, " The Auriferous Gravels of the Sierra Nevada," *Memoirs of the Museum of Comparative Zoölogy at Harvard College*, Cambridge, 1880, vol. vi.

[2] In an essay published in 1882 on " Europe before the Arrival of Man " (*Excursions of an Evolutionist*, i.), I argued that if we are to find traces of the " missing link," or primordial stock of primates from which man has been derived, we must undoubtedly look for it in the Miocene. I am pleased at finding the same opinion lately expressed by one of the highest living authorities. The case is thus stated by Alfred Russel Wallace. " The evidence we now possess of the exact nature of the resemblance of man to the various

Whatever may be the final outcome of the
Calaveras controversy, there can be no doubt as

species of anthropoid apes, shows us that he has little special
affinity for any one rather than another species, while he
differs from them all in several important characters in which
they agree with each other. The conclusion to be drawn
from these facts is, that his points of affinity connect him with
the whole group, while his special peculiarities equally sepa-
rate him from the whole group, and that he must, therefore,
have diverged from the common ancestral form before the
existing types of anthropoid apes had diverged from each
other. Now this divergence almost certainly took place as
early as the Miocene period, because in the Upper Miocene
deposits of western Europe remains of two species of ape
have been found allied to the gibbons, one of them, dryopi-
thecus, nearly as large as a man, and believed by M. Lartet
to have approached man in its dentition more than the existing apes. We seem hardly, therefore, to have reached in
the Upper Miocene the epoch of the common ancestor of
man and the anthropoids." (*Darwinism*, p. 455, London,
1889.) Mr. Wallace goes on to answer the objection of
Professor Boyd Dawkins, " that man did not probably exist
in Pliocene times, because almost all the known mammalia of
that epoch are distinct species from those now living on the
earth, and that the same changes of the environment which
led to the modification of other mammalian species would
also have led to a change in man." This argument, at
first sight apparently formidable, quite overlooks the fact that
in the evolution of man there came a point after which variations in his intelligence were seized upon more and more exclusively by natural selection, to the comparative neglect of
physical variations. After that point man changed but little in
physical characteristics, except in size and complexity of brain.
This is the theorem first propounded by Mr. Wallace in the

14

to the existence of man in North America far back in early Pleistocene times. The men of the River-drift, who long dwelt in western Europe during the milder intervals of the Glacial period, but seem to have become extinct towards the end of it, are well known to palæontologists through their bones and their rude tools. Contemporaneously with these Europeans of the River-drift there certainly lived some kind of men, of a similar low grade of culture, in the Mississippi valley and on both the Atlantic and Pacific slopes of North America. Along with these ancient Americans lived some terrestrial mammals that still survive, such as the elk, reindeer, prairie wolf, bison, musk-ox, and beaver; and many that have long been extinct, such as the mylodon, megatherium, megalonyx, mastodon, Siberian elephant, mammoth, at least six or seven species of ancestral horse, a huge bear similar to the cave bear of ancient Europe, a lion similar to the European cave lion, and a tiger as large as the modern tiger of Bengal.

Pleistocene men and mammals

Now while the general relative positions of

Anthropological Review, May, 1864; restated in his *Contributions to Natural Selection*, chap. ix., in 1870; and further extended and developed by me in connection with the theory of man's origin first suggested in my lectures at Harvard in 1871, and worked out in *Cosmic Philosophy*, part ii., chapters xvi., xxi., xxii.

those stupendous abysses that hold the oceans do not appear to have undergone any considerable change since an extremely remote geological period, their shallow marginal portions have been repeatedly raised so as to add extensive territories to the edges of continents, and in some cases to convert archipelagoes into continents, and to join continents previously separated. Such elevation is followed in turn by an era of subsidence, and almost everywhere either the one process or the other is slowly going on. If you look at a model in relief of the continents and ocean-floors, such as may be seen at the Museum of Comparative Zoölogy in Cambridge, showing the results Elevation and of a vast number of soundings in all subsidence parts of the world, you cannot fail to be struck with the shallowness of Bering Sea; it looks like a part of the continent rather than of the ocean, and indeed it is just that, — an area of submerged continent. So in the northern Atlantic there is a lofty ridge running from France to Greenland. The British islands, the Orkney, Shetland, and Færoe groups, and Iceland are the parts of this ridge high enough to remain out of water. The remainder of it is shallow sea. Again and again it has been raised, together with the floor of the German Ocean, so as to become dry land. Both before and since the time when those stone tools were

dropped into the red gravel from which Mr.
Cresson took them the other day, the northwestern part of Europe has been solid continent for more than a hundred miles to the west
of the French and Irish coasts, the Thames and
Humber have been tributaries to the Rhine,
which emptied into the Arctic Ocean, and across
the Atlantic ridge one might have walked to
the New World dryshod.[1] In similar wise the
northwestern corner of America has repeatedly
been joined to Siberia through the elevation of
Bering Sea.

There have therefore been abundant opportunities for men to get into America from the
Old World without crossing salt water. Probably this was the case with the ancient inhabitants of the Delaware and Little Miami
valleys; it is not at all likely that men who
used their kind of tools knew much about
going on the sea in boats.

Whether the Indians are descended from this
ancient population or not, is a question with
which we have as yet no satisfactory method of
dealing. It is not unlikely that these glacial
men may have perished from off the face of the
earth, having been crushed and sup- Waves of
planted by stronger races. There may migration
have been several successive waves of migration,

[1] See, for example, the map of Europe in early post-
glacial times, in James Geikie's *Prehistoric Europe*.

of which the Indians were the latest.[1] There is time enough for a great many things to happen in a thousand centuries. It will doubtless be long before all the evidence can be brought in and ransacked, but of one thing we may feel pretty sure : the past is more full of changes than we are apt to realize. Our first theories are usually too simple, and have to be enlarged and twisted into all manner of shapes in order to cover the actual complication of facts.[2]

[1] " There are three human crania in the Museum, which were found in the gravel at Trenton, one several feet below the surface, the others near the surface. These skulls, which are of remarkable uniformity, are of small size and of oval shape, differing from all other skulls in the Museum. In fact, they are of a distinct type, and hence of the greatest importance. So far as they go they indicate that palæolithic man was exterminated, or has become lost by admixture with others during the many thousand years which have passed since he inhabited the Delaware valley." F. W. Putnam, "The Peabody Museum," *Proceedings of the American Antiquarian Society*, 1889, New Series, vol. vi. p. 189.

[2] An excellent example of this is the expansion and modification undergone during the past twenty years by our theories of the Aryan settlement of Europe. See Benfey's preface to Fick's *Woerterbuch der Indogermanischen Grundsprache*, 1868 ; Geiger, *Zur Entwickelungsgeschichte der Menschheit*, 1871 ; Cuno, *Forschungen im Gebiete der alten Voelkerkunde*, 1871 ; Schmidt, *Die Verwandtschaftsverhältnisse der Indogermanischen Sprachen*, 1872 ; Poesche, *Die Arier*, 1878 ; Lindenschmit, *Handbuch der deutschen Alterthumskunde*, 1880 ; Penka, *Origines Ariacæ*, 1883 ; and *Die Herkunft der Arier*, 1886 ; Spiegel, *Die arische Periode*

In this connection the history of the Eskimos introduces us to some interesting problems.
Mention has been made of the River-drift men
who lived in Europe during the milder intervals of the Glacial period. At such times they
made their way into Germany and Britain,
along with leopards, hyænas, and African elephants. But as the cold intervals came on and
the edge of the polar ice-sheet crept southward
and mountain glaciers filled up the valleys,
these men and beasts retreated into Africa ; and
their place was taken by a sub-arctic The Cave
race of men known as the Cave men, men of
along with the reindeer and arctic fox Europe in the
Glacial
and musk-sheep. More than once period
with the secular alternations of temperature did
the River-drift men thus advance and retreat
and advance again, and as they advanced the
Cave men retreated, both races yielding to an
enemy stronger than either, — to wit, the hos-
tile climate. At length all traces of the River-

und ihre Zustande, 1887 ; Rendal, *Cradle of the Aryans*,
1889 ; Schrader, *Sprachvergleichung und Urgeschichte*,
1883, and second edition translated into English, with the
title, *Prehistoric Antiquities of the Aryan Peoples*, 1890.
Schrader's is an epoch-making book. An attempt to defend
the older and simpler views is made by Max Müller, *Biographies of Words and the Home of the Aryas*, 1888 ; see
also Van den Gheyn, *L'origine européenne des Aryas*, 1889.
The whole case is well summed up by Isaac Taylor, *Origin
of the Aryans*, 1889.

drift men vanish, but what of the Cave men? They have left no representatives among the present populations of Europe, but the musk-sheep, which always went and came with the Cave men, is to-day found only in sub-arctic America among the Eskimos, and the fossilized bones of the musk-sheep lie in a regular trail across the eastern hemisphere, from the Pyrenees through Germany and Russia and all the vast length of Siberia. The stone arrow-heads, the sewing-needles, the necklaces and amulets of cut teeth, and the daggers made from antler, used by the Eskimos, resemble so minutely the implements of the Cave men, that if recent Eskimo remains were to be put into the Pleistocene caves of France and England they would be indistinguishable in appearance from the remains of the Cave men which are now found there.[1] There is another striking point of resemblance. The Eskimos have a talent for artistic sketching of men and beasts, and scenes in which men and beasts figure, which is absolutely unrivalled among rude peoples. One need but look at the sketches by common Eskimo fishermen which illustrate Dr. Henry Rink's fascinating book on Danish Greenland, to realize that this rude Eskimo art has a character as pronounced and unmistakable in its way as the much higher art of the Japanese.

[1] See Dawkins, *Early Man in Britain*, pp. 233–245.

Now among the European remains of the Cave men are many sketches of mammoths, cave bears, and other animals now extinct, and hunting scenes so artfully and vividly portrayed as to bring distinctly before us many details of daily life in an antiquity so vast that in comparison with it the interval between the pyramids of Egypt and the Eiffel tower shrinks into a point. Such a talent is unique among savage peoples. It exists only among the living Eskimos and the ancient Cave men ; and when considered in connection with so many other points of agreement, and with the indisputable fact that the Cave men were a sub-arctic race, it affords a strong presumption in favour of the opinion of that great palæontologist, Professor Boyd Dawkins, that the Eskimos of North America are to-day the sole survivors of the race that made their homes in the Pleistocene caves of western Europe.[1]

The Eskimos are probably a remnant of the Cave men

[1] According to Dr. Rink the Eskimos formerly inhabited the central portions of North America, and have retreated or been driven northward ; he would make the Eskimos of Siberia an offshoot from those of America, though he freely admits that there are grounds for entertaining the opposite view. Dr. Abbott is inclined to attribute an Eskimo origin to some of the palæoliths of the Trenton gravel. On the other hand, Mr. Clements Markham derives the American Eskimos from those of Siberia. It seems to me that these views may be comprehended and reconciled in a wider one.

If we have always been accustomed to think
of races of men only as they are placed on

I would suggest that during the Glacial period the ancestral
Eskimos may have gradually become adapted to arctic conditions of life ; that in the mild interglacial intervals they
migrated northward along with the musk-sheep ; and that
upon the return of the cold they migrated southward again,
keeping always near the edge of the ice-sheet. Such a southward migration would naturally enough bring them in one
continent down to the Pyrenees, in the other down to the
Alleghanies ; and naturally enough the modern inquirer has
his attention first directed to the indications of their final retreat, *both* northward in America and northeastward from
Europe through Siberia. This is like what happened with
so many plants and animals. Compare Darwin's remarks on
" Dispersal in the Glacial Period," *Origin of Species*, chap.
xii.

The best books on the Eskimos are those of Dr. Rink,
Tales and Traditions of the Eskimo, Edinburgh, 1875 ;
Danish Greenland, London, 1877 ; *The Eskimo Tribes,
their Distribution and Characteristics, especially in regard to
Language*, Copenhagen, 1887. See also Franz Boas,
" The Central Eskimo," *Sixth Report of the Bureau of
Ethnology*, Washington, 1888, pp. 399–669 ; W. H. Dall,
Alaska and its Resources, 1870 ; Markham, " Origin and
Migrations of the Greenland Esquimaux," *Journal of the
Royal Geographical Society*, 1865 ; Cranz, *Historie von
Groenland*, Leipsic, 1765 ; Petitot, *Traditions indiennes du
Canada nord-ouest*, Paris, 1886 ; Pilling's *Bibliography of
the Eskimo Language*, Washington, 1887 ; Wells and Kelly,
*English-Eskimo and Eskimo-English Vocabularies, with
Ethnographical Memoranda concerning the Arctic Eskimos
in Alaska and Siberia*, Washington, 1890 ; Carstensen's
Two Summers in Greenland, London, 1890.

modern maps, it at first seems strange to think of England and France as ever having been inhabited by Eskimos. Facts equally strange may be cited in abundance from zoölogy and botany. The camel is found to-day only in Arabia and Bactria; yet in all probability the camel originated in America,[1] and is an intruder into what we are accustomed to call his native deserts, just as the people of the United States are European intruders upon the soil of America. So the giant trees of Mariposa Grove are now found only in California, but there was once a time when they were as common in Europe[2] as maple-trees to-day in a New England village.

Familiarity with innumerable facts of this sort, concerning the complicated migrations and distribution of plants and animals, has entirely altered our way of looking at the question as to the origin of the American Indians. As already observed, we can hardly be said to possess sufficient data for determining whether they are descended from the Pleistocene inhabitants of America, or have come in some later wave of migration from the Old World. Nor can we as yet determine whether they were earlier or later

[1] Wallace, *Geographical Distribution of Animals*, vol. ii. p. 155.

[2] Asa Gray, "Sequoia and its History," in his *Darwiniana*, pp. 205–235.

comers than the Eskimos. But since we have got rid of that feeling of speculative necessity above referred to, for bringing the red men from Asia within the historic period, it has become more and more clear that they have dwelt upon American soil for a very long time. The aboriginal American, as we know him, with his language and legends, his physical and mental peculiarities, his social observances and customs, is most emphatically a native and not an imported article. He belongs to the American continent as strictly as its opossums and armadillos, its maize and its golden-rod, or any members of its aboriginal fauna and flora belong to it. In all probability he came from the Old World at some ancient period, whether pre-glacial or post-glacial, when it was possible to come by land ; and here in all probability, until the arrival of white men from Europe, he remained undisturbed by later comers, unless the Eskimos may have been such. There is not a particle of evidence to suggest any connection or intercourse between aboriginal America and Asia within any such period as the last twenty thousand years, except in so far as there may perhaps now and then have been slight surges of Eskimo tribes back and forth across Bering Strait.

The Indians must surely be regarded as an

There was probably no connection or intercourse by water between ancient America and the Old World

ANCIENT AMERICA

entirely different stock from the Eskimos. On the other hand, the most competent American ethnologists are now pretty thoroughly agreed that all the aborigines south of the Eskimo region, all the way from Hudson's Bay to Cape Horn, belong to one and the same race. It was formerly supposed that the higher culture of the Aztecs, Mayas, and Peruvians must indicate that they were of different race from the more barbarous Algonquins and Dakotas; and a speculative necessity was felt for proving that, whatever may have been the case with the other American peoples, this higher culture at any rate must have been introduced within the historic period from the Old World.[1] This feeling was caused partly by the fact that, owing to crude and loosely framed conceptions of the real points of difference between civilization and barbarism, this Central American culture was absurdly exaggerated. As the further study of the uncivilized parts of the world has led to more accurate and precise conceptions, this kind of speculative necessity has ceased to be felt. There is an increasing disposition among scholars to agree

There is one great American "red" race

[1] Illustrations may be found in plenty in the learned works of Brasseur de Bourbourg : *Histoire des nations civilisées du Méxique et de l' Amérique centrale*, 4 vols., Paris, 1857–58 ; *Popol Vuh*, Paris, 1861 ; *Quatre lettres sur le Méxique*, Paris, 1868 ; *Le manuscrit Troano*, Paris, 1870, etc.

25

that the warrior of Anahuac and the shepherd of the Andes were just simply Indians, and that their culture was no less indigenous than that of the Cherokees or Mohawks.

To prevent any possible misconception of my meaning, a further word of explanation may be needed at this point. The word "race" is used in such widely different senses that there is apt to be more or less vagueness about it. The difference is mainly in what logicians call extension; sometimes the word covers very little ground, sometimes a great deal. We say that the people of England, of the United States, and of New South Wales belong to one and the same race; and we say that an Englishman, a Frenchman, and a Greek belong to three different races. There is a sense in which both these statements are true. But there is also a sense in which we may say that the Englishman, the Frenchman, and the Greek belong to one and the same race; and that is when we are contrasting them as white men with black men or yellow men. Now we may correctly say that a Shawnee, an Ojibwa, and a Kickapoo belong to one and the same Algonquin race; that a Mohawk and a Tuscarora belong to one and the same Iroquois race; but that an Algonquin differs from an Iroquois somewhat

Different senses in which the word "race" is used

as an Englishman differs from a Frenchman. No doubt we may fairly say that the Mexicans encountered by Cortes differed in race from the Iroquois encountered by Champlain, as much as an Englishman differs from an Albanian or a Montenegrin. But when we are contrasting aboriginal Americans with white men or yellow men, it is right to say that Mexicans and Iroquois belong to the same great red race.

In some parts of the world two strongly contrasted races have become mingled together, or have existed side by side for centuries without intermingling. In Europe the big blond Aryan-speaking race has mixed with the small brunette Iberian race, producing the endless varieties in stature and complexion which may be seen in any drawing-room in London or New York. In Africa south of Sahara, on the other hand, we find, interspersed among negro tribes but kept perfectly distinct, that primitive dwarfish race with yellow skin and tufted hair to which belong the Hottentots and Bushmen, the Wambatti lately discovered by Mr. Stanley, and other tribes.[1] Now in America south of Hudson's Bay the case seems to have been quite otherwise, and more as it would have been

---

[1] See Werner, "The African Pygmies," *Popular Science Monthly*, September, 1890, — a thoughtful and interesting article.

in Europe if there had been only Aryans, or in Africa if there had been only blacks.[1]

The belief that the people of the Cordilleras must be of radically different race from other Indians was based upon the vague notion that grades of culture have some necessary connection with likenesses and differences of race. There is no such necessary connection.[2] Between the highly civilized Japanese and their barbarous Mandshu cousins the difference in culture is much greater than the difference between

No necessary connection between differences in culture and differences in race

---

[1] This sort of illustration requires continual limitation and qualification. The case in ancient America was not *quite* as it would have been in Europe if there had been only Aryans there. The semi-civilized people of the Cordilleras were relatively brachycephalous as compared with the more barbarous Indians north and east of New Mexico. It is correct to call this a distinction of race if we mean thereby a distinction developed upon American soil, a differentiation within the limits of the red race, and not an intrusion from without. In this sense the Caribs also may be regarded as a distinct sub-race ; and, in the same sense, we may call the Kafirs a distinct sub-race of African blacks. See, as to the latter, Tylor, *Anthropology*, p. 89.

[2] As Sir John Lubbock well says, " Different races in similar stages of development often present more features of resemblance to one another than the same race does to itself in different stages of its history." (*Origin of Civilization*, p. 11.) If every student of history and ethnology would begin by learning this lesson, the world would be spared a vast amount of unprofitable theorizing.

Mohawks and Mexicans; and the same may be said of the people of Israel and Judah in contrast with the Arabs of the desert, or of the imperial Romans in comparison with their Teutonic kinsmen as described by Tacitus.

At this point, in order to prepare ourselves the more clearly to understand sundry facts with which we shall hereafter be obliged to deal, especially the wonderful experiences of the Spanish conquerors, it will be well to pause for a moment and do something towards defining the different grades of culture through Grades which men have passed in attaining to of culture the grade which can properly be called civilization. Unless we begin with clear ideas upon this head we cannot go far towards understanding the ancient America that was first visited and described for us by Spaniards. The various grades of culture need to be classified, and that most original and suggestive scholar, the late Lewis Morgan, of Rochester, made a brilliant attempt in this direction, to which the reader's attention is now invited.

Below *Civilization* Mr. Morgan[1] distinguishes two principal grades or stages of culture, namely *Savagery* and *Barbarism*. There is much looseness and confusion in the popular use of these terms, and this is liable to become

[1] See his great work on *Ancient Society*, New York, 1877.

a fruitful source of misapprehension in the case of any statement involving either of them.

Distinction between Savagery and Barbarism

When popular usage discriminates between them it discriminates in the right direction ; there is a vague but not uncertain feeling that savagery is a lower stage than barbarism. But ordinarily the discrimination is not made and the two terms are carelessly employed as if interchangeable. Scientific writers long since recognized a general difference between savagery and barbarism, but Mr. Morgan was the first to suggest a really useful criterion for distinguishing between them. His criterion is the making of pottery ; and his reason for selecting it is that the making of pottery is something that presupposes village life and more or less progress in the simpler arts. The earlier methods of boiling food were either putting it into holes in the ground lined with skins and then using heated stones, or else

Origin of pottery

putting it into baskets coated with clay to be supported over a fire. The clay served the double purpose of preventing liquids from escaping and protecting the basket against the flame. It was probably observed that the clay was hardened by the fire, and thus in course of time it was found that the clay would answer the purpose without the basket.[1] Whoever first

[1] See the evidence in Tylor, *Researches into the Early History of Mankind,* pp. 269–272 ; cf. Lubbock, *Prehis-*

made this ingenious discovery led the way from savagery to barbarism. Throughout the present work we shall apply the name " savages " only to uncivilized people who do not make pottery.

But within each of these two stages Mr. Morgan distinguishes three subordinate stages, or Ethnic Periods, which may be called either lower, middle, and upper status, or older, middle, and later periods. The lower status of savagery was that wholly prehistoric Lower status stage when men lived in their original of savagery restricted habitat and subsisted on fruit and nuts. To this period must be assigned the beginning of articulate speech. All existing races of men had passed beyond it at an unknown antiquity.

Men began to pass beyond it when they discovered how to catch fish and how to use fire. They could then begin (following coasts and rivers) to spread over the earth. The Middle status middle status of savagery, thus intro- of savagery duced, ends with the invention of that compound weapon, the bow and arrow. The natives of Australia, who do not know this weapon, are still in the middle status of savagery.[1]

toric Times, p. 573 ; and see Cushing's masterly " Study of Pueblo Pottery," etc., _Reports of Bureau of Ethnology_, iv., 473–521.

[1] Lumholtz, _Among Cannibals_, London, 1889, gives a vivid picture of aboriginal life in Australia.

The invention of the bow and arrow, which marks the upper status of savagery, was not only a great advance in military art, but it also Upper status of savagery vastly increased men's supply of food by increasing their power of killing wild game. The lowest tribes in America, such as those upon the Columbia River, the Athabaskans of Hudson's Bay, the Fuegians and some other South American tribes, are in the upper status of savagery.

The transition from this status to the lower status of barbarism was marked, as before observed, by the invention of pottery. The end of the lower status of barbarism was marked in the Old World by the domestication of animals other than the dog, which was probably domesticated at a much earlier period as an aid to the hunter. The domestication of horses and asses, Lower status of barbarism: it ended differently in the two hemispheres oxen and sheep, goats and pigs, marks of course an immense advance. Along with it goes considerable development of agriculture, thus enabling a small territory to support many people. It takes a wide range of country to support hunters. In the New World, except in Peru, the only domesticated animal was the dog. Horses, oxen, and the other animals mentioned did not exist in America, during the historic period, until they were brought over from Europe by the Spaniards. In ancient American society there was no such thing as a pastoral stage of development,[1] and the absence of domesticable animals from the western hemisphere may well be reckoned as very important among the causes which retarded the progress of mankind in this part of the world.

On the other hand the ancient Americans had a cereal plant peculiar to the New World, which made comparatively small demands upon the intelligence and industry of the cultivator. Maize or " Indian corn " has played a most important part in the history of the New World, as regards both the red men and the white men. It could be planted without clearing or ploughing the soil. It was only necessary to girdle the trees with a stone hatchet, so as to destroy their leaves and let in the sunshine. A few scratches and digs were made in the ground with a stone digger, and the seed once dropped in took care of itself. The ears could hang for weeks after ripening, and could be picked off with- out meddling with the stalk ; there was no need of threshing and win- nowing. None of the Old World cereals can be cultivated without much more industry and in- telligence. At the same time, when Indian corn is sown in tilled land it yields with little labour

Importance of Indian corn

[1] The case of Peru, which forms an apparent but not real exception to this general statement, will be considered below in chap. ix.

33

more than twice as much food per acre as any other kind of grain. This was of incalculable advantage to the English settlers of New England, who would have found it much harder to gain a secure foothold upon the soil if they had had to begin by preparing it for wheat and rye without the aid of the beautiful and beneficent American plant.[1] The Indians of the Atlantic coast of North America for the most part lived in stockaded villages, and cultivated their corn along with beans, pumpkins, squashes, and tobacco; but their cultivation was of the rudest sort,[2] and population was too sparse for much progress towards civilization. But Indian corn, when sown in carefully tilled and irrigated land, had much to do with the denser population, the increasing organization of labour, and the higher development in the arts, which characterized the confederacies of Mexico and Central America and all the pueblo Indians of the southwest. The potato played a somewhat similar part in Peru. Hence it seems proper to take the regular employment of tillage with irrigation as marking the end of the lower period of barbarism in the

[1] See Shaler, "Physiography of North America," in Winsor's *Narr. and Crit. Hist.*, vol. iv. p. xiii.

[2] "No manure was used," says Mr. Parkman, speaking of the Hurons, "but at intervals of from ten to twenty years, when the soil was exhausted and firewood distant, the village was abandoned and a new one built." *Jesuits in North America*, p. xxx.

34

New World. To this Mr. Morgan adds the use of adobe-brick and stone in architecture, which also distinguished the Mexicans and their neighbours from the ruder tribes of North and South America. All these ruder tribes, except the few already mentioned as in the upper period of savagery, were somewhere within the lower period of barbarism. Thus the Algonquins and Iroquois, the Creeks, the Dakotas, etc., when first seen by white men, were within this period; but some had made much further progress within it than others. For example, the Algonquin tribe of Ojibwas had little more than emerged from savagery, while the Creeks and Cherokees had made considerable advance towards the middle status of barbarism.

Let us now observe some characteristics of this extremely interesting middle period. It began, we see, in the eastern hemi- Middle status of barbarism sphere with the domestication of other animals than the dog, and in the western hemisphere with cultivation by irrigation and the use of adobe-brick and stone for building. It also possessed another feature which distinguished it from earlier periods, in the materials of which its tools were made. In the periods of savagery hatchets and spear-heads were made of rudely chipped stones. In the lower period of barbarism the chipping became more and more

skilful until it gave place to polishing. In the
middle period tools were greatly multiplied,
improved polishing gave sharp and accurate
points and edges, and at last metals began to be
used as materials preferable to stone. In America the metal used was copper, and in some spots
where it was very accessible there were instances
of its use by tribes not in other respects above
the lower status of barbarism, — as for example,
the " mound-builders." In the Old World the
metal used was the alloy of copper and tin
familiarly known as bronze, and in its working
it called for a higher degree of intelligence than
copper.

Towards the close of the middle period of
barbarism the working of metals became the
Working of most important element of progress,
metals and the period may be regarded as
ending with the invention of the process of
smelting iron ore. According to this principle
of division, the inhabitants of the lake villages
of ancient Switzerland, who kept horses and
oxen, pigs and sheep, raised wheat and ground
it into flour, and spun and wove linen garments,
but knew nothing of iron, were in the middle
status of barbarism. The same was true of the
ancient Britons before they learned the use of
iron from their neighbours in Gaul. In the
New World the representatives of the middle
status of barbarism were such peoples as the

Zuñis, the Aztecs, the Mayas, and the Peruvians.

The upper status of barbarism, in so far as it implies a knowledge of smelting iron, was never reached in aboriginal America. In the Old World it is the stage which had been reached by the Greeks of the Homeric poems [1] and the Germans in the

Upper status of barbarism

---

[1] In the interesting architectural remains unearthed by Dr. Schliemann at Mycenæ and Tiryns, there have been found at the former place a few iron keys and knives, at the latter one iron lance-head ; but the form and workmanship of these objects mark them as not older than the beginning of the fifth century B. C., or the time of the Persian wars. With these exceptions the weapons and tools found in these cities, as also in Troy, were of bronze and stone. Bronze was in common use, but obsidian knives and arrow-heads of fine workmanship abound in the ruins. According to Professor Sayce, these ruins must date from 2000 to 1700 B. C. The Greeks of that time would accordingly be placed in the middle status of barbarism. (See Schliemann's *Mycenæ*, pp. 75, 364; *Tiryns*, p. 171.) In the state of society described in the Homeric poems the smelting of iron was well known, but the process seems to have been costly, so that bronze weapons were still commonly used. (Tylor, *Anthropology*, p. 279.) The Romans of the regal period were ignorant of iron. (Lanciani, *Ancient Rome in the Light of Recent Discoveries*, Boston, 1888, pp. 39–48.) The upper period of barbarism was shortened for Greece and Rome through the circumstance that they learned the working of iron from Egypt and the use of the alphabet from Phœnicia. Such copying, of course, affects the symmetry of such schemes as Mr. Morgan's, and allowances have to be made for it. It is curious that both Greeks

time of Cæsar. The end of this period and the beginning of true civilization is marked by the invention of a phonetic alphabet and the production of written records. This brings within the pale of civilization such people as the ancient Phœnicians, the Hebrews after the exodus, the ruling classes at Nineveh and Babylon, the Aryans of Persia and India, and the Japanese. But clearly it will not do to insist too narrowly upon the phonetic character of the alphabet. Where people acquainted with iron have enshrined in hieroglyphics so much matter of historic record and literary interest as the Chinese and the ancient Egyptians, they too must be classed as civilized ; and this Mr. Morgan by implication admits.

Beginning of civilization

and Romans seem to have preserved some tradition of the Bronze Age : —

> τοῖς δ' ἦν χάλκεα μὲν τεύχεα, χάλκεοι δέ τε οἶκοι,
> χαλκῷ δ' εἰργάζοντο · μέλας δ' οὐκ ἔσκε σίδηρος.
>
> HESIOD, *Opp. Di.* 134.

> Arma antiqua manus ungues dentesque fuerunt
> Et lapides et item silvarum fragmina rami,
> Et flamma atque ignes, postquam sunt cognita primum.
> Posterius ferri vis est, ærisque reperta.
> Et prior æris erat, quam ferri cognitus usus, etc.
>
> Lucretius, v. 1283.

Perhaps, as Munro suggests, Lucretius was thinking of Hesiod ; but it does not seem improbable that in both cases there may have been a genuine tradition that their ancestors used bronze tools and weapons before iron, since the change was comparatively recent, and sundry religious observances tended to perpetuate the memory of it.

38

This brilliant classification of the stages of early culture will be found very helpful if we only keep in mind the fact that in all wide generalizations of this sort the case is liable to be somewhat unduly simplified. The story of human progress is really not quite so easy to decipher as such descriptions would make it appear, and when we have laid down rules of this sort we need not be surprised if we now and then come upon facts that will not exactly fit into them. In such an event it is best not to try to squeeze or distort the unruly facts, but to look and see if our rules will not bear some little qualification. The faculty for generalizing is a good servant but a bad master. If we observe this caution we shall find Mr. Morgan's work to be of great value. It will be observed that, with one exception, his restrictions leave the area of civilization as wide as that which we are accustomed to assign to it in our ordinary speaking and thinking. That exception is the case of Mexico, Central America, and Peru. We have so long been accustomed to gorgeous accounts of the civilization of these countries at the time of their discovery by the Spaniards that it may at first shock our preconceived notions to see them set down as in the " middle status of barbarism," one stage higher than Mohawks, and one stage lower than the warriors of the Iliad. This does indeed mark a change since Dr. Draper expressed the opinion that the Mexicans and Peruvians were morally and "Civilizations" of Mexico and Peru intellectually superior to the Europeans of the sixteenth century.[1] The reaction from the state of opinion in which such an extravagant remark was even possible has been attended with some controversy; but on the whole Mr. Morgan's main position has been steadily and rapidly gaining ground, and it is becoming more and more clear that if we are to use language correctly when we speak of the civilizations of Mexico and Peru, we really mean civilizations of an extremely archaic type, considerably more archaic than that of Egypt in the time of the Pharaohs. A "civilization" like that of the Aztecs, without domestic animals or iron tools, with trade still in the primitive stage of barter, with human sacrifices, and with cannibalism, has certainly some of the most vivid features of barbarism. Along with these primitive features, however, there seem to have been — after making all due allowances — some features of luxury and splendour such as we are wont to associate with civilization. The Aztecs, moreover, though doubtless a full ethnical period behind the ancient Egyptians in general advancement, had worked out a system of hieroglyphic writing, and had

[1] See his *Intellectual Development of Europe*, New York, 1863, pp. 448, 464.

begun to put it to some literary use. It would seem that a people may in certain special points reach a level of attainment higher than the level which they occupy in other points. The Cave men of the Glacial period were ignorant of pottery, and thus had not risen above the upper status of savagery; but their artistic talent, upon which we have remarked, was not such as we are wont to associate with savagery. Other instances will occur to us in the proper place.

The difficulty which people usually find in realizing the true position of the ancient Mexican culture arises partly from the misconceptions which have until recently distorted the facts, and partly from the loose employment of terms above noticed. It is quite correct to speak of the Australian black-fellows as "savages," but nothing is more common than to hear the same epithet employed to characterize Shawnees and Mohawks; and to call those Indians "savages" is quite misleading. So on the other hand the term "civilization" is often so loosely used as to cover a large territory belonging to "barbarism." One does not look for scientific precision in newspapers, but they are apt to reflect popular habits of thought quite faithfully, and for that reason it is proper here to quote from one. In a newspaper account of Mr. Cushing's recent discoveries of buried towns, works of irri-

Loose use of the words "savagery" and "civilization"

gation, etc., in Arizona, we are first told that
these are the remains of a " splendid prehistoric
civilization," and the next moment we are told,
in entire unconsciousness of the contradiction,
that the people who constructed these works
had only stone tools. Now to call a people
" civilized " who have only stone tools is utterly
misleading. Nothing but confusion of ideas
and darkening of counsel can come from such
a misuse of words. Such a people may be in a
high degree interesting and entitled to credit for
what they have achieved, but the grade of culture which they have reached is not " civilization."

With " savagery " thus encroaching upon its
area of meaning on the one side, and " civilization " encroaching on the other, the word " barbarism," as popularly apprehended, is left in a
vague and unsatisfactory plight. If we speak of
Montezuma's people as barbarians one stage
further advanced than Mohawks, we are liable
Value and   to be charged with calling them " sav-
importance   ages." Yet the term " barbarism " is
of the term
" barba-   a very useful one ; indispensable, in-
rism "   deed, in the history of human progress. There is no other word which can serve
in its stead as a designation of the enormous interval which begins with the invention of pottery
and ends with the invention of the alphabet.
The popular usage of the word is likely to be-

come more definite as it comes to be more generally realized how prodigious that interval has been. When we think what a considerable portion of man's past existence has been comprised within it, and what a marvellous transformation in human knowledge and human faculty has been gradually wrought between its beginning and its end, the period of barbarism becomes invested with most thrilling interest, and its name ceases to appear otherwise than respectable. It is Mr. Morgan's chief title to fame that he has so thoroughly explored this period and described its features with such masterly skill.

It is worth while to observe that Mr. Morgan's view of the successive stages of culture is one which could not well have been marked out in all its parts except by a student of American archæology. Aboriginal America is the richest field in the world for the study of barbarism. Its people present every gradation in social life during three ethnical periods, — the upper period of savagery and the lower and middle periods of barbarism, — so that the process of development may be most systematically and instructively studied. Until we have become familiar with ancient American society, and so long as our view is confined to the phases of progress in the Old World, the demarcation

The status of barbarism is most completely exemplified in ancient America

43

between civilized and uncivilized life seems too abrupt and sudden; we do not get a correct measure of it. The oldest European tradition reaches back only through the upper period of barbarism.[1] The middle and lower periods have lapsed into utter oblivion, and it is only modern archæological research that is beginning to recover the traces of them. But among the red men of America the social life of ages more remote than that of the lake villages of Switzerland is in many particulars preserved for us to-day, and when we study it we begin to realize as never before the continuity of human development, its enormous duration, and the almost infinite accumulation of slow efforts by which progress has been achieved. Ancient America is further instructive in presenting the middle status of barbarism in a different form from that which it assumed in the eastern hemisphere. Its most conspicuous outward manifestations, instead of tents and herds, were strange and imposing edifices of stone, so that it was quite natural that observers interpreting it from a basis of European experience should mistake it for civilization. Certain aspects of that middle period may be studied to-day in New Mexico and Arizona, as phases of the older periods

[1] Now and then, perhaps, but very rarely, it just touches the close of the middle period, as, *e. g.*, in the lines from Hesiod and Lucretius above quoted.

may still be found among the wilder tribes, even after all the contact they have had with white men. These survivals from antiquity will not permanently outlive that contact, and it is important that no time should be lost in gathering and putting on record all that can be learned of the speech and arts, the customs and beliefs, everything that goes to constitute the philology and anthropology of the red men. For the intelligent and vigorous work of this sort now conducted by the Bureau of Ethnology of the Smithsonian Institution, under the direction of Major Powell, no praise can be too strong and no encouragement too hearty.

Survivals of bygone epochs of culture

A brief enumeration of the principal groups of Indians will be helpful in enabling us to comprehend the social condition of ancient America. The groups are in great part defined by differences of language, which are perhaps a better criterion of racial affinity in the New World than in the Old, because there seems to have been little or nothing of that peculiar kind of conquest with incorporation resulting in complete change of speech which we sometimes find in the Old World; as, for example, when we see the Celto-Iberian population of Spain and the Belgic, Celtic, and Aquitanian populations of Gaul forgetting their native tongues, and

numerous were the Dakotas, comprising the Sioux, Poncas, Omahas, Iowas, Kaws, Otoes, and Missouris. From the headwaters of the Mississippi their territory extended westward on both sides of the Missouri for a thousand miles. One of their tribes, the Winnebagos, had crossed the Mississippi and pressed into the region between that river and Lake Michigan.

A second group, very small in numbers but extremely interesting to the student of ethnology, comprises the Minnitarees and Mandans on the upper Missouri.[1] The remnants of these tribes now live together in the same village, and in personal appearance, as well as in intelligence, they are described as superior to any other red men north of New Mexico. From their first discovery, by the brothers La Vérendrye in 1742, down to Mr. Catlin's visit nearly a century later, there was no change in their condition,[2] but shortly after-

The Minnitarees and Mandans

---

[1] An excellent description of them, profusely illustrated with coloured pictures, may be found in Catlin's *North American Indians*, vol. i. pp. 66–207, 7th ed., London, 1848; the author was an accurate and trustworthy observer. Some writers have placed these tribes in the Dakota group because of the large number of Dakota words in their language ; but these are probably borrowed words, like the numerous French words in English.

[2] See Francis Parkman's paper, "The Discovery of the Rocky Mountains," *Atlantic Monthly*, June, 1888. [Mr. Parkman's paper was later included, though with considerable

wards, in 1838, the greater part of them were swept away by smallpox. The excellence of their horticulture, the framework of their houses, and their peculiar religious ceremonies early attracted attention. Upon Mr. Catlin they made such an impression that he fancied there must be an infusion of white blood in them ; and after the fashion of those days he sought to account for it by a reference to the legend of Madoc, a Welsh prince who was dimly imagined to have sailed to America about 1170. He thought that Madoc's party might have sailed to the Mississippi and founded a colony which ascended that river and the Ohio, built the famous mounds of the Ohio valley, and finally migrated to the upper Missouri.[1] To this speculation was appended the inevitable list of words which happen to sound somewhat alike in Mandan and in Welsh. In the realm of free fancy everything is easy. That there was a Madoc who went somewhere in 1170 is quite possible, but as shrewd old John Smith said about it, " where this place was no history can show." [2] But one

revision and amplification, in *A Half-Century of Conflict*, where it appears in this new form as chapter xvi. Mr. Parkman, when putting his material into final shape, modified somewhat his statement that there had been no change in the condition of the Mandans.]

[1] *North American Indians*, vol. ii., Appendix A.

[2] Smith's *Generall Historie of Virginia, New England and the Summer Isles*, p. 1, London, 1626.

part of Mr. Catlin's speculation may have hit somewhat nearer the truth. It is possible that the Minnitarees or the Mandans, or both, may be a remnant of some of those Mound-builders in the Mississippi valley concerning whom something will presently be said.

The third group in this western region consists of the Pawnees and Arickarees,[1] of the Platte valley in Nebraska, with a few kindred tribes farther to the south.

Pawnees, etc.

Of the three groups eastward of the Mississippi we may first mention the Maskoki, or Muskhogees, consisting of the Choctaws, Chickasaws, Seminoles, and others, with the Creek confederacy.[2] These tribes were intelligent and powerful, with a culture well advanced towards the end of the lower period of barbarism.

Maskoki family

[1] For the history and ethnology of these interesting tribes, see three learned papers by J. B. Dunbar, in *Magazine of American History*, vol. iv. pp. 241–281; vol. v. pp. 321–342; vol. viii. pp. 734–756; also Grinnell's *Pawnee Hero Stories and Folk-Tales*, New York, 1889.

[2] These tribes of the Gulf region were formerly grouped, along with others not akin to them, as "Mobilians." The Cherokees were supposed to belong to the Maskoki family, but they have lately been declared an intrusive offshoot from the Iroquois stock. The remnants of another alien tribe, the once famous Natchez, were adopted into the Creek confederacy. For a full account of these tribes, see Gatschet, *A Migration Legend of the Creek Indians*, vol. i., Philadelphia, 1884.

The Algonquin family, bordering at its southern limits upon the Maskoki, had a vast range northeasterly along the Atlantic coast until it reached the confines of Labrador, and northwesterly through the region of the Great Lakes and as far as the Churchill River [1] to the west of Hudson's Bay. In other words, the Algonquins were bounded on the south by the Maskoki,[2] on the west by the Dakotas, on the northwest by the Athabaskans, on the northeast by Eskimos, and on the east by the ocean. Between Lake Superior and the Red River of the North the Crees had their hunting grounds, and closely related to them were the Pottawatomies, Ojibwas, and Ottawas. One offshoot, including the Blackfeet, Cheyennes, and Arrapahos, roamed as far west as the Rocky Mountains. The great triangle between the upper Mississippi and the Ohio was occupied by the Menomonees and Kickapoos, the Sacs and Foxes, the Miamis and Illinois, and the Shawnees. Along the coast region the principal Algonquin tribes were the Powhatans of Virginia, the Lenape or Delawares, the Munsees or Minisinks of the mountains about the Susquehanna, the Mohegans on the Hudson,

Algonquin family of tribes

[1] Howse, *Grammar of the Cree Language*, London, 1865, p. vii.

[2] Except in so far as the Cherokees and Tuscaroras, presently to be mentioned, were interposed.

the Adirondacks between that river and the St. Lawrence, the Narragansetts and their congeners in New England, and finally the Micmacs and Wabenaki far down East, as the last name implies. There is a tradition, supported to some extent by linguistic evidence,[1] that the Mohegans, with their cousins the Pequots, were more closely related to the Shawnees than to the Delaware or coast group. While all the Algonquin tribes were in the lower period of barbarism, there was a noticeable gradation among them, the Crees and Ojibwas of the far North standing lowest in culture, and the Shawnees, at their southernmost limits, standing highest.

We have observed the Dakota tribes pressing eastward against their neighbours and sending out an offshoot, the Winnebagos, across the Mississippi River. It has been supposed that the Huron-Iroquois group of tribes was a more remote offshoot from the Dakotas. This is very doubtful; but in the thirteenth or fourteenth century the general trend of the Huron-Iroquois movement seems to have been eastward, either in successive swarms, or in a single swarm, which became divided and scattered by segmentation, as was common with all Indian tribes. They seem early to have proved their superiority over the Algonquins in bravery and intelligence.

Huron-Iroquois family of tribes

[1] Brinton, *The Lenape and their Legends*, p. 30.

Their line of invasion seems to have run eastward to Niagara, and thereabouts to have bifurcated, one line following the valley of the St. Lawrence, and the other that of the Susquehanna. The Hurons established themselves in the peninsula between the lake that bears their name and Lake Ontario. South of them and along the northern shore of Lake Erie were settled their kindred, afterwards called the "Neutral Nation."[1] On the southern shore the Eries planted themselves, while the Susquehannocks pushed on in a direction sufficiently described by their name. Farthest of all penetrated the Tuscaroras, even into the pine forests of North Carolina, where they maintained themselves in isolation from their kindred until 1715. These invasions resulted in some displacement of Algonquin tribes, and began to sap the strength of the confederacy or alliance in which the Delawares had held a foremost place.

But by far the most famous and important of the Huron-Iroquois were those that followed the northern shore of Lake Ontario into the valley of the St. Lawrence. In that direction their progress was checked by the Algonquin tribe of Adirondacks, but they succeeded in re-

[1] Because they refused to take part in the strife between the Hurons and the Five Nations. Their Indian name was Attiwandarons. They were unsurpassed for ferocity. See Parkman, *Jesuits in North America*, p. xliv.

taining a foothold in the country for a long time; for in 1535 Jacques Cartier found on the site which he named Montreal an Iroquois village which had vanished before Champlain's arrival seventy years later. Those Iroquois who were thrust back in the struggle for the St. Lawrence valley, early in the fifteenth century, made their way across Lake Ontario and established themselves at the mouth of the Oswego River. They were then in three small tribes, — the Mohawks, Onondagas, and Senecas, — but as they grew in numbers and spread eastward to the Hudson and westward to the Genesee, the intermediate tribes of Oneidas and Cayugas were formed by segmentation.[1] About 1450 the five

The Five Nations

tribes — afterwards known as the Five Nations — were joined in a confederacy in pursuance of the wise counsel which Hayowentha, or Hiawatha,[2] according to the

---

[1] Morgan, *Ancient Society*, p. 125.

[2] Whether there was ever such a person as Hiawatha is, to say the least, doubtful. As a traditional culture-hero his attributes are those of Ioskeha, Michabo, Quetzalcoatl, Viracocha, and all that class of sky-gods to which I shall again have occasion to refer. See Brinton's *Myths of the New World*, p. 172. When the Indian speaks of Hiawatha whispering advice to Daganoweda, his meaning is probably the same as that of the ancient Greek when he attributed the wisdom of some mortal hero to whispered advice from Zeus or his messenger Hermes. Longfellow's famous poem is based upon Schoolcraft's book entitled *The Hiawatha Legends*,

legend, whispered into the ears of the Onondaga sachem, Daganoweda. This union of their resources combined, with their native bravery and cunning, and their occupation of the most commanding military position in eastern North America, to render them invincible among red men. They exterminated their old enemies the Adirondacks, and pushed the Mohegans over the mountains from the Hudson River to the Connecticut. When they first encountered white men in 1609 their name had become a terror in New England, insomuch that as soon as a single Mohawk was caught sight of by the Indians in that country, they would raise the cry from hill to hill, "A Mohawk! a Mohawk!" and forthwith would flee like sheep before wolves, never dreaming of resistance.[1]

After the Five Nations had been supplied with firearms by the Dutch their power increased with portentous rapidity.[2] At first they sought to persuade their neighbours of kindred blood and speech, the Eries and others, to join their confederacy ; and failing in this they went to

which is really a misnomer, for the book consists chiefly of Ojibwa stories about Manabozho, son of the West Wind. There was really no such legend of Hiawatha as that which the poet has immortalized. See Hale, *The Iroquois Book of Rites*, pp. 36, 180–183.

[1] Cadwallader Colden, *History of the Five Nations*, New York, 1727.

[2] Morgan, *League of the Iroquois*, p. 12.

war and exterminated them.[1] Then they overthrew one Algonquin tribe after another until
in 1690 their career was checked by the French.
By that time they had reduced to a tributary
condition most of the Algonquin tribes, even to
the Mississippi River. Some writers have spoken of the empire of the Iroquois, and it has
been surmised that, if they had not been inter-
fered with by white men, they might have
played a part analogous to that of the Romans
in the Old World ; but there is no real similarity between the two cases. The Romans acquired their mighty strength by incorporating
vanquished peoples into their own body politic.[2]
No American aborigines ever had a glimmer-
ing of the process of state-building after the
Roman fashion. No incorporation resulted
from the victories of the Iroquois. Where their
burnings and massacres stopped short of extermination, they simply took tribute, which was
as far as state-craft had got in the lower period
of barbarism. General Walker has summed
up their military career in a single sentence :

[1] All except the distant Tuscaroras, who in 1715 migrated
from North Carolina to New York, and joining the Iroquois
league made it the Six Nations. All the rest of the outlying
Huron-Iroquois stock was wiped out of existence before the
end of the seventeenth century, except the remnant of Hurons since known as Wyandots.

[2] See my *Beginnings of New England*, chap. i.

"They were the scourge of God upon the aborigines of the continent."[1]

The six groups here enumerated — Dakota, Mandan, Pawnee, Maskoki, Algonquin, Iroquois — made up the great body of the aborigines of North America who at the time of the Discovery lived in the lower status of barbarism. All made pottery of various degrees of rudeness. Their tools and weapons were of the Neolithic type, — stone either polished or accurately and artistically chipped. For the most part they lived in stockaded villages, and culti-

Horticulture must be distinguished from field agriculture

vated maize, beans, pumpkins, squashes, sunflowers, and tobacco. They depended for subsistence partly upon such vegetable products, partly upon hunting and fishing, the women generally attending to the horticulture, the men to the chase. *Horticulture* is an appropriate designation for this stage in which the ground is merely scratched with stone spades and hoes. It is incipient agriculture, but should be carefully distinguished from the *field agriculture* in which extensive pieces of land are subdued by the plough. The assistance of domestic animals is needed before such work can be carried far, and it does not appear that there was an approach to field agriculture in any part of pre-

[1] F. A. Walker, "The Indian Question," *North American Review*, April, 1873, p. 370.

Columbian America except Peru, where men were harnessed to the plough, and perhaps occasionally llamas were used in the same way.[1] Where subsistence depended upon rude horticulture eked out by game and fish, it required a large territory to support a sparse population. The great diversity of languages contributed to maintain the isolation of tribes and prevent extensive confederation. Intertribal warfare was perpetual, save now and then for truces of brief duration. Warfare was attended by wholesale massacre. As many prisoners as could be managed were taken home by their captors; in some cases they were adopted into the tribe of the latter as a means of increasing its fighting strength, otherwise they were put to death with lingering torments.[2] There was

Perpetual warfare

[1] See Humboldt, *Ansichten der Natur*, 3d ed., Stuttgart, 1849, vol. i. p. 203.

[2] "Women and children joined in these fiendish atrocities, and when at length the victim yielded up his life, his heart, if he were brave, was ripped from his body, cut in pieces, broiled, and given to the young men, under the belief that it would increase their courage; they drank his blood, thinking it would make them more wary; and finally his body was divided limb from limb, roasted or thrown into the seething pot, and hands and feet, arms and legs, head and trunk, were all stewed into a horrid mess and eaten amidst yells, songs, and dances." Jeffries Wyman, in *Seventh Report of Peabody Museum*, p. 37. For details of the most appalling character, see Butterfield's *History of the Girtys*, pp. 176–182; Stone's *Life of Joseph Brant*, vol.

nothing which afforded the red men such exquisite delight as the spectacle of live human flesh lacerated with stone knives or hissing under the touch of firebrands, and for elaborate ingenuity in devising tortures they have never been equalled.[1]   Cannibalism was quite com-

ii. pp. 31, 32 ; Dodge's *Plains of the Great West,* p. 418, and *Our Wild Indians,* pp. 525–529 ; Parkman's *Jesuits in North America,* pp. 387–391 ; and many other places in Parkman's writings.

[1] One often hears it said that the cruelty of the Indians was not greater than that of mediæval Europeans, as exemplified in judicial torture and in the horrors of the Inquisition. But in such a judgment there is lack of due discrimination. In the practice of torture by civil and ecclesiastical tribunals in the Middle Ages, there was a definite moral purpose which, however lamentably mistaken or perverted, gave it a very different character from torture wantonly inflicted for amusement. The atrocities formerly attendant upon the sack of towns, as *e. g.* Beziers, Magdeburg, etc., might more properly be regarded as an illustration of the survival of a spirit fit only for the lowest barbarism : and the Spanish conquerors of the New World themselves often exhibited cruelty such as even Indians seldom surpass. See below, vol. iii. p. 267. In spite of such cases, however, it must be held that for artistic skill in inflicting the greatest possible intensity of excruciating pain upon every nerve in the body, the Spaniard was a bungler and a novice as compared with the Indian. See Dodge's *Our Wild Indians,* pp. 536–538. Colonel Dodge was in familiar contact with Indians for more than thirty years, and writes with fairness and discrimination.

In truth the question as to comparative cruelty is not so much one of race as of occupation, except in so far as race is moulded by long occupation. The "old Adam,"

monly practised.[1] The scalps of slain enemies
were always taken, and until they had attained

i. e. the inheritance from our brute ancestors, is very strong
in the human race. Callousness to the suffering of others than
self is part of this brute inheritance, and under the influence
of certain habits and occupations this germ of callousness may
be developed to almost any height of devilish cruelty. In the
lower stages of culture the lack of political aggregation on a
large scale is attended with incessant warfare in the shape in
which it comes home to everybody's door. This state of
things keeps alive the passion of revenge and stimulates cruelty
to the highest degree. As long as such a state of things en-
dures, as it did in Europe to a limited extent throughout the
Middle Ages, there is sure to be a dreadful amount of cruelty.
The change in the conditions of modern warfare has been a
very important factor in the rapidly increasing mildness and
humanity of modern times. See my *Beginnings of New England*, chap. v. Something more will be said hereafter with
reference to the special causes concerned in the cruelty and
brutality of the Spaniards in America. Meanwhile it may be
observed in the present connection, that the Spanish taskmasters who mutilated and burned their slaves were not
representative types of their own race to anything like the
same extent as the Indians who tortured Brébeuf or Crawford.
If the fiendish Pedrarias was a Spaniard, so too was the saintly
Las Casas. The latter type would be as impossible among
barbarians as an Aristotle or a Beethoven. Indeed, though
there are writers who would like to prove the contrary, it
may be doubted whether that type has ever attained to per-
fection except under the influence of Christianity.

[1] See the evidence collected by Jeffries Wyman, in *Seventh
Report of Peabody Museum*, pp. 27–37 ; cf. Wake, *Evolution of Morality*, vol. i. p. 243. Many illustrations are
given by Mr. Parkman. In this connection it may be ob-

such trophies the young men were not likely
to find favour in the eyes of women. The
Indian's notions of morality were those that
belong to that state of society in which the tribe
is the largest well-established political aggregate. Murder without the tribe was meritorious
unless it entailed risk of war at an obvious dis-
advantage ; murder within the tribe was either
revenged by blood-feud or compounded by a
present given to the victim's kinsmen. Such
rudimentary *wergild* was often reckoned in
wampum, or strings of beads made of a kind
of mussel-shell, and put to divers uses, as personal ornament, mnemonic record, and finally
money. Religious thought was in the fetich-
istic or animistic stage,[1] while many tribes had
risen to a vague conception of tutelar deities
embodied in human or animal forms. Myth-
tales abounded, and the folk-lore of the red
men is found to be extremely interesting and

served that the name " Mohawk " means " Cannibal." It
is an Algonquin word, applied to this Iroquois tribe by their
enemies in the Connecticut valley and about the lower Hudson. The name by which the Mohawks called themselves
was " Caniengas," or " People-at-the-Flint." See Hale,
The Iroquois Book of Rites, p. 173.

[1] For accounts and explanations of animism, see Tylor's
Primitive Culture, London, 1871, 2 vols. ; Caspari, *Urge-
schichte der Menschheit,* Leipsic, 1877, 2 vols. ; Spencer's
Principles of Sociology, part i.; and my *Myths and Myth-
Makers,* chap. vii.

instructive.[1] Their religion consisted mainly in a devout belief in witchcraft. No well-defined priestly class had been evolved; the so-called "medicine men" were mere conjurers, though possessed of considerable influence.

But none of the characteristics of barbarous society above specified will carry us so far towards realizing the gulf which divides it from civilized society as the imperfect development of its domestic relations. The importance of this subject is such as to call for a few words of special elucidation.

Thirty years ago, when Sir Henry Maine

[1] No time should be lost in gathering and recording every scrap of this folk-lore that can be found. The American Folk-Lore Society, founded chiefly through the exertions of my friend Mr. W. W. Newell, and organized January 4, 1888, is already doing excellent work and promises to become a valuable aid, within its field, to the work of the Bureau of Ethnology. Of the *Journal of American Folk-Lore*, published for the society by Messrs. Houghton, Mifflin & Co., nine numbers have appeared [1891], and the reader will find them full of valuable information. One may also profitably consult Knortz's *Mährchen und Sagen der nordamerikanischen Indianer*, Jena, 1871 ; Brinton's *Myths of the New World*, N. Y., 1868, and his *American Hero-Myths*, Phila., 1882; Leland's *Algonquin Legends of New England*, Boston, 1884; Mrs. Emerson's *Indian Myths*, Boston, 1884. Some brief reflections and criticisms of much value, in relation to aboriginal American folk-lore, may be found in Curtin's *Myths and Folk-Lore of Ireland*, pp. 12–27.

published that magnificent treatise on "Ancient
Law," which, when considered in all its potency
of suggestiveness, has perhaps done more than
any other single book of our century towards
placing the study of history upon a scientific
basis, he began by showing that in
primitive society the individual is   Ancient Law
nothing and the state nothing, while the family-
group is everything, and that the progress of
civilization politically has consisted on the one
hand in the aggregation and building up of
family-groups through intermediate tribal or-
ganizations into states, and on the other hand
in the disentanglement of individuals from the
family thraldom. In other words, we began by
having no political communities larger than
clans, and no bond of political union except
blood-relationship, and in this state of things
the individual, as to his rights and obligations,
was submerged in the clan. We at length come
to have great nations like the English or the
French, in which blood-relationship as a bond
of political union is no longer indispensable or
even much thought of, and in which the individual citizen is the possessor of legal rights
and subject to legal obligations. No one in
our time can forget how beautifully Sir Henry
Maine, with his profound knowledge of early
Aryan law and custom, from Ireland to Hindustan, delineated the slow growth of individual

ownership of property and individual responsibility for delict and crime out of an earlier stage in which ownership and responsibility belonged only to family-groups or clans.

In all these brilliant studies Sir Henry Maine started with the patriarchal family as we find it at the dawn of history among all peoples of Aryan and Semitic speech, — the patriarchal family of the ancient Roman and the ancient Jew, the family in which kinship is reckoned through males, and in which all authority centres in the eldest male, and descends to his eldest son. Maine treated this patriarchal family as primitive; but his great book had hardly appeared when other scholars, more familiar than he with races in savagery or in the lower status of barbarism, showed that his view was too restricted. We do not get back to primitive society by studying Greeks, Romans, and Jews, peoples who had nearly emerged from the later period of barbarism when we first know them.[1] Their patri-

The patriarchal family not primitive

---

[1] Until lately our acquaintance with human history was derived almost exclusively from literary memorials, among which the Bible, the Homeric poems, and the Vedas, carried us back about as far as literature could take us. It was natural, therefore, to suppose that the society of the times of Abraham or Agamemnon was " primitive," and the wisest scholars reasoned upon such an assumption. With vision thus restricted to civilized man and his ideas and works, people felt free to speculate about uncivilized races (generally grouped

archal family was perfected in shape during the later period of barbarism, and it was preceded by a much ruder and less definite form of family-group in which kinship was reckoned only through the mother, and the headship never descended from father to son. As so often happens, this discovery was made almost simultaneously by two investigators, each working in ignorance of what the other was doing. In 1861, the same year in which " Ancient Law " was published, Professor Bachofen, of Basel, published his famous book, " Das Mutterrecht," of "Mother-right" which his co-discoverer and rival, after taking exception to some of his statements, thus cordially writes : " It remains, however, after all qualifications and deductions, that Bachofen, before any one else, discovered the fact that a system of kinship through mothers only had anciently everywhere prevailed before the tie of blood between father and child had found a place in systems of relationships. And the honour of that discovery, the importance of which, as affording a new starting-point for all

together indiscriminately as " savages ") according to any *a priori* whim that might happen to captivate their fancy. But the discoveries of the last half-century have opened such stupendous vistas of the past that the age of Abraham seems but as yesterday. The state of society described in the book of Genesis had five entire ethnical periods, and the greater part of a sixth, behind it ; and its institutions were, comparatively speaking, modern.

65

history, cannot be overestimated, must without stint or qualification be assigned to him." [1] Such are the generous words of the late John Ferguson McLennan, who had no knowledge of Bachofen's work when his own treatise on "Primitive Marriage" was published in 1865. Since he was so modest in urging his own claims, it is due to the Scotch lawyer's memory to say that, while he was inferior in point of erudition to the Swiss professor, his book is

Primitive marriage — characterized by greater sagacity, goes more directly to the mark, and is less encumbered by visionary speculations of doubtful value. [2] Mr. McLennan proved, from evidence collected chiefly from Australians and South Sea Islanders, and sundry non-Aryan tribes of Hindustan and Thibet, that systems of kinship in which the father is ignored exist to-day, and he furthermore discovered unmistakable and very significant traces of the former existence of such a state of things among the Mongols, the Greeks and Phœnicians, and the ancient Hebrews. By those who were inclined to regard Sir Henry Maine's views as final, it was argued that Mr. McLennan's facts were

[1] McLennan's *Studies in Ancient History, comprising a reprint of Primitive Marriage,* etc. London, 1876, p. 421.

[2] There is much that is unsound in it, however, as is often inevitably the case with books that strike boldly into a new field of inquiry.

of a sporadic and exceptional character. But when the evidence from this vast archaic world of America began to be gathered in and interpreted by Mr. Morgan, this argument fell to the ground, and as to the point chiefly in contention, Mr. McLennan was proved to be right. Throughout aboriginal America, with one or two exceptions, kinship was reckoned through females only, and in the exceptional instances the vestiges of that system were so prominent as to make it clear that the change had been but recently effected. During the past fifteen years, evidence has accumulated from various parts of the world, until it is beginning to appear as if it were the patriarchal system that is exceptional, having been reached only by the highest races.[1]

The system of reckoning kinship through females only

[1] A general view of the subject may be obtained from the following works: Bachofen, *Das Mutterrecht*, Stuttgart, 1871, and *Die Sage von Tanaquil*, Heidelberg, 1870; McLennan's *Studies in Ancient History*, London, 1876, and *The Patriarchal Theory*, London, 1884; Morgan's *Systems of Consanguinity* (Smithsonian Contributions to Knowledge, vol. xvii.), Washington, 1871, and *Ancient Society*, New York, 1877; Robertson Smith, *Kinship and Marriage in Early Arabia*, Cambridge, Eng., 1885; Lubbock, *Origin of Civilization*, 5th ed., London, 1889; Giraud-Teulon, *La Mère chez certains peuples de l'antiquité*, Paris, 1867, and *Les Origines de la Famille*, Geneva, 1874; Starcke (of Copenhagen), *The Primitive Family*, London, 1889. Some criticisms upon McLennan and Morgan may be found in Maine's later works, *Early History of Institutions*, London,

Sir Henry Maine's work has lost none of its value, only, like all human work, it is not final; it needs to be supplemented by the further study of savagery as best exemplified in Australia and some parts of Polynesia, and of barbarism as best exemplified in America. The subject is, moreover, one of great and complicated difficulty, and leads incidentally to many questions for solving which the data at our command are still inadequate. It is enough for us now to observe in general that while there are plenty of instances of change from the system of reckoning kinship only through females, to the system of reckoning through males, there do not appear to have been any instances of change in the reverse direction; and that in ancient America the earlier system was prevalent.

If now we ask the reason for such a system of reckoning kinship and inheritance, so strange according to all our modern notions, the true answer doubtless is that which was given by prudent (πεπνυμένος) Telemachus to the goddess Athene when she asked him to tell her truly if he was the son of Odysseus : " My mother says I am his son, for my part, I don't know ; one never knows of one's

Original reason for the system

1875, and *Early Law and Custom*, London, 1883. By far the ablest critical survey of the whole field is that in Spencer's *Principles of Sociology*, vol. i. pp. 621–797.

self who one's father is." [1] Already, no doubt,
in Homer's time there was a gleam of satire
about this answer, such as it would show on a
modern page; but in more primitive times it
was a very serious affair. From what we know
of the ideas and practices of uncivilized tribes
all over the world, it is evident that the sacred-
ness of the family based upon indissoluble marriage is a thing of comparatively modern growth.
If the sexual relations of the Australians, as observed to-day,[2] are an improvement upon an
antecedent state of things, that antece-   The primeval
dent state must have been sheer pro-   human horde
miscuity. There is ample warrant for supposing,
with Mr. McLennan, that at the beginning of
the lower status of savagery, long since every-

[1] Ἀλλ' ἄγε μοι τόδε εἰπὲ καὶ ἀτρεκέως κατάλεξον,
εἰ δὴ ἐξ αὐτοῖο τόσος παῖς εἰς Ὀδυσῆος.
αἰνῶς γὰρ κεφαλήν τε καὶ ὄμματα καλὰ ἔοικας
κείνῳ, ἐπεὶ θαμὰ τοῖον ἐμισγόμεθ' ἀλλήλοισιν,
πρίν γε τὸν ἐς Τροίην ἀναβήμεναι, ἔνθα περ ἄλλοι
Ἀργείων οἱ ἄριστοι ἔβαν κοίλης ἐπὶ νηυσίν·
ἐκ τοῦ δ' οὔτ' Ὀδυσῆα ἐγὼν ἴδον οὔτ' ἐμὲ κεῖνος.
Τὴν δ' αὖ Τηλέμαχος πεπνυμένος ἀντίον ηὔδα
τοιγὰρ ἐγώ τοι, ξεῖνε, μάλ' ἀτρεκέως ἀγορεύσω.
μήτηρ μέν τ' ἐμέ φησι τοῦ ἔμμεναι, αὐτὰρ ἔγωγε
οὐκ οἶδ'· οὐ γάρ πώ τις ἑὸν γόνον αὐτὸς ἀνέγνω.
Odyssey, i. 206.

[2] Lumholtz, *Among Cannibals*, p. 213; Lubbock, *Origin of
Civilization*, p. 107 ; Morgan, *Ancient Society*, part iii., ch. iii.
" After battle it frequently happens among the native tribes of
Australia that the wives of the conquered, of their own free-will,
go over to the victors ; reminding us of the lioness which, quietly
watching the fight between two lions, goes off with the con-
queror." Spencer, *Principles of Sociology*, vol. i. p. 632.

where extinct, the family had not made itself distinctly visible, but men lived in a horde very much like gregarious brutes.[1] I have shown that the essential difference between this primeval human horde and a mere herd of brutes consisted in the fact that the gradual but very great prolongation of infancy had produced two effects : the lengthening of the care of children tended to differentiate the horde into family-groups, and the lengthening of the period of youthful mental plasticity made it more possible for a new generation to improve upon the ideas and customs of its predecessors.[2] In these two

[1] The notion of the descent of the human race from a single " pair," or of different races from different " pairs," is a curious instance of transferring modern institutions into times primeval. Of course the idea is absurd. When the elder Agassiz so emphatically declared that " pines have originated in forests, heaths in heaths, grasses in prairies, bees in hives, herrings in shoals, buffaloes in herds, men in nations " (*Essay on Classification*, London, 1859, p. 58), he made, indeed, a mistake of the same sort, so far as concerns the origin of Man, for the nation is a still more modern institution than the family ; but in the other items of his statement he was right, and as regards the human race he was thinking in the right direction when he placed *multitude* instead of *duality* at the beginning. If instead of that extremely complex and highly organized multitude called " nation " (in the plural), he had started with the extremely simple and almost unorganized multitude called " horde " (in the singular), the statement for Man would have been correct. Such views were hardly within the reach of science thirty years ago.

[2] *Outlines of Cosmic Philosophy*, part ii., chaps. xvi.,

concomitant processes — the development of
the family and the increase of mental plasticity,
or ability to adopt new methods and strike out
into new paths of thought — lies the whole explanation of the moral and intellectual superiority of men over dumb animals. But in each case
the change was very gradual.[1] The true savage
is only a little less unteachable than the beasts
of the field. The savage family is at first barely
discernible amid the primitive social chaos in
which it had its origin. Along with polyandry
and polygyny in various degrees and forms, instances of exclusive pairing, of at least a temporary character, are to be found among the lowest
existing savages, and there are reasons Earliest fam-
for supposing that such may have been ily-group:
the case even in primeval times. But the clan
it was impossible for strict monogamy to flourish
in the ruder stages of social development; and
the kind of family-group that was first clearly
and permanently differentiated from the primeval horde was not at all like what civilized people
would recognize as a family. It was the *gens* or

xxi., xxii.; *Excursions of an Evolutionist*, xii.; *Darwinism,
and other Essays*, iii.; *The Destiny of Man*, §§ iii.-ix.

[1] The slowness of the development has apparently been
such as befits the transcendent value of the result. Though
the question is confessedly beyond the reach of science, may
we not hold that civilized man, the creature of an infinite
past, is the child of eternity, maturing for an inheritance of
immortal life?

71

clan, as we find it exemplified in all stages from the middle period of savagery to the middle period of barbarism. The *gens* or *clan* was simply — to define it by a third synonym — the *kin;* it was originally a group of males and females who were traditionally aware of their common descent reckoned in the female line. At this stage of development there was quite generally though not universally prevalent the custom of " exogamy," by which a man was forbidden to marry a woman of his own clan. Among such Australian tribes as have been studied, this primitive restriction upon promiscuity seems to be about the only one.

"Exogamy"

Throughout all the earlier stages of culture, and even into the civilized period, we find society organized with the clan for its ultimate unit, although in course of time its character becomes greatly altered by the substitution of kinship in the paternal, for that in the maternal line. By long-continued growth and repeated segmentation the primitive clan was developed into a more complex structure, in which a group of clans constituted a *phratry* or brotherhood, and a group of phratries constituted a *tribe.* This threefold grouping is found so commonly in all parts of the world as to afford good ground for the belief that it has been universal. It was long ago familiar to historians in the case of Greece and Rome, and of our

Phratry and tribe

founded was not the family but the exogamous
clan.

I have been at some pains to elucidate this
point because the house-life of the American
aborigines found visible, and in some instances
very durable, expression in a remarkable style
of house-architecture. The manner in which the
Indians built their houses grew directly out of
the requirements of their life. It was an unmistakably characteristic architecture, and while it
exhibits manifold unlikenesses in detail, due to
differences in intelligence as well as to
the presence or absence of sundry materials, there is one underlying principle always manifest. That underlying
principle is adaptation to a certain
mode of communal living such as all American
aborigines that have been carefully studied are
known to have practised. Through many grada-
tions, from the sty of the California savage up
to the noble sculptured ruins of Uxmal and
Chichen-Itza, the principle is always present.
Taken in connection with evidence from other
sources, it enables us to exhibit a gradation of
stages of culture in aboriginal North America,
with the savages of the Sacramento and Columbia valleys at the bottom, and the Mayas of
Yucatan at the top; and while in going from
one end to the other a very long interval was

Intimate connection of aboriginal architecture with social life

rule, was occupied by related families, the mothers and their children belonging to the same gens, while their husbands and the fathers of these children belonged to other gentes; consequently the gens or clan of the mother largely predominated in the household. Whatever was taken in the hunt or raised by cultivation by any member of the household . . . was for the common benefit. Provisions were made a common stock within the household."[1]

" Over every such household a matron presided, whose duty it was to supervise its domestic economy. After the single daily meal had been cooked at the different fires within the house, it was her province to divide the food from the kettle to the several families according to their respective needs. What remained was placed in the custody of another person until she again required it."[2]

Not only the food was common property, but many chattels, including the children, belonged to the gens or clan. When a young

[1] The Iroquois ceased to build such houses before the beginning of the present century. I quote Mr. Morgan's description at length, because his book is out of print and hard to obtain. It ought to be republished, and in octavo, like his *Ancient Society*, of which it is a continuation.

[2] Lucien Carr, " On the Social and Political Position of Woman among the Huron-Iroquois Tribes," *Reports of Peabody Museum*, vol. iii. p. 215.

woman got married she brought her husband home with her. Though thenceforth an inmate of this household he remained an alien to her clan. " If he proved lazy and failed to do his share of the providing, woe be to him. No matter how many children, or whatever goods he might have in the house, he might at any time be ordered to pick up his blanket and Summary budge; and after such orders it would divorce not be healthful for him to disobey; the house would be too hot for him; and unless saved by the intercession of some aunt or grandmother [of his wife] he must retreat to his own clan, or, as was often done, go and start a new matrimonial alliance in some other. . . . The female portion ruled the house." [1]

Though there was but one freshly cooked meal, taken about the middle of the day, any member of the household when hungry could be helped from the common stock. Hospitality was universal. If a person from one of the other communal households, or a stranger from another tribe (in time of peace), were to visit the house, the women would immediately offer him food, and it was a Hospitality breach of etiquette to decline to eat it. This cus-

---

[1] This was not incompatible with the subjection of women to extreme drudgery and ill-treatment. For an instructive comparison with the case among the tribes of the Far West, see Dodge, *Our Wild Indians,* chap. xvi.

tom was strictly observed all over the continent and in the West India Islands, and was often remarked upon by the early discoverers, in whose minds it was apt to implant idyllic notions that were afterwards rudely disturbed. The prevalence of hospitality among uncivilized races has long been noted by travellers, and is probably in most cases, as it certainly was in ancient America, closely connected with communism in living.

The clan, which practised this communism, had its definite organization, officers, rights, and duties. Its official head was the " sachem," whose functions were of a civil nature. The sachem was elected by the clan and must be a member of it, so that a son could not be chosen to succeed his father, but a sachem could be succeeded by his uterine brother or by his sister's son, and in this way customary lines of succession could and often did tend to become established. The clan also elected its " chiefs," whose functions were military; the number of chiefs was proportionate to that of the people composing the clan, usually one chief to every fifty or sixty persons. The clan could depose its sachem or any of its chiefs. Personal property, such as weapons, or trophies, or rights of user in the garden-plots, was inheritable in the female line, and thus stayed within the clan. The members were re-

Structure of the clan

ciprocally bound to help, defend, and avenge one
another. The clan had the right of adopting
strangers to strengthen itself. It had the right
of naming its members, and these names were
always obviously significant, like Little Turtle,
Yellow Wolf, etc.; of names like our Richard
or William, with the meaning lost, or obvious
only to scholars, no trace is to be found in aboriginal America. The clan itself, too, always
had a name, which was usually that of some
animal, as Wolf, Eagle, or Salmon, and a rude
drawing or pictograph of the creature served
as a "totem" or primitive heraldic device. A
mythological meaning was attached to this emblem. The clan had its own common religious
rites and common burial place. There was a
clan-council, of which women might be members; there were instances, indeed, of its being
composed entirely of women, whose position
was one of much more dignity and influence
than has commonly been supposed. Instances
of squaw sachems were not so very rare.[1]

---

[1] Among the Wyandots there is in each clan a council
composed of four squaws, and this council elects the male
sachem who is its head. Therefore the tribal-council, which
is the aggregate of the clan-councils, consists one fifth of men
and four fifths of women. See Powell, "Wyandot Government : a Short Study of Tribal Society," in *First Annual
Report of the Bureau of Ethnology*, Washington, 1881, pp.
59–69 ; and also Mr. Carr's interesting essay above cited.

The number of clans in a tribe naturally bore some proportion to the populousness of the tribe, varying from three, in the case of the Delawares, to twenty or more, as in the case of the Ojibwas and Creeks. There were usually eight or ten, and these were usually grouped into two or three phratries. The phratry seems to have originated in the segmentation of the overgrown clan, for in some cases exogamy was originally practised as between the phratries and afterwards the custom died out while it was retained as between their constituent clans.[1] The system of naming often indicates this origin of the phratry, though seldom quite so forcibly as in the case of the Mohegan tribe, which was thus composed:[2] —

Origin and
structure of
the phratry

I. Wolf Phratry.

Clans: 1. Wolf, 2. Bear, 3. Dog, 4. Opossum.

II. Turtle Phratry.

Clans: 5. Little Turtle, 6. Mud Turtle, 7. Great Turtle, 8. Yellow Eel.

III. Turkey Phratry.

Clans: 9. Turkey, 10. Crane, 11. Chicken.

Here the senior clan in the phratry tends to

[1] H. H. Bancroft, *Native Races of the Pacific States,* vol. i. p. 109.

[2] Morgan, *Houses and House-Life,* p. 16.

keep the original clan-name, while the junior clans have been guided by a sense of kinship in choosing their new names. This origin of the phratry is further indicated by the fact that the phratry does not always occur ; sometimes the clans are organized directly into the tribe. The phratry was not so much a governmental as a religious and social organization. Its most important function seems to have been supplementing or reinforcing the action of the single clan in exacting compensation for murder; and this point is full of interest because it helps us to understand how among our Teutonic forefathers the " hundred " (the equivalent of the phratry) became charged with the duty of prosecuting criminals. The Greek phratry had a precisely analogous function.[1]

The Indian tribe was a group of people distinguished by the exclusive possession of a dialect in common. It possessed a tribal name and occupied a more or less clearly defined territory ; there were also tribal religious rites. Its supreme government was vested in the council of its clan-chiefs and sachems ;

Structure of the tribe

---

[1] See Freeman, *Comparative Politics*, p. 117 ; Stubbs, *Const. Hist.*, vol. i. pp. 98–104 ; Grote, *History of Greece*, vol. iii. pp. 74, 88. It is interesting to compare Grote's description with Morgan's (*Anc. Soc.*, pp. 71, 94) and note both the closeness of the general parallelism and the character of the specific variations.

and as these were thus officers of the tribe as well as of the clan, the tribe exercised the right of investing them with office, amid appropriate solemnities, after their election by their respective clans. The tribal-council had also the right to depose chiefs and sachems. In some instances, not always, there was a head chief or military commander for the tribes, elected by the tribal-council. Such was the origin of the office which, in most societies of the Old World, gradually multiplied its functions and accumulated power until it developed into true kingship. Nowhere in ancient North America did it quite reach such a stage.

Among the greater part of the aborigines no higher form of social structure was attained than the tribe. There were, however, several instances of permanent confederation, of which the two most interesting and most highly developed were the League of the Iroquois, mentioned above, and the Mexican confederacy, presently to be considered. The principles upon which the Iroquois league was founded have been thoroughly and minutely explained by Mr. Morgan.[1] It originated in a union of five

Cross-relationships between clans and tribes : the Iroquois confederacy

---

[1] In his *League of the Iroquois*, Rochester, 1851, a book now out of print and excessively rare. A brief summary is given in his *Ancient Society*, chap. v., and in his *Houses and House-Life*, pp. 23–41. Mr. Morgan was adopted into the

tribes composed of clans in common, and speaking five dialects of a common language. These tribes had themselves arisen through the segmentation of a single overgrown tribe, so that portions of the original clans survived in them all. The Wolf, Bear, and Turtle clan were common to all the five tribes ; three other clans were common to three of the five. " All the members of the same gens [clan], whether Mohawks, Oneidas, Onondagas, Cayugas, or Senecas, were brothers and sisters to each other in virtue of their descent from the same common [female] ancestor, and they recognized each other as such with the fullest cordiality. When they met, the first inquiry was the name of each other's gens, and next the immediate pedigree of each other's sachems ; after which they were able to find, under their peculiar system of consanguinity, the relationship in which they stood to each other. . . . This cross-relationship between persons of the same gens in the different tribes is still preserved and recognized among them in all its original force. It explains the tenacity with which the fragments of the old confederacy still cling together."[1] Acknow-

Seneca tribe, and his life work was begun by a profound and exhaustive study of this interesting people.

[1] *Houses and House-Life*, p. 33. At the period of its greatest power, about 1675, the people of the confederacy were about 25,000 in number. In 1875, according to

ledged consanguinity is to the barbarian a sound
reason, and the only one conceivable, for permanent political union; and the very existence
of such a confederacy as that of the Five Nations was rendered possible only through the
permanence of the clans or communal households which were its ultimate units. We have
here a clue to the policy of these Indians
towards the kindred tribes who refused to join
their league. These tribes, too, so far as is
known, would seem to have contained the same
clans. After a separation of at least four hundred years the Wyandots have still five of their
eight clans in common with the Iroquois. When

official statistics (see table appended to Dodge's *Plains of the
Great West*, pp. 441–448), there were in the state of New
York 198 Oneidas, 203 Onondagas, 165 Cayugas, 3043
Senecas, and 448 Tuscaroras, — in all 4057. Besides
these there were 1279 Oneidas on a reservation in Wisconsin, and 207 Senecas in the Indian Territory. The Mohawks are not mentioned in the list. During the Revolution-
ary War, and just afterwards, the Mohawks migrated into
Upper Canada (Ontario), for an account of which the reader
may consult the second volume of Stone's *Life of Brant*.
Portions of the other tribes also went to Canada. In New
York the Oneidas and Tuscaroras were converted to Christianity by Samuel Kirkland and withheld from alliance with
the British during the Revolution; the others still retain their
ancient religion. They are for the most part farmers and are
now increasing in numbers. Their treatment by the state of
New York has been honourably distinguished for justice and
humanity.

88

the Eries and other tribes would not join the
league of their kindred, the refusal smacked of
treason to the kin, and we can quite understand
the deadly fury with which the latter turned
upon them and butchered every man, woman,
and child except such as they saw fit to adopt
into their own clans.

Each of the Five Tribes retained its local
self-government. The supreme government of
the confederacy was vested in a General Council of fifty sachems, " equal in rank and authority." The fifty sachemships were created in
perpetuity in certain clans of the several tribes ;
whenever a vacancy occurred, it was filled by
the clan electing one of its own members ; a
sachem once thus elected could be deposed by
the clan-council for good cause ; " but the right
to invest these sachems with office was reserved
to the General Council." These fifty
sachems of the confederacy were Structure of
the confed-
likewise sachems in their respective eracy
tribes, " and with the chiefs of these tribes
formed the council of each, which was supreme
over all matters pertaining to the tribe exclusively." The General Council could not con-
vene itself, but could be convened by any one
of the five tribal-councils. The regular meeting
was once a year in the autumn, in the valley of
Onondaga, but in stirring times extra sessions
were frequent. The proceedings were opened

maternal ancestry. The house-architecture was as much a constituent part of the fabric as the council of sachems. There is a transparency about the system that is very different from the obscurity we continually find in Europe and Asia, where different strata of ideas and institutions have been superimposed one upon another and crumpled and distorted with as little apparent significance or purpose as the porches and gables of a so-called " Queen Anne " house.[1] Conquest in the Old World has resulted in the commingling and manifold fusion of peoples in very different stages of development. In the New World there has been very little of that sort of thing. Conquest in ancient America was pretty much all of the Iroquois type, entailing in its milder form the imposition of tribute, in its more desperate form the extermination of a tribe with the adoption of its remnants into the similarly constituted tribe of the conquerors. There was therefore but little modification of the social structure while the people, gradually acquiring new arts, were passing through savagery and into a more or less advanced stage of barbarism.

[1] For instance, the whole discussion in Gomme's *Village Community*, London, 1890, an excellent book, abounds with instances of this crumpling.

The symmetry of the structure and the relation of one institution to another is thus distinctly apparent.

The communal household and the political structure built upon it, as above described in the case of the Iroquois, seem to have existed all over ancient North America, with agreement in fundamental characteristics and variation in details and degree of development. There are many corners as yet imperfectly explored, but hitherto, in so far as research has been rewarded with information, it all points in the same general direction. Among the tribes above enumerated as either in savagery or in the lower status of barbarism, so far as they have been studied, there seems to be a general agreement, as to the looseness of the marriage tie, the clan with descent in the female line, the phratry, the tribe, the officers and councils, the social equality, the community in goods (with exceptions already noted), and the wigwam or house adapted to communal living.

The extreme of variation consistent with adherence to the common principle was to be found in the shape and material of the houses. Those of the savage tribes were but sorry huts. The long house was used by the Powhatans and other Algonquin tribes. The other most highly developed type may be illustrated by the circular frame houses of the Mandans.[1] These houses were from forty to sixty feet in diameter.

A dozen or more posts, each about eight inches in diameter, were set in the ground, " at equal distances in the circumference of a circle, and rising about six feet above the level of the floor." The tops of the posts were connected by horizontal stringers ; and outside each post a slanting wooden brace sunk in the ground about four feet distant served as a firm support to the structure. The spaces between these braces were filled by tall wooden slabs, set with the same slant and resting against the stringers. Thus the framework of the outer wall was completed. To support the roof four posts were set in the ground about ten feet apart in the form of a square, near the centre of the building. They were from twelve to fifteen feet in height, and were connected at the top by four stringers forming a square. The rafters rested upon these stringers and upon the top of the circular wall below. The rafters were covered with willow matting, and upon this was spread a layer of prairie grass. Then both wall and roof, from the ground up to the summit, were covered with earth, solid and hard, to a thickness of at least two feet. The rafters projected above the square framework

[1] Morgan, *Houses and House-Life*, pp. 126–129 ; Catlin's *North Amer. Indians*, i. 81 *ff*.

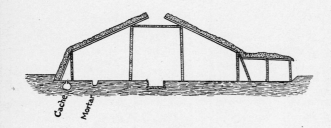

Cache

Mortar

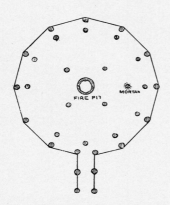

FIRE PIT

MORTAR

VIEW, CROSS–SECTION, AND GROUND-PLAN OF
MANDAN ROUND HOUSE

at the summit, so as to leave a circular opening in the centre about four feet in diameter.
This hole let in a little light, and let out some
of the smoke from the fire which blazed under-
neath in a fire-pit lined with stone slabs set on
edge. The only other aperture for light was the
doorway, which was a kind of vestibule or passage some ten feet in length. Curtains of buffalo
robes did duty instead of doors. The family
compartments were triangles with base at the
outer wall, and apex opening upon the central
hearth; and the partitions were hanging mats
or skins, which were tastefully fringed and or-
namented with quill-work and pictographs.[1] In
the lower Mandan village, visited by Catlin,
there were about fifty such houses, each able
to accommodate from thirty to forty persons.
The village, situated upon a bold bluff at a
bend of the Missouri River, and surrounded by
a palisade of stout timbers more than ten feet
in height, was very strong for defensive purposes. Indeed, it was virtually impregnable to
Indian methods of attack, for the earth-covered
houses could not be set on fire by blazing arrows, and just within the palisade ran a trench
in which the defenders could securely skulk,
while through the narrow chinks between the
timbers they could shoot arrows fast enough to
keep their assailants at a distance. This purpose

[1] Catlin, i. 83.

was further secured by rude bastions, and considering the structure as a whole one cannot help admiring the ingenuity which it exhibits. It shows a marked superiority over the conceptions of military defence attained by the Iroquois or any other Indians north of New Mexico. Besides the communal houses the village contained its "medicine lodge," or council house, and an open area for games and ceremonies. In the spaces between the houses were the scaffolds for drying maize, buffalo meat, etc., ascended by well-made portable ladders. Outside the village, at a short distance on the prairie, was a group of such scaffolds upon which the dead were left to moulder, somewhat after the fashion of the Parsees.[1]

We are now prepared to understand some essential points in the life of the groups of Indians occupying the region of the Cordilleras, both north and south of the Isthmus of Darien, all the way from Zuñi to Quito. The principal groups are the Moquis and Zuñis of Arizona and New Mexico, the Nahuas or Nahuatlac tribes of Mexico, the Mayas, Quichés, and kindred peoples of Central America; and beyond the isthmus, the Chibchas of New Granada, and sundry peoples comprised within the

The Indians of the pueblos, — in the middle status of barbarism

[1] Catlin, i. 90.

domain of the Incas. With regard to the ethnic relationships of these various groups, opinion is still in a state of confusion ; but it is not necessary for our present purpose that we should pause to discuss the numerous questions thus arising. Our business is to get a clear notion in outline of the character of the culture to which these peoples had attained at the time of the Discovery. Here we observe, on the part of all, a very considerable divergence from the average Indian level which we have thus far been describing.

This divergence increases as we go from Zuñi towards Cuzco, reaching its extreme, on the whole, among the Peruvians, though in some respects the nearest approach to civilization was made by the Mayas. All these peoples were at least one full ethnical period nearer to true civilization than the Iroquois, — and a vast amount of change and improvement is involved in the conception of an entire ethnical period. According to Mr. Morgan, one more such period would have brought the average level of these Cordilleran peoples to as high a plane as that of the Greeks described in the Odyssey. Let us now observe the principal points involved in the change, bearing in mind that it implies a considerable lapse of time. While the date 1325, at which the city of Mexico was founded, is the earliest date in the history of that country which can be regarded as securely established, it was preceded by a long series of generations of migration and warfare, the confused and fragmentary record of which historians have tried — hitherto with scant success — to unravel. To develop such a culture as that of the Aztecs out of an antecedent culture similar to that of the Iroquois must of course have taken a long time.

It will be remembered that the most conspicuous distinctive marks of the grade of culture attained by the Cordilleran peoples were

Horticulture with irrigation, and architecture with adobe

two, — the cultivation of maize in large quantities by irrigation, and the use of adobe-brick or stone in building. Probably there was at first, to some extent, a causal connection between the former and the latter. The region of the Moqui-Zuñi culture is a region in which arid plains become richly fertile when water from neighbouring cliffs or peaks is directed down upon them. It is mainly an affair of sluices, not of pump or well, which seem to have been alike beyond the ken of aboriginal Americans of whatever grade. The change of occupation involved in raising large crops of corn by the aid of sluices would facilitate an increase in density of population, and would encourage a preference for agricultural over predatory life. Such changes would be likely to favour the development of defensive military art. The Mohawk's surest defence lay in the terror which his prowess created hundreds of miles away. One can easily see how the forefathers of our Moquis and Zuñis may have come to prefer the security gained by living more closely together and building impregnable fortresses.

The earthen wall of the Mandan, supported on a framework of posts and slabs, seems to me curiously and strikingly suggestive of the incipient pottery made by surrounding a basket with a coating of clay.[1] When it was discovered how to make the earthen bowl or dish without the basket, a new era in progress was begun. So when it was discovered that an earthen wall could be fashioned to answer the requirements of housebuilders without the need of a permanent wooden framework, another great step was taken. Again the consequences were great enough to make it mark the beginning of a new ethnical period. If we suppose the central portion of our continent, the Mississippi and Missouri valleys, to have been occupied at some time by tribes familiar with the Mandan style of building; and if we further suppose a gradual extension or migration of this population, or some part of it, westward into the mountain region; that would be a movement into a region in which timber was scarce, while adobe clay was abundant. Under

Possible origin of adobe architecture

[1] See above, p. 30.

such circumstances the useful qualities of that peculiar clay could not fail to be soon discovered. The simple exposure to sunshine would quickly convert a Mandan house built with it into an adobe house; the coating of earth would become a coating of brick. It would not then take long to ascertain that with such adobe-brick could be built walls at once light and strong, erect and tall, such as could not be built with common clay. In some such way as this I think the discovery must have been made by the ancestors of the Zuñis, and others who have built pueblos. After the pueblo style of architecture, with its erect walls and terraced stories, had become developed, it was an easy step, when the occasion suggested it, to substitute for the adobe-brick coarse rubble-stones embedded in adobe. The final stage was reached in Mexico and Yucatan, when soft coralline limestone was shaped into blocks with a flint chisel and laid in courses with adobe-mortar.

The pueblos of New Mexico and Arizona are among the most interesting structures in the world. Several are still inhabited by the descendants of the people who were living in them at the time of the Spanish Discovery, and their primitive customs and habits of thought have Mr. Cushing been preserved to the present day with at Zuñi but little change. The long sojourn of Mr. Cushing, of the Bureau of Ethnology,

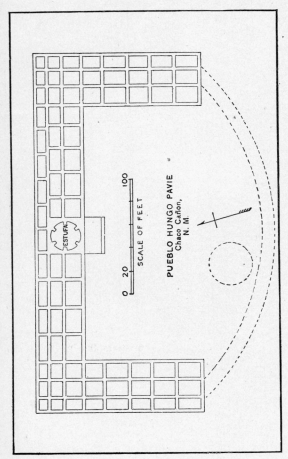

PUEBLO HUNGO PAVIE
Chaco Cañon,
N. M.

SCALE OF FEET
0   20   100

ESTUFA

GROUND-PLAN OF PUEBLO HUNGO PAVIE

in the Zuñi pueblo, has already thrown a flood of light upon many points in American archæology.[1] As in the case of American aborigines generally, the social life of these people is closely connected with their architecture, and the pueblos which are still inhabited seem to furnish us with the key to the interpretation of those that we find deserted or in ruins, whether in Arizona or in Guatemala.

In the architecture of the pueblos one typical form is reproduced with sundry variations in detail. The typical form is that of a solid block of buildings making three sides of an extensive rectangular enclosure or courtyard. On the inside, facing upon the courtyard, the structure is but one story in height; on the outside, looking out upon the surrounding country, it rises to three, or perhaps even five or six stories. From inside to outside the flat roofs rise in a series of terraces, so that the floor of the second row is continuous with the roof of the first, the floor of the third row is continuous with the roof of the second,

Typical structure of the pueblo

---

[1] See his articles in the *Century Magazine*, Dec., 1882, Feb., 1883, May, 1883 ; and his papers on "Zuñi Fetiches," *Reports of the Bureau of Ethnology*, ii. 9–45 ; "A Study of Pueblo Pottery as Illustrative of Zuñi Culture Growth," id. iv. 473–521 ; see also Mrs. Stevenson's paper, "Religious Life of a Zuñi Child," id. v. 539–555 ; Sylvester Baxter, "An Aboriginal Pilgrimage," *Century Magazine*, Aug., 1882.

and so on. The fourth side of the rectangle is formed by a solid block of one-story apartments, usually with one or two narrow gateways overlooked by higher structures within the enclosure. Except these gateways there is no entrance from without; the only windows are frowning loopholes, and access to the several apartments is gained through skylights reached by portable ladders. Such a structure is what our own forefathers would have naturally called a "burgh," or fortress; it is in one sense a house, yet in another sense a town;[1] its divisions are not so much houses as compartments; it is a joint-tenement affair, like the Iroquois long houses, but in a higher stage of development.

So far as they have been studied, the pueblo Indians are found to be organized in clans, with descent in the female line, as in the case of the ruder Indians above described. In the event of marriage the young husband goes to live with his wife, and she may turn him out of doors if he deserves it.[2] The ideas of property seem still

[1] Cf. Greek οἶκος, "house," with Latin *vicus*, "street" or "village," Sanskrit *vesa*, "dwelling-place," English *wick*, "mansion" or "village."

[2] "With the woman rests the security of the marriage ties; and it must be said, in her high honour, that she rarely abuses the privilege; that is, never sends her husband ' to the home of his fathers,' unless he richly deserves it." But should not Mr. Cushing have said " home of his mothers," or perhaps of " his sisters and his cousins and his aunts " ? For a moment

Restoration of Pueblo Hungo Pavie

limited to that of possessory right, with the ultimate title in the clan, except that portable articles subject to individual owner- Pueblo society ship have become more numerous.

In government the council of sachems reappears with a principal sachem, or cacique, called by the Spaniards " gobernador." There is an organized priesthood, with distinct orders, and a ceremonial more elaborate than those of the ruder Indians. In every pueblo there is to be found at least one " estufa," or council house, for governmental or religious transactions. Usually there are two or three or more such estufas. In mythology, in what we may call pictography or rudimentary hieroglyphics, as well as in ordinary handicrafts, there is a marked advance beyond the Indians of the lower status of barbarism, after making due allowances for such things as the people of the pueblos have learned from white men.[1]

From the pueblos still existing, whether in-

afterwards he tells us, " To her belong all the children ; and descent, including inheritance, is on her side." *Century Magazine*, May, 1883, p. 35.

[1] For example, since the arrival of the Spaniards some or perhaps all of the pueblos have introduced chimneys into their apartments ; but when they were first visited by Coronado, he found the people wearing cotton garments, and Franciscan friars in 1581 remarked upon the superior quality of their shoes. In spinning and weaving, as well as in the grinding of meal, a notable advance had been made.

habited or in ruins, we may eventually get some sort of clue to the populations of ancient towns visited by the Spanish discoverers.[1] The pueblo of Zuñi seems to have had at one time a population of 5000, but it has dwindled to less than 2000. Of the ruined pueblos, built of stone with adobe-mortar, in the valley of the Rio Chaco, the Pueblo Hungo Pavie contained 73 apartments in the first story, 53 in the second, and 29 in the third, with an average size of 18 feet by 13, and would have accommodated about 1000 Indians. In the same valley Pueblo Bonito, with four stories, contained not less than 640 apartments, with room enough for a population of 3000 ; within a third of a mile from this huge structure stood Pueblo Chettro Kettle, with 506 apartments. The most common variation from the rectangular shape was that in which a terraced semicircle was substituted for the three terraced sides, as in Pueblo Bonito, or the whole rectangular design was converted into an ellipse, as in Pueblo Peñasca Blanca. There are indications that these fortresses were not in all cases built at one time, but that, at least in some cases, they grew by gradual accretions.[2] The smallness

Wonderful ancient pueblos in the Chaco valley

---

[1] At least a better one than Mr. Prescott had when he naïvely reckoned five persons to a household. *Conquest of Mexico*, ii. 97.

[2] Morgan, *Houses and House-Life*, chap. vii.

Restoration of Pueblo Bonito

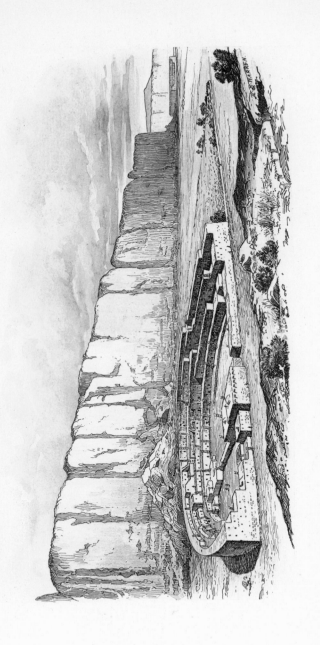

of the distances between those in the Chaco valley suggests that their inhabitants must have been united in a confederation ; and one can easily see that an actual juxtaposition or partial coalescence of such communities would have made a city of very imposing appearance. The pueblos are always found situated near a river, and their gardens, lying outside, are easily accessible to sluices from neighbouring cliffs or mesas. But in some cases, as the Wolpi pueblo of the Moquis, the whole stronghold is built upon the summit of the cliff; there is a coalescence of communal structures, each enclosing a courtyard, in which there is a spring for the water-supply ; and the irrigated gardens are built in terrace-form just below on the bluff, and protected by solid walls. From this curious pueblo another transition takes us to the extraordinary cliff-houses found in the Chelly, Mancos, and McElmo cañons, and elsewhere, — veritable human eyries perched in crevices or clefts of the perpendicular rock, accessible only by dint of a toilsome and perilous climb; places of refuge, perhaps for fragments of tribes overwhelmed by more barbarous invaders, yet showing in their dwelling-rooms and estufas marks of careful building and tasteful adornment.[1]

The Moqui pueblos

The cliff pueblos

[1] For careful descriptions of the ruined pueblos and cliff-houses, see Nadaillac's *Prehistoric America,* chap. v., and

The pueblo of Zuñi is a more extensive and complex structure than the ruined pueblos on the Chaco River. It is not so much an enormous communal house as a small town formed of a number of such houses crowded together, **Pueblo of Zuñi** with access from one to another along their roof-terraces. Some of the structures are of adobe-brick, others of stone embedded in adobe-mortar and covered with plaster. There are two open plazas or squares in the town, and several streets, some of which are covered ways passing beneath the upper stories of houses. The effect, though not splendid, must be very picturesque, and would doubtless astonish and bewilder visitors unprepared for such a sight. When Coronado's men discovered Zuñi in 1540, although that style of building was no longer a novelty to them, they compared the place to Granada.

Now it is worthy of note that Cortes made the same comparison in the case of Tlascala, one **Pueblo of Tlascala** of the famous towns at which he stopped on his march from Vera Cruz to the city of Mexico. In his letter to the Emperor Charles V., he compared Tlascala to Gra-

Short's *North Americans of Antiquity*, chap. vii. The latter sees in them the melancholy vestiges of a people gradually "succumbing to their unpropitious surroundings — a land which is fast becoming a howling wilderness, with its scourgeing sands and roaming savage Bedouin — the Apaches."

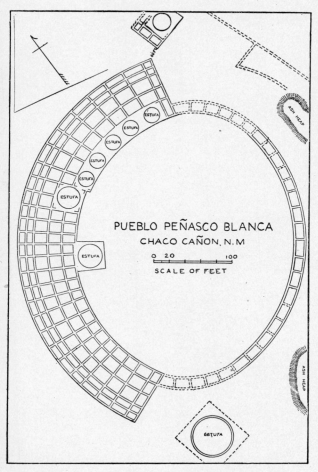

PUEBLO PEÑASCO BLANCA
CHACO CAÑON, N.M

0 20 100
SCALE OF FEET

ESTUFA

ASH HEAP

GROUND–PLAN OF PUEBLO PEÑASCA BLANCA

nada, "affirming that it was larger, stronger, and more populous than the Moorish capital at the time of the conquest, and quite as well built." [1] Upon this Mr. Prescott observes, "we shall be slow to believe that its edifices could have rivalled those monuments of Oriental magnificence, whose light aerial forms still survive after the lapse of ages, the admiration of every traveller of sensibility and taste. The truth is that Cortes, like Columbus, saw objects through the warm medium of his own fond imagination, giving them a higher tone of colouring and larger dimensions than were strictly warranted by the fact." Or, as Mr. Bandelier puts it, when it comes to general statements about numbers and dimensions, "the descriptions of the conquerors cannot be taken as facts, only as the expression of feelings, honestly entertained but uncritical." From details given in various Spanish descriptions, including those of Cortes himself, it is evident that there could not have been much difference in size between Tlascala and its neighbour Cholula. The population of the latter town has often been given as from 150,000 to 200,000;

---

[1] " La qual ciudad . . . es muy mayor que Granada, y muy mas fuerte, y de tan buenos edificios, y de mucha mas gente, que Granada tenia al tiempo que se gaño." Cortes, *Relacion segunda al Emperador*, ap. Lorenzana, p. 58, cited in Prescott's *Conquest of Mexico*, vol. i. p. 401 (7th ed., London, 1855).

but, from elaborate archæological investigations made on the spot in 1881, Mr. Bandelier concludes that it cannot have greatly exceeded 30,000, and this number really agrees with the estimates of two very important Spanish authorities, Las Casas and Torquemada, when correctly understood.[1] We may therefore suppose that the population of Tlascala was about 30,000. Now the population of the city of Granada, at the time of its conquest by Ferdinand and Isabella, is said by the greatest of Spanish historians[2] to have been about 200,000. It would thus appear

[1] See Bandelier's *Archæological Tour in Mexico*, Boston, 1885, pp. 160–164. Torquemada's words, cited by Bandelier, are "Quando entraron los Españoles, dicen que tenia mas de quarenta mil vecinos esta ciudad." *Monarquía indiana*, lib. iii. cap. xix. p. 281. A prolific source of error is the ambiguity in the word *vecinos*, which may mean either "inhabitants" or "householders." Where Torquemada meant 40,000 inhabitants, uncritical writers fond of the marvellous have understood him to mean 40,000 houses, and multiplying this figure by 5, the average number of persons *in a modern family*, have obtained the figure 200,000. But 40,000 houses peopled after the old Mexican fashion, with at least 200 persons in a house (to put it as low as possible), would make a city of 8,000,000 inhabitants! Las Casas, in his *Destruycion de las Indias*, vii., puts the population of Cholula at about 30,000. I observe that Llorente (in his *Œuvres de Las Casas*, tom. i. p. 38) translates the statement correctly. I shall recur to this point below, vol. iii. p. 57.

[2] Mariana, *Historia de España*, Valencia, 1795, tom. viii. p. 317.

that Cortes sometimes let his feelings run away
with him; and, all things considered, small
blame to him if he did! In studying the story
of the Spanish conquest of America, liberal
allowance must often be made for inaccuracies
of statement that were usually pardonable and
sometimes inevitable.

But when Cortes described Tlascala as " quite
as well built " as Granada, it is not at all likely
that he was thinking about that exquisite
Moorish architecture which in the mind of Mr.
Prescott or any cultivated modern writer is the
first thing to be suggested by the name. The
Spaniards of those days did not admire the
artistic work of " infidels; " they covered up
beautiful arabesques with a wash of dirty plaster,
and otherwise behaved very much like the Puritans who smashed the "idolatrous" statues in
English cathedrals. When Cortes looked at
Tlascala, and Coronado looked at Zuñi, and
both soldiers were reminded of Granada, they
were probably looking at those places with a
professional eye as fortresses hard to capture;
and from this point of view there was doubtless
some justice in the comparison.

In the description of Tlascala by the Spaniards who first saw it, with its dark and narrow
streets, its houses of adobe, or " the better sort "
of stone laid in adobe-mortar, and its flat and
terraced roofs, one is irresistibly reminded of

one cannot properly call a theory but rather an incoherent medley of notions about barbaric society. Nothing could be further from *feudalism*, in which the relation of landlord and tenant is a fundamental element, than the society of the American aborigines, in which that relation was utterly unknown and inconceivable. This more primitive form of society is not improperly called *gentilism*, inasmuch as it is based upon the gens or clan, with communism in living, and with the conception of individual ownership of property undeveloped. It was gentilism that everywhere prevailed throughout the myriads of unrecorded centuries during which the foremost races of mankind struggled up through savagery and barbarism into civilization, while weaker and duller races lagged behind at various stages on the way. The change from "gentile" society to political society as we know it was in some respects the most important change that has occurred in human affairs since men became human. It might be roughly defined as the change from personal to territorial organization. It was accomplished when the stationary clan became converted into the township, and the stationary tribe into the small state;[1] when the concep-

Contrast between feudalism and gentilism

Change from gentile society to political society

[1] The small states into which tribes were at first transformed have in many cases survived to the present time as

tion of individual property in land was fully
acquired; when the tie of physical kinship
ceased to be indispensable as a bond for holding a society together; when the *clansman* became a *citizen*. This momentous change was
accomplished among the Greeks during a period
beginning shortly before the first Olympiad
(B. C. 776), and ending with the reforms of
Kleisthenes at Athens (B. C. 509); among the
Romans it was accomplished by the series of
legislative changes beginning with those ascribed
to Servius Tullius (about B. C. 550), and perfected by the time of the first Punic War (B. C.
264–241). In each case about three centuries
was required to work the change.[1] If now the

portions of great states or nations. The shires or counties of
England, which have been reproduced in the United States,
originated in this way, as I have briefly explained in my little
book on *Civil Government in the United States*, p. 49.
When you look on the map of England, and see the town of
Icklingham in the county of *Suffolk*, it means that this place
was once the "home" of the "Icklings" or "children of
Ickel," a clan which formed part of the tribe of Angles
known as "South folk." So the names of Gaulish tribes
survived as names of French provinces, *e. g. Auvergne* from
the *Arverni, Poitou* from the *Pictavi, Anjou* from the *Ande-
cavi, Béarn* from the *Bigerrones*, etc.

[1] "It was no easy task to accomplish such a fundamental
change, however simple and obvious it may now seem. . . .
Anterior to experience, a township, as the unit of a political
system, was abstruse enough to tax the Greeks and Romans
to the depths of their capacities before the conception was

reader, familiar with European history, will reflect upon the period of more than a thousand years which intervened between the date last named and the time when feudalism became thoroughly established, if he will recall to mind the vast and powerful complication of causes which operated to transform civil society from the aspect which it wore in the days of Regulus and the second Ptolemy to that which it had assumed in the times of Henry the Fowler or Fulk of Anjou, he will begin to realize how much " feudalism " implies, and what a wealth of experience it involves, above and beyond the change from "gentile" to "civil" society. It does not appear that any people in ancient America ever approached very near to this earlier change. None had fairly begun to emerge from gentilism; none had advanced so far as the Greeks of the first Olympiad or the Romans under the rule of the Tarquins.

The first eminent writer to express a serious doubt as to the correctness of the earlier views of Mexican civilization was that sagacious Scotchman, William Robertson.[1] The illustrious statesman and philologist, Albert Gallatin, founder of the American Ethnological Society,

formed and set in practical operation." Morgan, *Ancient Society*, p. 218.

[1] Robertson's *History of America*, 9th ed. vol. iii. pp. 274, 281.

published in the first volume of its " Transactions " an essay which recognized the danger of trusting the Spanish narratives without very careful and critical scrutiny.[1] It is to be observed that Mr. Gallatin approached the subject with somewhat more knowledge of aboriginal life in America than had been possessed by previous writers. A similar scepticism was expressed by Lewis Cass, who also knew a great deal about Indians.[2] Next came Mr. Morgan,[3] the man of path-breaking ideas, whose minute and profound acquaintance with Indian life was joined with a power of penetrating the hidden impli-

Suspicions as to the erroneousness of the Spanish accounts

[1] " Notes on the Semi-civilized Nations of Mexico, Yucatan, and Central America," *American Ethnological Society's Transactions*, vol. i., New York, 1852. There is a brief account of Mr. Gallatin's pioneer work in American philology and ethnology in Stevens's *Albert Gallatin*, pp. 386–396.

[2] Cass, "Aboriginal Structures," *North Amer. Review*, Oct., 1840.

[3] Mr. R. A. Wilson's *New History of the Conquest of Mexico*, Philadelphia, 1859, denounced the Spanish conquerors as wholesale liars, but as his book was ignorant, uncritical, and full of wild fancies, it produced little effect. It was demolished, with neatness and despatch, in two articles in the *Atlantic Monthly*, April and May, 1859, by the eminent historian John Foster Kirk, whose *History of Charles the Bold* is in many respects a worthy companion to the works of Prescott and Motley. Mr. Kirk had been Mr. Prescott's secretary.

cations of facts so keen and so sure as to amount to genius. Mr. Morgan saw the nature of the delusion under which the Spaniards laboured; he saw that what they mistook for feudal castles owned by great lords, and inhab-

Detection and explanation of the errors, by Lewis Morgan

ited by dependent retainers, were really huge communal houses, owned and inhabited by clans, or rather by segments of overgrown clans. He saw this so vividly that it betrayed him now and then into a somewhat impatient and dogmatic manner of statement; but that was a slight fault, for what he saw was not the outcome of dreamy speculation but of scientific insight. His researches, which reduced " Montezuma's empire " to a confederacy of tribes dwelling in pueblos, governed by a council of chiefs, and collecting tribute from neighbouring pueblos, have been fully sustained by subsequent investigation.

The state of society which Cortes saw has, indeed, passed away, and its monuments and hieroglyphic records have been in great part destroyed. Nevertheless some monuments and some hieroglyphic records remain, and the people are still there. Tlascalans and Aztecs, descendants in the eleventh or twelfth generation from the men whose bitter feuds gave such a golden opportunity to Cortes, still dwell upon the soil of Mexico, and speak the language in which Montezuma made his last harangue to the furious people. There is, moreover, a great mass of literature in Spanish, besides more or less in Nahuatl, written during the century following the conquest, and the devoted missionaries and painstaking administrators, who wrote books about the country in which they were working, were not engaged in a wholesale conspiracy for deceiving mankind. From a really critical study of this literature, combined with archæological investigation, much may be expected; and a noble beginning has already been made. A more extensive acquaintance with Mexican literature would at times have materially modified Mr. Morgan's conclusions, though without altering their general drift. At this point the work has been taken up by Mr. Adolf Bandelier, of Highland, Illinois, to whose rare sagacity and untiring industry as a field archæologist is joined such a thorough knowledge of Mexican literature as few men before him have possessed. Armed with such resources, Mr. Bandelier is doing for the ancient history of America work as significant as that which Mommsen has done for Rome, or Baur for the beginnings of Christianity. When a sufficient mass of facts and incidents have once been put upon record, it is hard for ignorant misconception to bury the truth in a pit so deep but that the delving gen-

Adolf Bandelier's researches

ius of critical scholarship will sooner or later drag it forth into the light of day.[1]

At this point in our exposition a very concise summary of Mr. Bandelier's results will suffice to enable the reader to understand their import. What has been called the "empire of Montezuma" was in reality a confederacy of three tribes, the Aztecs, Tezcucans, and Tlacopans,[2] dwelling in three large composite pueblos situated very near together in one of the strongest defensive positions ever occupied by Indians. This Aztec confederacy extended its "sway" over a considerable portion of the Mexican peninsula, but that "sway" could not correctly be described as "empire,"

The Aztec confederacy

[1] A summary of Mr. Bandelier's principal results, with copious citation and discussion of original Spanish and Nahuatl sources, is contained in his three papers, " On the art of war and mode of warfare of the ancient Mexicans," — " On the distribution and tenure of land, and the customs with respect to inheritance, among the ancient Mexicans," — " On the social organization and mode of government of the ancient Mexicans," *Peabody Museum Reports*, vol. ii., 1876–79, pp. 95–161, 385–448, 557–699.

[2] In the Iroquois confederacy the Mohawks enjoyed a certain precedence or seniority, the Onondagas had the central council-fire, and the Senecas, who had the two head war-chiefs, were much the most numerous. In the Mexican confederacy the various points of superiority seem to have been more concentrated in the Aztecs ; but spoils and tribute were divided into five portions, of which Mexico and Tezcuco each took two, and Tlacopan one.

for it was in no sense a military occupation of the country. The confederacy did not have garrisons in subject pueblos or civil officials to administer their affairs for them. It simply sent some of its chiefs about from one pueblo to another to collect tribute. This tax consisted in great part of maize and other food, and each tributary pueblo reserved a certain portion of its tribal territory to be cultivated for the benefit of the domineering confederacy. If a pueblo proved delinquent or recalcitrant, Aztec warriors swooped down upon it in stealthy midnight assault, butchered its inhabitants and emptied its granaries, and when the paroxysm of rage had spent itself, went exulting homeward, carrying away women for concubines, men to be sacrificed, and such miscellaneous booty as could be conveyed without wagons or beasts to draw them.[1] If the sudden assault, with scaling ladders, happened to fail, the assailants were likely to be baffled, for there was no artillery, and so little food could be carried that a siege meant starvation for the besiegers.

The tributary pueblos were also liable to be summoned to furnish a contingent of warriors to the war-parties of the confederacy, under the same penalties for delinquency as in the case of refusal of tribute. In such cases it was quite

[1] The wretched prisoners were ordinarily compelled to carry the booty.

common for the confederacy to issue a peremptory summons, followed by a declaration of war. When a pueblo was captured, the only way in which the vanquished people could stop the massacre was by holding out signals of submission ; a parley then sometimes adjusted the affair, and the payment of a year's tribute in advance induced the conquerors to depart, but captives once taken could seldom if ever be ransomed. If the parties could not agree upon terms, the slaughter was renewed, and sometimes went on until the departing victors left naught behind them but ruined houses belching from loop-hole and doorway lurid clouds of smoke and flame upon narrow silent streets heaped up with mangled corpses.

The sway of the Aztec confederacy over the Mexican peninsula was thus essentially similar to the sway of the Iroquois confederacy over a great part of the tribes between the Connecticut River and the Mississippi. It was simply the levying of tribute, — a system of plunder enforced by terror. The so-called empire was " only a partnership formed for the purpose of carrying on the business of warfare, and that intended, not for the extension of territorial ownership, but only for an increase of the means of subsistence." [1] There was none of that coalescence and incorporation of peoples which occurs after the

[1] Bandelier, *op. cit.* p. 563.

change from gentilism to civil society has been effected. Among the Mexicans, as elsewhere throughout North America, the tribe remained intact as the highest completed political integer.

The Aztec tribe was organized in clans and phratries, and the number of clans would indicate that the tribe was a Aztec clans very large one.[1] There were twenty clans, called in the Nahuatl language " calpullis." We may fairly suppose that the average size of a clan was larger than the average tribe of Algonquins or Iroquois ; but owing to the compact " city " life, this increase of numbers did not result in segmentation and scattering, as among Indians

---

[1] The notion of an immense population groaning under the lash of taskmasters and building huge palaces for idle despots must be dismissed. The statements which refer to such a vast population are apt to be accompanied by incompatible statements. Mr. Morgan is right in throwing the burden of proof upon those who maintain that a people without domestic animals or field agriculture could have been so numerous (*Anc. Soc.*, p. 195). On the other hand, I believe Mr. Morgan makes a grave mistake in the opposite direction, in underestimating the numbers that could be supported upon Indian corn even under a system of horticulture without the use of the plough. Some pertinent remarks on the extraordinary reproductive power of maize in Mexico may be found in Humboldt, *Essai politique sur la Nouvelle Espagne*, Paris, 1811, tom. iii. pp. 51–60 ; the great naturalist is of course speaking of the yield of maize in ploughed lands, but, after making due allowances, the yield under the ancient system must have been well-nigh unexampled in barbaric agriculture.

in the lower status. Each Aztec clan seems to have occupied a number of adjacent communal houses, forming a kind of precinct, with its special house or houses for official purposes, corresponding to the *estufas* in the New Mexican pueblos. The houses were the common property of the clan, and so was the land which its members cultivated ; and such houses and land could not be sold or bartered away by the clan, or in anywise alienated. The idea of " real estate " had not been developed ; the clan simply exercised a right of occupancy, and — as among some ruder Indians — its individual members exercised certain limited rights of user in particular garden-plots.

The clan was governed by a clan-council, consisting of chiefs (*tecuhtli*) elected by the clan, and inducted into office after a cruel religious ordeal, in which the candidate was bruised, tortured, and half starved. An executive department was more clearly differentiated from the council than among the Indians of the lower status. The clan (*calpulli*) had an official head, or sachem, called the *calpullec* ; and also a military commander called the *ahcacautin*, or " elder brother." The *ahcacautin* was also a kind of peace officer, or constable, for the precinct occupied by the clan, and carried about with him a staff of office ; a tuft of white feathers attached to this staff betokened that his er-

Clan officers

rand was one of death. The clan elected its
calpullec and *ahcacautin*, and could depose them
for cause.[1]

The members of the clan were reciprocally
bound to aid, defend, and avenge one another;
but wergild was no longer accepted, and the
penalty for murder was death. The clan exercised the right of naming its members. Such
names were invariably significant (as *Nezahual-
coyotl*, "Hungry Coyote," *Axayacatl*, "Face-
in-the-Water," etc.), and more or less
"medicine," or superstitious association, was attached to the name. The
clans also had their significant names and totems.
Each clan had its peculiar religious rites, its
priests or medicine-men who were members of
the clan-council, and its temple or medicine-
house. Instead of burying their dead the Mexican tribes practised cremation; there was,
therefore, no common cemetery, but the funeral
ceremonies were conducted by the clan.

The clans of the Aztecs, like those of many
other Mexican tribes, were organized into four
phratries; and this divided the city of Mexico,
as the Spaniards at once remarked,
into four quarters. The phratry had
acquired more functions than it possessed in the
lower status. Besides certain religious and social

[1] Compare this description with that of the institutions of
Indians in the lower status, above, p. 82.

duties, and besides its connection with the pun-
ishment of criminals, the Mexican phratry was
an organization for military purposes.[1] The four
phratries were four divisions of the tribal host,
each with its captain. In each of the quarters
was an arsenal, or " dart-house," where weapons were stored, and from which they were
handed out to war-parties about to start on an
expedition.

The supreme government of the Aztecs was
vested in the tribal-council composed of twenty
members, one for each clan. The
member, representing a clan, was not
its *calpullec*, or " sachem ; " he was one of the
tecuhtli, or clan-chiefs, and was significantly
called the " speaker " (*tlatoani*). The tribal-council, thus composed of twenty speakers, was
called the *tlatocan*, or " place of speech." [2] At

The tribal-council

---

[1] In this respect it seems to have had some resemblance to
the Roman *centuria* and Teutonic *hundred*. So in prehistoric
Greece we may perhaps infer from Nestor's advice to Agamemnon that a similar organization existed : —

κρῖν' ἄνδρας κατὰ φῦλα, κατὰ φρήτρας, Ἀγάμεμνον,
ὡς φρήτρη φρήρτηφιν ἀρήγῃ, φῦλα δὲ φύλοις.
Iliad, ii. 362.

But the phratry seems never to have reached so high a development among the Greeks as among the Romans and the early
English.

[2] Compare *parliament* from *parler*. These twenty were
the " grandees," " counsellors," and " captains " mentioned
by Bernal Diaz as always in Montezuma's company ; " y
siempre á la contina estaban en su compañía veinte grandes

least as often as once in ten days the council as-
sembled at the *tecpan*, or official house of the
tribe, but it could be convened whenever occasion required, and in cases of emergency was
continually in session. Its powers and duties
were similar to those of an ancient English shire-
mote, in so far as they were partly directive and
partly judicial. A large part of its business was
settling disputes between the clans. It superintended the ceremonies of investiture with which
the chiefs and other officers of the clans were
sworn into office. At intervals of eighty days
there was an " extra session " of the *tlatocan*, attended also by the twenty " elder brothers,"
the four phratry-captains, the two executive
chiefs of the tribe, and the leading priests, and
at such times a reconsideration of an unpopu-
lar decision might be urged ; but the authority
of the *tlatocan* was supreme, and from its final
decision there could be no appeal.[1]

The executive chiefs of the tribe were two in
number, as was commonly the case in ancient
America. The tribal sachem, or civil executive,

señores y consejeros y capitanes," etc. *Historia verdadera,*
ii. 95. See Bandelier, *op. cit.* p. 646.

[1] Mr. Bandelier's note on this point gives an especially apt
illustration of the confusion of ideas and inconsistencies of
statement amid which the early Spanish writers struggled to
understand and describe this strange society : *op. cit.* p.
651.

to settle. But in all probability the office grew up through the successive acquisition of ritual, judicial, and civil functions by the military commander. The paramount necessity of consulting the tutelar deities before fighting resulted in making the general a priest competent to perform sacrifices and interpret omens ;[1] he thus naturally became the most important among priests ; an increased sanctity invested his person and office ; and by and by he acquired control over the dispensation of justice, and finally over the whole civil administration. One step more was needed to develop the *basileus* into a despot, like the king of Persia, and that was to let him get into his hands the law-making power, involving complete control over taxation. When the Greeks and Romans became dissatisfied with the increasing powers of their kings, they destroyed the office. The Romans did not materially di-

---

[1] Such would naturally result from the desirableness of securing unity of command. If Demosthenes had been in sole command of the Athenian armament in the harbour of Syracuse, and had been a *basileus*, with priestly authority, who can doubt that some such theory of the eclipse as that suggested by Philochorus would have been adopted, and thus one of the world's great tragedies averted ? See Grote, *Hist. Greece*, vol. vii. chap. lx. M. Fustel de Coulanges, in his admirable book *La Cité antique*, pp. 205–210, makes the priestly function of the king primitive, and the military function secondary ; which is entirely inconsistent with what we know of barbarous races.

minish its functions, but put them into commission, by entrusting them to two consuls of equal authority elected annually. The Greeks, on the other hand, divided the royal functions among different officers, as *e. g.* at Athens among the nine archons.[1]

The typical kingship in mediæval Europe, after the full development of the feudal system, was very different indeed from the kingship in early Greece and Rome. In the Mid- Mediæval
dle Ages all priestly functions had kingship
passed into the hands of the Church.[2] A king like Charles VII. of France, or Edward III. of England, was military commander, civil magistrate, chief judge, and *supreme landlord;* the people were his tenants. That was the kind of king

---

[1] It is worthy of note that the archon who retained the priestly function was called *basileus,* showing perhaps that at that time this had come to be most prominent among the royal functions, or more likely that it was the one with which reformers had some religious scruples about interfering. The Romans, too, retained part of the king's priestly function in an officer called *rex sacrorum,* whose duty was at times to offer a sacrifice in the forum, and then run away as fast as legs could carry him, — ἣν θύσας ὁ βασιλεὺς, κατὰ τάχος ἄπεισι φεύγων ἐξ ἀγορᾶς (!) Plutarch, *Quæst. Rom.* 63.

[2] Something of the priestly quality of "sanctity," however, surrounded the king's person; and the ceremony of anointing the king at his coronation was a survival of the ancient rite which invested the head war-chief with priestly attributes.

with which the Spanish discoverers of Mexico were familiar.

Now the Mexican *tlacatecuhtli*, or " chief-of-men," was much more like Agamemnon in point of kingship than like Edward III. He was not supreme landlord, for landlordship did not exist in Mexico. He was not chief judge or civil magistrate ; those functions belonged to the " snake-woman." Mr. Bandelier regards the " chief-of-men " as simply a military commander ; but for reasons which I shall state hereafter,[1] it seems quite clear that he exercised certain very important priestly functions, although beside him there was a kind of high-priest or medicine-chief. If I am right in holding that Montezuma was a " priest-commander," then incipient royalty in Mexico had advanced at least one stage beyond the head war-chief of the Iroquois, and remained one stage behind the *basileus* of the Homeric Greeks.

Montezuma was a " priest-commander "

The *tlacatecuhtli*, or " chief-of-men," was elected by an assembly consisting of the tribal-council, the " elder brothers " of the several clans, and certain leading priests. Though the office was thus elective, the choice seems to

[1] They can be most conveniently stated in connection with the story of the conquest of Mexico ; see below, vol. iii. p. 72. When Mr. Bandelier completes his long-promised paper on the ancient Mexican religion, perhaps it will appear that he has taken these facts into the account.

have been practically limited to a particular clan, and in the eleven chiefs who were chosen from 1375 to 1520 a certain principle or custom of succession seems to be plainly indicated.[1] There was a further

Mode of succession to the office

limit to the order of succession. Allusion has been made to the four phratry-captains commanding the quarters of the city. Their cheerful titles were " man of the house of darts," " cutter of men," " bloodshedder," and " chief of the eagle and cactus." These captains were military chiefs of the phratries, and also magistrates charged with the duty of maintaining order and enforcing the decrees of the council in their respective quarters. The " chief of the eagle and cactus " was chief executioner, — Jack Ketch. He was not eligible for the office of " chief-of-men ; " the three other phratry-captains were eligible. Then there was a member of the priesthood entitled " man of the dark house." This person, with the three eligible captains, made a quartette, and one of this privileged four *must* succeed to the office of " chief-of-men."

The eligibility of the " man of the dark house "

[1] I cannot follow Mr. Bandelier in discrediting Clavigero's statement that the office of *tlacatecuhtli* " should always remain in the house of Acamapitzin," inasmuch as the eleven who were actually elected were all closely akin to one another. In point of fact it *did* remain " in the house of Acamapitzin."

may be cited here as positive proof that sometimes the " chief-of-men " could be a " priest-
commander." That in all cases he acquired
priestly functions after election, even when he
did not possess them before, is indicated by the
fact that at the ceremony of his induction into
office he ascended to the summit of the pyra-
mid sacred to the war-god Huitzilopochtli,
where he was anointed by the high-priest with
a black ointment, and sprinkled with sanctified
water ; having thus become consecrated he took
a censer of live coals and a bag of copal, and as
his first official act offered incense to the war-
god.[1]

As the " chief-of-men " was elected, so too he
could be deposed for misbehaviour. He was *ex
officio* a member of the tribal-council, and he had
his official residence in the *tecpan*, or tribal house,
where the meetings of the council were held,
and where the hospitalities of the tribe were extended to strangers. As an administrative officer,
the " chief-of-men " had little to do within the
limits of the tribe ; that, as already observed,
was the business of the " snake-woman." But

[1] H. H. Bancroft, *Native Races of the Pacific States*, vol.
ii. p. 145. Hence the accounts of the reverent demeanour
of the people toward Montezuma, though perhaps overcol-
oured, are not so absurd as Mr. Morgan deemed them. Mr.
Morgan was sometimes too anxious to reduce Montezuma to
the level of an Iroquois war-chief.

outside of the confederacy the " chief-of-men " exercised administrative functions. He superintended the collection of tribute. Each of the three confederate tribes appointed, Manner of collecting tribute through its tribal-council, agents to visit the subjected pueblos and gather in the tribute. These agents were expressively termed *calpixqui*, " crop-gatherers." As these men were obliged to spend considerable time in the vanquished pueblos in the double character of tax-collectors and spies, we can imagine how hateful their position was. Their security from injury depended upon the reputation of their tribes for ruthless ferocity.[1] The tiger-like confederacy was only too ready to take offence ; in the lack of a decent pretext it often went to war without one, simply in order to get human victims for sacrifice.

Once appointed, the tax-gatherers were directed by the " chief-of-men." The tribute was chiefly maize, but might be anything the conquerors chose to demand, — weapons, fine pottery or feather-work, gold ornaments, or female

[1] As I have elsewhere observed in a similar case : " Each summer there came two Mohawk elders, secure in the dread that Iroquois prowess had everywhere inspired ; and up and down the Connecticut valley they seized the tribute of weapons and wampum, and proclaimed the last harsh edict issued from the savage council at Onondaga." *Beginnings of New England*, p. 148.

slaves. Sometimes the tributary pueblo, instead of sacrificing all its prisoners of war upon its own altars, sent some of them up to Mexico as part of its tribute. The ravening maw of the horrible deities was thus appeased, not by the pueblo that paid the blackmail, but by the power that extorted it, and thus the latter obtained a larger share of divine favour. Generally the unhappy prisoners were forced to carry the corn and other articles. They were convoyed by couriers who saw that everything was properly delivered at the *tecpan*, and also brought information by word of mouth and by picture-writing from the *calpixqui* to the " chief-of-men." When the newly arrived Spaniards saw these couriers coming and going they fancied that they were " ambassadors." This system of tribute-taking made it necessary to build roads, and this in turn facilitated, not only military operations, but trade, which had already made some progress albeit of a simple sort. These " roads " might perhaps more properly be called Indian trails,[1] but they served their purpose.

[1] See Salmeron's letter of August 13, 1531, to the Council of the Indies, cited in Bandelier, *op. cit.* p. 696. The letter recommends that to increase the security of the Spanish hold upon the country the roads should be made practicable for beasts and wagons. They were narrow paths running straight ahead up hill and down dale, sometimes crossing narrow ravines upon heavy stone culverts.

The general similarity of the Aztec confederacy to that of the Iroquois, in point of social structure, is thus clearly manifest. Along with this general similarity we have observed some points of higher development, such as one might expect to find in traversing the entire length of an ethnical period. Instead of stockaded villages, with houses of bark or of clay supported upon a wooden frame-work, we have pueblos of adobe-brick or stone, in various stages of evolution, the most advanced of which present the appearance of castellated cities. Along with the systematic irrigation and increased dependence upon horticulture, we find evidences of greater density of population ; and we see in the victorious confederacy a more highly developed organization for adding to its stock of food and other desirable possessions by the systematic plunder of neighbouring weaker communities. Naturally such increase in numbers and organization entails some increase in the number of officers and some differentiation of their functions, as illustrated in the representation of the clans (*calpulli*) in the tribal-council (*tlatocan*), by speakers (*tlatoani*) chosen for the purpose, and not by the official heads (*calpullec*) of the clan. Likewise in the military commander-in-chief (*tlacatecuhtli*) we observe a marked increase in dignity, and — as I have already suggested and

Aztec and Iroquois confederacies contrasted

hope to maintain — we find that his office has been clothed with sacerdotal powers, and has thus taken a decided step toward kingship of the ancient type, as depicted in the Homeric poems.

No feature of the advance is more noteworthy than the development of the medicine-men into an organized priesthood.[1] The presence of this priesthood and its ritual was proclaimed to the eyes of the traveller in ancient Mexico by the numerous tall truncated pyramids (*teocallis*), on the flat summits of which men, women, and children were sacrificed to the gods. This custom of human sacrifice seems to have been a characteristic of the middle period of barbarism, and to have survived, with diminishing frequency, into the upper period. There are abundant traces of its existence throughout the early Aryan world, from Britain to Hindustan, as well as among the ancient Hebrews and their kindred.[2] But

Aztec priesthood : human sacrifices

---

[1] The priesthood was not hereditary, nor did it form a caste. There was no hereditary nobility in ancient Mexico, nor were there any hereditary vocations, as " artisans," "merchants," etc. See Bandelier, *op. cit.* p. 599.

[2] See the copious references in Tylor's *Primitive Culture*, ii. 340–371 ; Mackay, *Religious Development of the Greeks and Hebrews*, ii. 406–434 ; Oort and Hooykaas, *The Bible for Young People*, i. 30, 189–193 ; ii. 102, 220 ; iii. 21, 170, 316, 393, 395 ; iv. 85, 226. Ghillany, *Die Men-*

among all these peoples, at the earliest times at which we can study them with trustworthy records, we find the custom of human sacrifice in an advanced stage of decline, and generally no longer accompanied by the custom of cannibalism in which it probably originated.[1] Among the Mexicans, however, when they were first visited by the Spaniards, cannibalism flourished as nowhere else in the world except perhaps in Fiji, and human sacrifices were conducted on such a scale as could not have been witnessed in Europe without going back more than forty centuries.

The custom of sacrificing captives to the gods was a marked advance upon the practice in the lower period of barbarism, when the prisoner, unless saved by adoption into the tribe of his captors, was put to death with lingering torments. There were occasions on which the Aztecs tortured their prisoners before sending them to the altar,[2] but in general the prisoner was well treated and highly fed, — fatted, in short, for the final banquet in which the wor-

schenopfer der alten Hebräer, Nuremberg, 1842, treats the subject with much learning.

[1] Spencer, Princip. Sociol., i. 287 ; Tylor, op. cit. ii. 345.

[2] Mr. Prescott, to avoid shocking the reader with details, refers him to the twenty-first canto of Dante's Inferno, Conquest of Mexico, vol. i. p. 64.

pant did not own this outcast labourer, any more than he owned his lot; he only possessed a limited right of user in both labourer and lot. To a certain extent it was "adverse" or exclusive possession. If the slave ran away or was obstinately lazy, he could be made to wear a wooden collar and sold without his consent; if it proved too troublesome to keep him, the collared slave could be handed over to the priests for sacrifice.[1] In this class of outcasts and their masters we have an interesting illustration of a rudimentary phase of slavery and of private property.

At this point it is worthy of note that in the development of the family the Aztecs had advanced considerably beyond the point attained by Shawnees and Mohawks, and a little way toward the point attained in the patriarchal family of the ancient Romans and Hebrews. The Aztec family In the Aztec clan (which was exogamous[2]) the change to descent in the male line seems to have been accomplished be-

[1] There was, however, in this extreme case, a right of sanctuary. If the doomed slave could flee and hide himself in the *tecpan* before the master or one of his sons could catch him, he became free and recovered his clan-rights; and no third person was allowed to interfere in aid of the pursuer. Torquemada, *Monarquía indiana*, ii. 564–566.

[2] Bancroft, *Native Races of the Pacific States*, vol. ii. p. 251.

fore the time of the Discovery. Apparently it had been recently accomplished. Names for designating family relationships remained in that primitive stage in which no distinction is made between father and uncle, grandchildren and cousins. The family was still too feebly established to count for much in the structure of society, which still rested firmly upon the clan.[1] Nevertheless the marriage bonds were drawn much tighter than among Indians of the lower status, and penalties for incontinence were more severe. The wife became her husband's property and was entitled to the protection of his clan. All matrimonial arrangements were controlled by the clan, and no member of it, male or female, was allowed to remain unmarried, except for certain religious reasons. The penalty for contumacy was expulsion from the clan, and the same penalty was inflicted for such sexual irregularities as public opinion, still in what we should call quite a primitive stage, condemned. Men and women thus expelled went to swell the numbers of that small class of outcasts already noted. With men the result, as we have seen, was a kind of slavery; with women it was prostitution; and it is curious to see that the same penalty, entailing such a result, was visited alike upon unseemly frailty and upon refusal to marry. In either case the

[1] Bandelier, *op. cit.* pp. 429, 570, 620.

food and raiment, and things of a similar character.

" But in whatever relates to Indian society and government, their social relations and plan of life, they are nearly worthless, because they learned nothing and knew nothing of either. We are at full liberty to reject them in these respects and commence anew ; using any facts they may contain which harmonize with what is known of Indian society." [1]

Perhaps it would have been better if the second of these rules had been somewhat differently worded ; for even with regard to the strange society and government, the Spanish writers have recorded an immense number of valuable facts, without which Mr. Bandelier's work would have been impossible. It is not so much the *facts* as the *interpretations* of the Spanish historians that are " nearly worthless," and even their misinterpretations are interesting and instructive when once we rightly understand them. Sometimes they really help us toward the truth.

The broad distinction, however, as stated in Mr. Morgan's pair of rules, is well taken. In regard to such a strange form of society the Spanish discoverers of Mexico could not help making mistakes, but in regard to utensils and dress their senses were not likely to deceive them, and their statements, according to Mr.

[1] Morgan, *Ancient Society*, p. 186, note.

Morgan, may be trusted. Very good. But as soon as Mr. Morgan had occasion to write about the social life of the Aztecs, he forgot his own rules and paid as little respect to the senses of eye-witnesses as to their judgment. This was amusingly illustrated in his famous essay on "Montezuma's Dinner."[1] When Bernal Diaz describes Montezuma as sitting on a low chair at a table covered with a white cloth, Mr. Morgan declares that it could not have been so, — there were no chairs or tables! On second thought he will admit that there may have been a wooden block hollowed out for a stool, but in the matter of a table he is relentless. So when Cortes, in his despatch to the emperor, speaks of the "wine-cellar" and of the presence of "secretaries" at dinner, Mr. Morgan observes, "Since cursive writing was unknown among the Aztecs, the presence of these secretaries is an amusing feature in the account. The wine-cellar also is remarkable for two reasons: firstly, because the level of the streets and courts was but four feet above the level of the water, which made cellars impossible; and, secondly, because the Aztecs had no knowledge of wine. An acid beer (*pulque*), made by fermenting the juice of the maguey, was a common beverage of the Az-

Mr. Morgan sometimes disregarded his own rules: "Montezuma's Dinner"

---

[1] *North Amer. Review,* April, 1876. The substance of i. was reproduced in his *Houses and House-Life,* chap. x.

tecs; but it is hardly supposable that even this was used at dinner." [1]

To this I would reply that the fibre of that same useful plant from which the Aztecs made their " beer " supplied them also with paper, upon which they were in the habit of writing, not indeed in cursive characters, but in hiero-glyphics. This kind of writing, as well as any other, accounts for the presence of secretaries, which seems to me, by the way, a very probable and characteristic feature in the narrative. From the moment the mysterious strangers landed, every movement of theirs had been recorded in hieroglyphics, and there is no reason why notes of what they said and did should not have been taken at dinner. As for the place where the *pulque* was kept, it was a venial slip of the pen to call it a " wine-cellar," even if it was not be-low the ground. The language of Cortes does not imply that he visited the " cellar; " he saw a crowd of Indians drinking the beverage, and supposing the great house he was in to be Mon-tezuma's, he expressed his sense of that person's hospitality by saying that " his wine-cellar was open to all." And really, is it not rather a captious criticism which in one breath chides Cortes for calling the beverage " wine," and in the next breath goes on to call it " beer " ? The *pulque* was neither the one nor the other; for

[1] *Houses and House-Life*, p. 241.

Año de onçe casas y de 1529
se partio nuño de guzman
para jalisco y endo a su
jeptat Aquella tiersa fin
jen que sale la culebra de el cielo
diziendo que les venia travajo
A los naturales y en dulos
cristianos Alla

REPRESENTATION OF SPANIARDS IN A MEXICAN
MANUSCRIPT, 1529

want of any other name a German might have
called it beer, a Spaniard would be more likely
to call it wine. And why is it "hardly supposable" that *pulque* was used at dinner? Why
should Mr. Morgan, who never dined with
Montezuma, know so much more about *such
things* than Cortes and Bernal Diaz, who did?[1]

The Spanish statements of facts are, of course,
not to be accepted uncritically. When we are
told of cut slabs of porphyry inlaid in the walls
of a room, we have a right to inquire   The reaction
how so hard a stone could be cut with   against uncritical and
flint or copper chisels,[2] and are ready   exaggerated
to entertain the suggestion that some   statements
other stone might easily have been mistaken for
porphyry. Such a critical inquiry is eminently
profitable, and none the less so when it brings
us to the conclusion that the Aztecs did succeed in cutting porphyry. Again, when we read
about Indian armies of 200,000 men, pertinent

[1] Mr. Andrew Lang asks some similar questions in his
Myth, Ritual, and Religion, vol. ii. p. 349, but in a tone of
impatient contempt which, as applied to a man of Mr. Morgan's calibre, is hardly becoming.

[2] For an excellent account of ancient Mexican knives and
chisels, see Dr. Valentini's paper on "Semi-Lunar and Cres-
cent-Shaped Tools," in *Proceedings of Amer. Antiq. Soc.*,
New Series, vol. iii. pp. 449–474. Compare the very interesting Spanish observations on copper hatchets and flint
chisels in Clavigero, *Historia antigua*, tom. i. p. 242 ; Men-
dieta, *Historia ecclesiastica indiana*, tom. iv. cap. xii.

cans, they were ignorant of iron, their society was organized upon the principle of gentilism, they were cannibals and sacrificed men and

" The more I study these characters the stronger becomes the conviction that they have grown out of a pictographic system similar to that common among the Indians of North America.'' Exactly so; and this is typical of every aspect and every detail of ancient American culture. It is becoming daily more evident that the old notion of an influence from Asia has not a leg to stand on.) See also a suggestive paper by the astronomer, E. S. Holden, " Studies in Central American Picture-Writing,'' *First Report of the Bureau of Ethnology*, pp. 205–245 ; Brinton, *Ancient Phonetic Alphabet of Yucatan*, New York, 1870 ; *Essays of an Americanist*, Philadelphia, 1890, pp. 193–304 ; Léon de Rosny, *Les écritures figuratives*, Paris, 1870 ; *L'interprétation des anciens textes Mayas*, Paris, 1875 ; *Essai sur le déchiffrement de l'écriture hiératique de l'Amérique Centrale*, Paris, 1876 ; Förstemann, *Erläuterungen der Maya Handschrift*, Dresden, 1886. The decipherment is as yet but partially accomplished. The Mexican system of writing is clearly developed from the ordinary Indian pictographs ; it could not have arisen from the Maya system, but the latter might well have been a further development of the Mexican system ; the Maya system had probably developed some characters with a phonetic value, *i. e.* was groping toward the alphabetical stage ; but how far this groping had gone must remain very doubtful until the decipherment has proceeded further. Dr. Isaac Taylor is too hasty in saying that " the Mayas employed twenty-seven characters which must be admitted to be alphabetic '' (Taylor, *The Alphabet*, vol. i. p. 24) ; this statement is followed by the conclusion that the Maya system of writing was " superior in simplicity and convenience to that employed . . . by the great Assyrian nation at the epoch of its greatest power

PRE–COLUMBIAN MEXICAN HIEROGLYPHS

From the Codice Cospiano

women to idols, some of which were identical with those of Mexico. The Mayas had no conception of property in land; their buildings were great communal houses, like pueblos; in

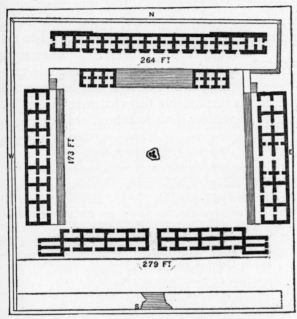

Ground-plan of so-called "House of the Nuns" at Uxmal

some cases these so-called palaces, at first supposed to be scanty remnants of vast cities, were themselves the entire "cities;" in other cases and glory." Dr. Taylor has been misled by Diego de Landa, whose work (*Relation des choses de l' Yucatan*, ed. Brasseur, Paris, 1864) has in it some pitfalls for the unwary.

their antiquity was perhaps suggested by the belief that certain colossal mahogany-trees growing between and over the ruins at Palenque must be nearly 2000 years old. But when M. de Charnay visited Palenque in 1859 he had the eastern side of the " palace " cleared of its dense vegetation in order to get a good photograph ; and when he revisited the spot in 1881 he found a sturdy growth of young mahogany the age of which he knew did not exceed twenty-two years. Instead of making a ring once a year, as in our sluggish and temperate zone, these trees had made rings at the rate of about one in a month ; their trunks were already more than two feet in diameter ; judging from this rate of growth the biggest giant on the place need not have been more than 200 years old, if as much.[1]

These edifices are not so durably constructed they are not the work of people who have passed away and whose history is lost, but that there are strong reasons to believe them the creations of the same races who inhabited the country at the time of the Spanish conquest, or some not very distant progenitors. And I would remark that we began our exploration without any theory to support. . . . Some are beyond doubt older than others ; some are known to have been inhabited at the time of the Spanish conquest, and others, perhaps, were really in ruins before ; . . . but in regard to Uxmal, at least, we believe that it was an existing and inhabited city at the time of the arrival of the Spaniards." Stephens, *Central America*, etc., vol. ii. p. 455.

[1] Charnay, *The Ancient Cities of the New World*, p. 260.

with the general plan of this book. I have not undertaken at present to go beyond the Isthmus of Darien, because this preliminary chapter is already disproportionately long, and after this protracted discussion the reader's attention may be somewhat relieved by an entire change of scene. Enough has been set forth to explain the narrative that follows, and to justify us henceforth in taking certain things for granted. The outline description of Mexico will be completed when we come to the story of its conquest by Spaniards, and then we shall be ready to describe some principal features of Peruvian society and to understand how the Spaniards conquered that country.

There is, however, one conspicuous feature of North American antiquity which has not yet received our attention, and which calls for a few words before we close this chapter. I refer to the mounds that are scattered over so large a part of the soil of the United States, and more particularly to those between the Mississippi River and the Alleghany Mountains, which have been the subject of so much theorizing, and in late years of so much careful study.[1] Vague and wild were

The "Mound-Builders"

[1] For original researches in the mounds one cannot do better than consult the following papers in the *Reports of the Bureau of Ethnology:* — 1. by W. H. Holmes, "Art in

the speculations once rife about the " Mound-Builders " and their wonderful civilization.

Shell of the Ancient Americans," ii. 181–305 ; " The Ancient Pottery of the Mississippi Valley," iv. 365–436 ; " Prehistoric Textile Fabrics of the United States," iii. 397–431 ; followed by an illustrated catalogue of objects collected chiefly from mounds, iii. 433–515 ; — 2. H. W. Henshaw, " Animal Carvings from the Mounds of the Mississippi Valley," ii. 121–166 ; — 3. Cyrus Thomas, " Burial Mounds of the Northern Section of the United States," v. 7–119 ; also three of the Bureau's " Bulletins " by Dr. Thomas, " The Problem of the Ohio Mounds," " The Circular, Square, and Octagonal Earthworks of Ohio," and " Work in Mound Exploration of the Bureau of Ethnology ; " also two articles by Dr. Thomas in the *Magazine of American History :* — " The Houses of the Mound-Builders," xi. 110–115 ; " Indian Tribes in Prehistoric Times," xx. 193–201. See also Horatio Hale, " Indian Migrations," in *American Antiquarian,* v. 18–28, 108–124 ; M. F. Force, *To What Race did the Mound-Builders belong ?* Cincinnati, 1875 ; Lucien Carr, *Mounds of the Mississippi Valley historically considered,* 1883 ; Nadaillac's *Prehistoric America,* ed. W. H. Dall, chaps. iii., iv. The earliest work of fundamental importance on the subject was Squier's *Ancient Monuments of the Mississippi Valley,* Philadelphia, 1848, being the first volume of the Smithsonian Contributions to Knowledge. — For statements of the theory which presumes either a race connection or a similarity in culture between the mound-builders and the pueblo Indians, see Dawson, *Fossil Men,* p. 55 ; Foster, *Prehistoric Races of the United States,* Chicago, 1873, chaps. iii., v.–x. ; Sir Daniel Wilson, *Prehistoric Man,* chap. x. The annual *Smithsonian Reports* for thirty years past illustrate the growth of knowledge and progressive changes of opinion on the subject. The biblio-

They were supposed to have been a race quite different from the red men, with a culture perhaps superior to our own, and more or less eloquence was wasted over the vanished " empire " of the mound-builders. There is no reason, however, for supposing that there ever was an empire of any sort in ancient North America, and no relic of the past has ever been seen at any spot on our planet which indicates the former existence of a vanished civilization even remotely approaching our own. The sooner the student of history gets his head cleared of all such rubbish, the better. As for the mounds, which are scattered in such profusion over the country west of the Alleghanies, there are some which have been built by Indians since the arrival of white men in America, and which contain knives and trinkets of European manufacture. There are many others which are much older, and in which the genuine remains sometimes indicate a culture like that of Shawnees or Senecas, and sometimes suggest something perhaps a little higher. With the progress of research the vast and vague notion of a distinct race of " Mound-Builders " became The notion narrowed and defined. It began to that they were like seem probable that the builders of the Aztecs ; the more remarkable mounds were tribes of

graphical account in Winsor's *Narr. and Crit. Hist.*, i. 397–412, is full of minute information.

Indians who had advanced beyond the average level in horticulture, and consequently in density of population, and perhaps in political and priestly organization. Such a conclusion seemed to be supported by the size of some of the "ancient garden-beds," often covering more than a hundred acres, filled with the low parallel ridges in which corn was planted. The mound people were thus supposed to be semi-civilized red men, like the Aztecs, and some of their elevated earthworks were explained as places for human sacrifice, like the pyramids of Mexico and Central America. It was thought that the "civilization" of the Cordilleran peoples might formerly have extended northward and eastward into the Mississippi valley, and might after a while have been pushed back by powerful hordes of more barbarous invaders. A further modification and reduction of this theory likened the mound-builders to the pueblo Indians of New Mexico. Such was the opinion of Mr. Morgan, who offered a very ingenious explanation of the extensive earthworks at High Bank, in Ross County, Ohio, as the fortified site of a pueblo.[1] Although there is no reason for supposing that the mound-builders practised irrigation (which would not be required in the Mississippi valley) or used adobe-brick, yet Mr. Morgan was inclined to admit them

[1] *Houses and House-Life*, chap. ix.

into his middle status of barbarism because of
the copper hatchets and chisels found in some
of the mounds, and because of the or like the
Zuñis
apparent superiority in horticulture
and the increased reliance upon it. He suggested that a people somewhat like the Zuñis
might have migrated eastward and modified
their building habits to suit the altered conditions of the Mississippi valley, where they dwelt
for several centuries, until at last, for some unknown reason, they retired to the Rocky Mountain region. It seems to me that an opinion
just the reverse of Mr. Morgan's would be
more easily defensible, — namely, that the ancestors of the pueblo Indians were a people of
building habits somewhat similar to the Mandans, and that their habits became modified in
adaptation to a country which demanded careful irrigation and supplied adobe-clay in abundance. If ever they built any of the mounds in
the Mississippi valley, I should be disposed to
place their mound-building period before their
pueblo period.

Recent researches, however, make it more and
more improbable that the mound-builders were
nearly akin to such people as the Zuñis or similar to them in grade of culture. Of late years
the exploration of the mounds has been carried
on with increasing diligence. More than 2000
mounds have been opened, and at least 38,000

ancient relics have been gathered from them:
such as quartzite arrow-heads and spades, green-
stone axes and hammers, mortars and pestles,
tools for spinning and weaving, and cloth, made
of spun thread and woven with warp and woof,
somewhat like a coarse sail-cloth. The water-
jugs, kettles, pipes, and sepulchral urns have
been elaborately studied. The net results of all
this investigation, up to the present time, have
been concisely summed up by Dr.
Cyrus Thomas.[1] The mounds were
not all built by one people, but by different tribes as clearly distinguishable
from one another as Algonquins are
distinguishable from Iroquois. These mound-
building tribes were not superior in culture to
the Iroquois and many of the Algonquins as
first seen by white men. They are not to be
classified with Zuñis, still less with Mexicans or
Mayas, in point of culture, but with Shawnees
and Cherokees. Nay more, — some of them
were Shawnees and Cherokees. The missionary
Johann Heckewelder long ago published the
Lenape tradition of the Tallegwi or Allighewi
people, who have left their name upon the

The mounds were probably built by different peoples in the lower status of barbarism;

[1] *Work in Mound Exploration of the Bureau of Ethnology,*
Washington, 1887. For a sight of the thousands of objects
gathered from the mounds, one should visit the Peabody Museum at Cambridge and the Smithsonian Institution at Washington.

Alleghany river and mountains.[1] The Tallegwi have been identified with the Cherokees, who are now reckoned among the most intelligent and progressive of Indian peoples.[2] The Cherokees were formerly classed in the Muskoki group, along with the Creeks and Choctaws, but a closer study of their language seems to show that they were a somewhat remote offshoot of the Huron-Iroquois stock. For a long time they occupied the country between the Ohio River and the Great Lakes, and probably built the mounds that are still to be seen there. Somewhere about the thirteenth or fourteenth century they were gradually pushed southward into the Muskoki region by repeated attacks from the Lenape and Hurons. The Cherokees were probably also the builders of the mounds of eastern Tennessee and western North Carolina. They retained their mound-building habits some time after the white men came upon the scene. On the other hand the mounds and box-shaped stone graves of Kentucky, Tennessee, and northern Georgia were

by Cherokees;

[1] Heckewelder, *History of the Indian Nations of Pennsylvania*, etc., Philadelphia, 1818; cf. Squier, *Historical and Mythological Traditions of the Algonquins*, a paper read before the New York Historical Society in June, 1848; also Brinton, *The Lenape and their Legends*, Philadelphia, 1885.

[2] For a detailed account of their later history, see C. C. Royce, "The Cherokee Nation," *Reports of Bureau of Ethnology*, v. 121–378.

probably the work of Shawnees, and the stone graves in the Delaware valley are to be ascribed to the Lenape. There are many rea-

sons for believing that the mounds of northern Mississippi were constructed by Chickasaws, and the burial tumuli and "effigy mounds" of Wisconsin by Winnebagos. The Minnitarees and Mandans were also very likely at one time a mound-building people.

If this view, which is steadily gaining ground, be correct, our imaginary race of " Mound-Builders " is broken up and vanishes, and henceforth we may content ourselves with speaking of the authors of the ancient earthworks as " Indians." There were times in the career of sundry Indian tribes when circumstances induced them to erect mounds as sites for communal houses or council houses, medicine-lodges or burial-places ; somewhat as there was a period in the history of our own forefathers in England when circumstances led them to build moated castles, with drawbridge and portcullis ; and there is no more occasion for assuming a mysterious race of " Mound-Builders " in America than for assuming a mysterious race of " Castle-Builders " in England.

Thus, at whatever point we touch the subject of ancient America, we find scientific opinion tending more and more steadily toward the conclusion that its people and their culture were indigenous. One of the most important lessons impressed upon us by a long study of comparative mythology is that human minds in different parts of the world, but under the influence of similar circumstances, develop similar ideas and clothe them in similar forms of expression. It is just the same with political institutions, with the development of the arts, with social customs, with culture generally.

Society in America at the time of the Discovery had reached stages similar to stages reached by eastern Mediterranean peoples fifty or sixty centuries earlier

To repeat the remark already quoted from Sir John Lubbock, — and it is well worth repeating, — " Different races in similar stages of development often present more features of resemblance to one another than the same race does to itself in different stages of its history." When the zealous Abbé Brasseur found things in the history of Mexico that reminded him of ancient Egypt, he hastened to the conclusion that Mexican culture was somehow " derived " from that of Egypt. It was natural enough for him to do so, but such methods of explanation are now completely antiquated. Mexican culture was no more Egyptian culture than a prickly-pear is a lotus. It was an outgrowth of peculiar American conditions acting upon the aboriginal American mind, and such of its features as remind us of ancient Egypt or prehistoric Greece show simply that it was approaching, though it had not reached, the standard attained in those Old World countries. From this point of view the resemblances become invested with surpassing interest. Ancient America, as we have seen, was a much more archaic world than the world of Europe and Asia, and presented in the time of Columbus forms of society that on the shores of the Mediterranean had been outgrown before the city of Rome was built. Hence the intense and peculiar fascination of American archæology, and its profound importance to the student of general history.

II

PRE–COLUMBIAN VOYAGES

THERE is something solemn and impressive in the spectacle of human life thus going on for countless ages in the Eastern and Western halves of our planet, each all unknown to the other and uninfluenced by it. The contact between the two worlds practically begins in 1492.

By this statement it is not meant to deny that occasional visitors may have come and did come before that famous date from the Old World to the New. On the contrary I am inclined to suspect that there may have been more such occasional visits than we have been wont to suppose. For the most part, however, the subject is shrouded in the mists of obscure narrative and fantastic conjecture. When it is argued that in the fifth century of the Christian era certain Buddhist missionary priests came from China by way of Kamtchatka and the _{The Chinese} Aleutian Islands, and kept on till they got to a country which they called Fusang, and which was really Mexico, one cannot reply that such a thing was necessarily and absolutely impossible ; but when other critics assure us that, after all, Fusang was really Japan, perhaps one feels a slight sense of relief.[1] So of the dim whispers of voyages to America undertaken by the Irish, in the days when the cloisters of sweet Innisfallen were a centre of piety and culture for northwestern Europe,[2] we may say that this sort of thing has not much to do with history, or history with it. Irish anchorites certainly went to Iceland in the seventh

The Irish

---

[1] This notion of the Chinese visiting Mexico was set forth by the celebrated Deguignes in 1761, in the *Mémoires de l'Académie des Inscriptions*, tom. xxviii. pp. 506–525. Its absurdity was shown by Klaproth, " Recherches sur le pays de Fou Sang," *Nouvelles annales des voyages*, Paris, 1831, 2e série, tom. xxi. pp. 53–68 ; see also Klaproth's introduction to *Annales des empereurs du Japon*, Paris, 1834, pp. iv–ix ; Humboldt, *Examen critique de l'histoire de la géographie du nouveau continent*, Paris, 1837, tom. ii. pp. 62–84. The fancy was revived by C. G. Leland (" Hans Breitmann "), in his *Fusang*, London, 1875, and was again demolished by the missionary, S. W. Williams, in the *Journal of the American Oriental Society*, vol. xi., New Haven, 1881.

[2] On the noble work of the Irish church and its missionaries in the sixth and seventh centuries, see Montalembert, *Les moines d'Occident*, tom. ii. pp. 465–661 ; tom. iii. pp. 79–332 ; Burton's *History of Scotland*, vol. i. pp. 234–277 ; and the instructive map in Miss Sophie Bryant's *Celtic Ireland*, London, 1889, p. 60. The notice of the subject in Milman's *Latin Christianity*, vol. ii. pp. 236–247, is entirely inadequate.

century,[1] and in the course of this book we shall have frequent occasion to observe that first and last there has been on all seas a good deal of blowing and drifting done. It is credibly reported that Japanese junks have been driven ashore on the coasts of Oregon and California; [2] and there is a story that in 1488 a certain Jean Cousin, of Dieppe, while sailing down the west coast of Africa, was caught in a storm and blown across to Brazil.[3] This was certainly quite possible, for it was not so very unlike what happened in 1500 to Pedro Alvarez de Cabral, as we shall hereafter see; [4] nevertheless, the evidence adduced in support

Cousin, of Dieppe

---

[1] The passion for solitude led some of the disciples of St. Columba to make their way from Iona to the Hebrides, and thence to the Orkneys, Shetlands, Færoes, and Iceland, where a colony of them remained until the arrival of the Northmen in 874. See Dicuil, *Liber de mensura Orbis Terræ* (A. D. 825), Paris, 1807 ; Innes, *Scotland in the Middle Ages*, p. 101 ; Lanigan, *Ecclesiastical History of Ireland*, chap. iii. ; Maurer, *Beiträge zur Rechtsgeschichte des Germanischen Nordens*, i. 35. For the legend of St. Brandan, see Gaffarel, *Les voyages de St. Brandan*, Paris, 1881.

[2] C. W. Brooks, of San Francisco, cited in Higginson, *Larger History of the United States*, p. 24.

[3] Desmarquets, *Mémoires chronologiques pour servir à l'histoire de Dieppe*, Paris, 1785, tom. i. pp. 91–98 ; Estancelin, *Recherches sur les voyages et découvertes des navigateurs normands*, etc., Paris, 1832, pp. 332–361.

[4] See below, vol. ii. p. 323.

of the story will hardly bear a critical examination.[1]

It is not my purpose to weary the reader with a general discussion of these and some other legends or rumours of pre-Columbian visitors to America. We may admit, at once, that " there is no good reason why any one of them may not have done " what is claimed, but at the same time the proof that any one of them *did* do it is very far from satisfactory.[2] Moreover the questions raised are often of small importance, and belong not so much to the serious workshop of history as to its limbo prepared for learned trifles, whither we will hereby relegate them.[3]

These stories are of little value;

But when we come to the voyages of the Northmen in the tenth and eleventh centuries,

[1] As Harrisse says, concerning the alleged voyages of Cousin and others, " Quant aux voyages du Dieppois Jean Cousin en 1488, de João Ramalho en 1490, et de João Vaz Cortereal en 1464 ou 1474, le lecteur nous pardonnera de les passer sous silence." *Christophe Colomb*, Paris, 1884, tom. i. p. 307.

[2] Winsor, *Narr. and Crit. Hist.*, i. 59.

[3] Sufficiently full references may be found in Watson's *Bibliography of the Pre-Columbian Discoveries of America*, appended to Anderson's *America not discovered by Columbus*, 3d ed., Chicago, 1883, pp. 121–164 ; and see the learned chapters by W. H. Tillinghast on " The Geographical Knowledge of the Ancients considered in relation to the Discovery of America," and by Justin Winsor on " Pre-Columbian Explorations," in *Narr. and Crit. Hist.*, vol. i.

it is quite a different affair. Not only is this a subject of much historic interest, but in dealing with it we stand for a great part of the time upon firm historic ground. but the case of the Northmen is entirely different The narratives which tell us of Vinland and of Leif Ericsson are closely intertwined with the authentic history of Norway and Iceland. In the ninth century of our era there was a process of political consolidation going on in Norway, somewhat as in England under Egbert and his successors. After a war of twelve years, King Harold Fairhair overthrew the combined forces of the Jarls, or small independent princes, in the decisive naval battle of Hafursfiord in the year 872. This resulted in making Harold the feudal landlord of Norway. Allodial tenures were abolished, and the Jarls were required to become his vassals. This consolidation of the kingdom was probably beneficial in its main consequences, but to many a proud spirit and crafty brain it made life in Norway unendurable. These bold Jarls and their Viking[1] followers, to whom, as to the ancient Greeks, the sea was not a barrier, but a highway,[2] had no

[1] The proper division of this Old Norse word is not into *vi-king*, but into *vĭk-ing*. The first syllable means a " bay " or " fiord," the second is a patronymic termination, so that " vikings " are " sons of the fiord," — an eminently appropriate and descriptive name.

[2] Curtius (*Griechischen Etymologie*, p. 237) connects

mind to stay at home and submit to unwonted thraldom. So they manned their dragon-prowed keels, invoked the blessing of Wodan, god of storms, upon their enterprise, and sailed away. Some went to reinforce their kinsmen who were making it so hot for Alfred in England [1] and for Charles the Bald in Gaul ; some had already visited Ireland and were establishing themselves at Dublin and Limerick ; others now followed and found homes for themselves in the Hebrides and all over Scotland north of glorious Loch Linnhe and the Murray frith ; some made their way through the blue Mediterranean to " Micklegard," the Great City of the Byzantine Emperor, and in his service wielded their stout axes against Magyar and Saracen ; [2] some found their

The Viking exodus from Norway

πόντος with πάτος ; compare the Homeric expressions ὑγρὰ κέλευθα, ἰχθυόεντα κέλευθα, etc.

[1] The descendants of these Northmen formed a very large proportion of the population of the East Anglian counties, and consequently of the men who founded New England. The East Anglian counties have been conspicuous for resistance to tyranny and for freedom of thought. See my *Beginnings of New England*, chap. ii.

[2] They were the Varangian guard at Constantinople, described by Sir Walter Scott in *Count Robert of Paris*. About this same time their kinsmen, the Russ, moving eastward from Sweden, were subjecting Slavic tribes as far as Novgorod and Kief, and laying the foundations of the power that has since, through many and strange vicissitudes, developed into

amphibious natures better satisfied upon the islands of the Atlantic ridge, — the Orkneys, Shetlands, and Færoes, and especially noble Iceland. There an aristocratic re- Founding of public soon grew up, owning slight Iceland, A. D. and indefinite allegiance to the kings 874 of Norway.[1] The settlement of Iceland was such a wholesale colonization of communities of picked men as had not been seen since ancient Greek times, and was not to be seen again until Winthrop sailed into Massachusetts Bay. It was not long before the population of Iceland exceeded 50,000 souls. Their sheep and cattle flourished, hay crops were heavy, a lively trade — with fish, oil, butter, skins, and wool, in exchange for meal and malt — was kept up with Norway, Denmark, and the British islands, political freedom was unimpaired,[2] justice was

Russia. See Thomsen, *The Relations between Ancient Russia and Scandinavia*, Oxford, 1877.

[1] Fealty to Norway was not formally declared until 1262.

[2] The settlement of Iceland is celebrated by Robert Lowe in verses which show that, whatever his opinion may have been in later years as to the use of a classical education, his own early studies must always have been a source of comfort to him : —

> Χαῖρε καί ἐν νεφέλαισι καί ἐν νιφάδεσσι βαρείαις
> Καὶ πυρὶ καὶ σεισμοῖς νῆσε σαλευομένη·
> Ἐνθάδε γὰρ βασιλῆος ὑπέρβιον ὕβριν ἀλύξας
> Δῆμος Ὑπερβορέων, κόσμου ἐπ᾽ ἐσχατιῇ,
> Αὐτάρκη βίοτον θείων τ᾽ ἐρεθίσματα Μουσῶν
> Καὶ θεσμοὺς ἀγνῆς εὗρεν ἐλευθερίας.

These verses are thus rendered by Sir Edmund Head (*Viga Glums Saga*, p. v) : —

(for the Middle Ages) fairly well administered, naval superiority kept all foes at a distance; and under such conditions the growth of the new community in wealth [1] and culture was surprisingly rapid. In the twelfth century, before literature had begun to blossom in the modern speech of France or Spain or Italy, there was a flourishing literature in prose and verse in Iceland. Especial attention was paid to history, and the " Landnáma-bók," or statistical and genealogical account of the early settlers, was the most complete and careful work of the kind which had ever been undertaken by any people down to quite recent times. Few persons

> " Hail, Isle ! with mist and snowstorms girt around,
> Where fire and earthquake rend the shattered ground, —
> Here once o'er furthest ocean's icy path
> The Northmen fled a tyrant monarch's wrath :
> Here, cheered by song and story, dwelt they free,
> And held unscathed their laws and liberty."

Laing (*Heimskringla,* vol. i. p. 57) couples Iceland and New England as the two modern colonies most distinctly " founded on principle and peopled at first from higher motives than want or gain."

[1] Just what was then considered wealth, for an individual, may best be understood by a concrete instance. The historian Snorro Sturleson, born in 1178, was called a rich man. " In one year, in which fodder was scarce, he lost 120 head of oxen without being seriously affected by it." The fortune which he got with his first wife Herdisa, in 1199, was equivalent nominally to $4000, or, according to the standard of to-day, about $80,000. Laing, *Heimskringla,* vol. i. pp. 191, 193.

in our day adequately realize the extent of the early Icelandic literature or its richness. The poems, legends, and histories earlier than the date when Dante walked and mused in the streets of Florence survive for us now in some hundreds of works, for the most part of rare and absorbing interest. The " Heimskringla," or chronicle of Snorro Sturleson, written about 1215, is one of the greatest history books in the world.[1]

Now from various Icelandic chronicles[2] we

[1] Laing's excellent English translation of it was published in London in 1844. The preliminary dissertation, in five chapters, is of great value. A new edition, revised by Prof. Rasmus Anderson, was published in London in 1889. Another charming book is Sir George Dasent's *Story of Burnt Njal*, Edinburgh, 1861, 2 vols., translated from the *Njals Saga*. Both the saga itself and the translator's learned introduction give an admirable description of life in Iceland at the end of the tenth century, the time when the voyages to America were made. It is a very instructive chapter in history.

The Icelanders of the present day retain the Old Norse language, while on the Continent it has been modified into Swedish and Norwegian-Danish. They are a well-educated people, and, in proportion to their numbers, publish many books.

[2] A full collection of these chronicles is given in Rafn's *Antiquitates Americanæ*, Copenhagen, 1837, in the original Icelandic, with Danish and Latin translations. This book is of great value for its full and careful reproduction of original texts ; although the rash speculations and the want of critical discernment shown in the editor's efforts to determine the precise situation of Vinland have done much to discredit the

learn that in 876, only two years after the island
commonwealth was founded, one of the set-

whole subject in the eyes of many scholars. That is, however, very apt to be the case with first attempts, like Rafn's,
and the obvious defects of his work should not be allowed to
blind us to its merits. In the footnotes to the present chapter
I shall cite it simply as " Rafn ; " as the exact phraseology
is often important, I shall usually cite the original Icelandic,
and (for the benefit of readers unfamiliar with that language)
shall also give the Latin version, which has been well made,
and quite happily reflects the fresh and pithy vigour of the
original. An English translation of all the essential parts may
be found in De Costa, *Pre-Columbian Discovery of America
by the Northmen*, 2d ed., Albany, 1890 ; see also Slafter,
Voyages of the Northmen to America, Boston, 1877 (Prince
Society). An Icelandic version, interpolated in Peringskiold's
edition of the *Heimskringla*, 1697, is translated in Laing,
vol. iii. pp. 344–361.

The first modern writer to call attention to the Icelandic
voyages to Greenland and Vinland was Arngrim Jónsson, in his
Crymogæa, Hamburg, 1610, and more explicitly in his *Speci-
men Islandiæ historicum*, Amsterdam, 1643. The voyages
are also mentioned by Campanius, in his *Kort beskrifning
om provincien Nya Swerige uti America*, Stockholm, 1702.
The first, however, to bring the subject prominently before
European readers was that judicious scholar Thormodus Torfæus, in his two books *Historia Vinlandiæ antiquæ*, and *Historia Gronlandiæ antiquæ*, Copenhagen, 1705 and 1706.
Later writers have until very recently added but little that is
important to the work of Torfæus. In the voluminous literature of the subject the discussions chiefly worthy of mention
are Forster's *Geschichte der Entdeckungen und Schiffahrten im
Norden*, Frankfort, 1784, pp. 44–88 ; and Humboldt, *Examen critique*, etc., Paris, 1837, tom. i. pp. 84–104 ; see,
also, Major, *Select Letters of Columbus*, London, 1847

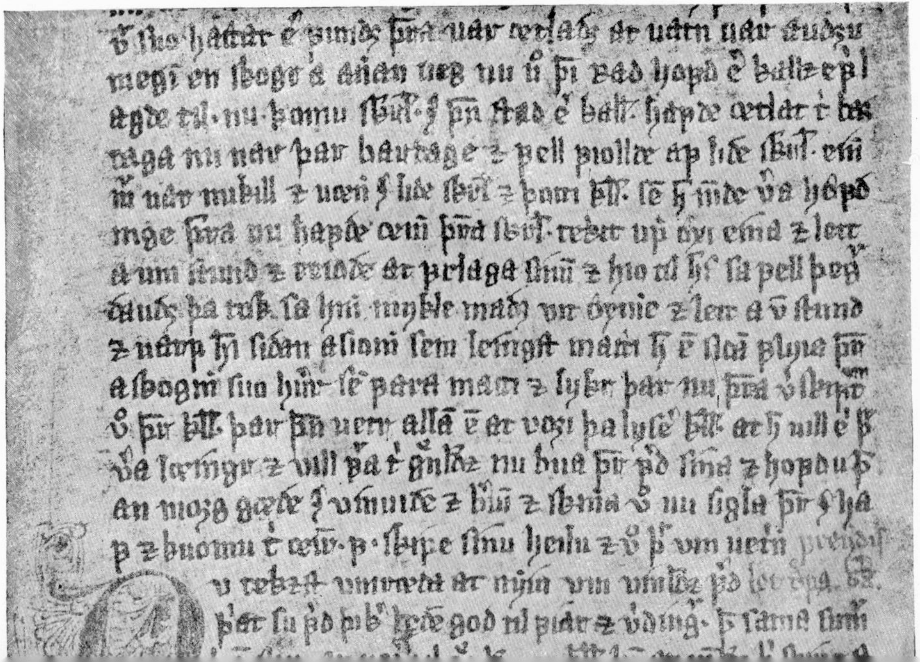

ICELANDIC MANUSCRIPT

One quarter of a page of the Flatey book

tlers named Gunnbjörn was driven by foul weather to some point on the coast of Greenland, where he and his crew contrived to pass the winter, their ship being locked in ice; when the spring set them free, they returned to Iceland. In the year 983

Discovery of Greenland, 876

(Hakluyt Soc.), pp. xii–xxi. The fifth chapter of Samuel Laing's preliminary dissertation to the *Heimskringla*, which is devoted to this subject, is full of good sense ; for the most part the shrewd Orkneyman gets at the core of the thing, though now and then a little closer knowledge of America would have been useful to him. The latest critical discussion of the sources, marking a very decided advance since Rafn's time, is the paper by Gustav Storm, professor of history in the University of Christiania, " Studier over Vinlandsreiserne," in *Aarbøger for Nordisk Oldkyndighed og Historie*, Copenhagen, 1887, pp. 293–372.

Since this chapter was written I have seen an English translation of the valuable paper just mentioned, " Studies on the Vineland Voyages," in *Mémoires de la société royale des antiquaires du Nord*, Copenhagen, 1888, pp. 307–370. I have therefore in most cases altered my footnote references below, making the page-numbers refer to the English version (in which, by the way, some parts of the Norwegian original are, for no very obvious reason, omitted). By an odd coincidence there comes to me at the same time a book fresh from the press, whose rare beauty of mechanical workmanship is fully equalled by its intrinsic merit, *The Finding of Wineland the Good — the History of the Icelandic Discovery of America*, edited and translated from the earliest records by Arthur Middleton Reeves, London, 1890. This beautiful quarto contains phototype plates of the original Icelandic vellums in the *Hauks-bók*, the MS. AM. 557, and the *Flateyar-bók*, together with the texts carefully edited, an admirable English

Eric the Red, a settler upon Öxney (Ox-island) near the mouth of Breidafiord, was outlawed for killing a man in a brawl. Eric then determined to search for the western land which Gunnbjörn had discovered. He set out with a few followers, and in the next three years these bold sailors explored the coasts of Greenland pretty thoroughly for a considerable distance on each side of Cape Farewell. At length they found a suitable place for a home, at the head of Igaliko fiord, not far from the site of the modern Julianeshaab.[1] It was fit work for Vikings to penetrate so deep a fiord and find out such a spot, hidden as it is by miles upon miles of craggy and ice-covered headlands. They proved their sagacity by pitching upon one of the pleasantest spots on the gaunt Greenland coast; and there upon a smooth grassy plain may still be seen the ruins of seventeen houses built of rough blocks of sandstone, their chinks caulked up with clay and gravel. In contrast with most of its bleak

translation, and several chapters of critical discussion decidedly better than anything that has gone before it. On reading it carefully through, it seems to me the best book we have on the subject in English, or perhaps in any language.

Since the above was written, the news has come of the sudden and dreadful death of Mr. Reeves, in the railroad disaster at Hagerstown, Indiana, February 25, 1891. Mr. Reeves was an American scholar of most brilliant promise, only in his thirty-fifth year.

[1] Rink, *Danish Greenland*, p. 6.

surroundings the place might well be called Greenland, and so Eric named it, for, said he, it is well to have a pleasant name if we would induce people to come hither. The name thus given by Eric to this chosen spot has been extended in modern usage to the whole of the vast continental region north of Davis Strait, for the greater part of which it is a flagrant misnomer.[1] In 986 Eric ventured back to Iceland, and was so successful in enlisting settlers for Greenland that on his return voyage he started with five and twenty ships. The loss from foul weather and icebergs was cruel. Eleven vessels were lost; the remaining fourteen, carrying probably from four to five hundred souls, arrived safely at the head of Igaliko fiord, and began building their houses at the place called Brattahlid. Their settlement presently extended over the head of

Eric's colony in Greenland, 986

---

[1] We thus see the treacherousness of one of the arguments cited by the illustrious Arago to prove that the Greenland coast must be colder now than in the tenth century. The Icelanders, he thinks, called it "a green land" because of its verdure, and therefore it must have been warmer than at present. But the land which Eric called green was evidently nothing more than the region about Julianeshaab, which still has plenty of verdure; and so the argument falls to the ground. See Arago, *Sur l'état thermométrique du globe terrestre*, in his *Œuvres*, tom. v. p. 243. There are reasons, however, for believing that Greenland was warmer in the tenth century than at present. See below, p. 203.

Tunnudliorbik fiord, the next deep inlet to the northwest; they called it Ericsfiord. After a while it extended westward as far as Immarti-nek, and eastward as far as the site of Friedrich-sthal; and another distinct settlement of less extent was also made about four hundred miles to the northwest, near the present site of God-thaab. The older settlement, which began at Igaliko fiord, was known as the East Bygd;[1]

[1] The map is reduced from Rafn's *Antiquitates Americanæ*, tab. xv. The ruins dotted here and there upon it have been known ever since the last rediscovery of Greenland in 1721, but until after 1831 they were generally supposed to be the ruins of the West Bygd. After the fifteenth century, when the old colony had perished, and its existence had become a mere literary tradition, there grew up a notion that the names East Bygd and West Bygd indicated that the two settlements must have been respectively eastward and westward of Cape Farewell ; and after 1721 much time was wasted in looking for vestiges of human habitations on the barren and ice-bound eastern coast. At length, in 1828–31, the exploring expedi-tion sent out by the Danish government, under the very able and intelligent Captain Graah, demonstrated that both settle-ments were west of Cape Farewell, and that the ruins here indicated upon the map are the ruins of the East Bygd. It now became apparent that a certain description of Greenland by Ivar Bardsen — written in Greenland in the fourteenth century, and generally accessible to European scholars since the end of the sixteenth, but not held in much esteem before Captain Graah's expedition — was quite accurate and ex-tremely valuable. From Bardsen's description, about which we shall have more to say hereafter, we can point out upon the map the ancient sites with much confidence. Of those mentioned in the present work, the bishop's church, or " ca-

184

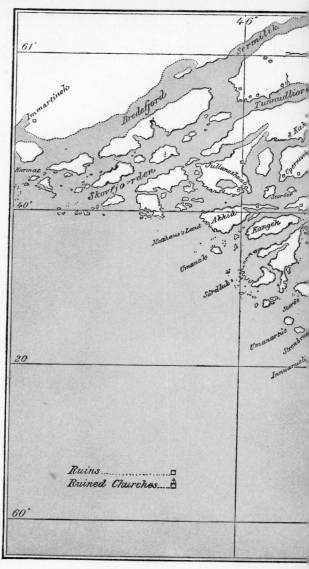

THE EAST BYGD, OR EASTERN SETT

the younger settlement, near Godthaab, was called the West Bygd.

This colonization of Greenland by the Northmen in the tenth century is as well established as any event that occurred in the Middle Ages. For four hundred years the fortunes of the Greenland colony formed a part, albeit a very humble part, of European history. Geographically speaking, Greenland is reckoned as a part of America, of the western hemisphere, and not of the eastern. The Northmen who settled in Greenland had, therefore, in this sense found their way to America. Nevertheless one rightly feels that in the history of geographical discovery an arrival of Europeans in Greenland is equivalent merely to reaching the vestibule or ante-chamber of the western hemisphere. It is an affair begun and ended outside of the great world of the red men.

thedral" (a view of which is given below, p. 257), was at Kakortok. The village of Gardar, which gave its name to the bishopric, was at Kaksiarsuk, at the northeastern extremity of Igaliko fiord. Opposite Kaksiarsuk, on the western fork of the fiord, the reader will observe a ruined church ; that marks the site of Brattahlid. The fiord of Igaliko was called by the Northmen Einarsfiord ; and that of Tunnudliorbik was their Ericsfiord. The monastery of St. Olaus, visited by Nicolò Zeno (see below, p. 276), is supposed by Mr. Major to have been situated near the Iisblink at the bottom of Tessermiut fiord, between the east shore of the fiord and the small lake indicated on the map.

But the story does not end here. Into the world of the red men the voyagers from Iceland did assuredly come, as indeed, after once getting a foothold upon Greenland, they could hardly fail to do. Let us pursue the remainder of the story as we find it in our Icelandic sources of information, and afterwards it will be proper to inquire into the credibility of these sources.

One of the men who accompanied Eric to Greenland was named Herjulf, whose son Bjarni, after roving the seas for some years, came home to Iceland in 986 to drink the Yuletide ale with his father. Finding him gone, he weighed anchor and started after him to Greenland, but encountered foggy weather, and sailed on for many days by guesswork without seeing sun or stars. When at length he sighted land it was a shore without mountains, showing only small heights covered with dense woods. It was evidently not the land of fiords and glaciers for which Bjarni was looking. So without stopping to make explorations he turned his prow to the north and kept on. The sky was now fair, and after scudding nine or ten days with a brisk breeze astern, Bjarni saw the icy crags of Greenland looming up before him, and after some further searching found his way to his father's new home.[1] On the route

Voyage of Bjarni Herjulfson, 986

[1] In Herjulfsfiord, at the entrance to which the modern Friedrichsthal is situated. Across the fiord from Friedrichsthal

he more than once sighted land on the lar-
board.

This adventure of Bjarni's seems not to have
excited general curiosity or to have awakened
speculation. Indeed, in the dense geographical
ignorance of those times there is no reason why it
should have done so. About 994 Bjarni was in
Norway, and one or two people expressed some
surprise that he did not take more pains to learn
something about the country he had seen ; but
nothing came of such talk till it reached the ears
of Leif, the famous son of Eric the Red. This
wise and stately man [1] spent a year or two in
Norway about 998. Roman missionary priests
were then preaching up and down the Conversion
land, and had converted the king, Olaf of the Northmen to Chris-
Tryggvesson, great-grandson of Har- tianity
old Fairhair. Leif became a Christian and was
baptized, and when he returned to Greenland
he took priests with him who converted many
people, though old Eric, it is said, preferred to go
in the way of his fathers, and deemed boisterous
Valhalla, with its cups of wassail, a place of better

a ruined church stands upon the cape formerly known as Her-
julfsness. See map.

[1] "Leifr var mikill madhr ok sterkr, manna sköruligastr at
sjá, vitr madhr ok gódhr hófsmadhr um alla hluti," *i. e.*
"Leif was a large man and strong, of noble aspect, prudent
and moderate in all things." Rafn, p. 33.

187

cheer than the New Jerusalem, with its streets of gold.

Leif's zeal for the conversion of his friends in Greenland did not so far occupy his mind as to prevent him from undertaking a voyage of discovery. His curiosity had been stimulated by what he had heard about Bjarni's experiences, and he made up his mind to go and see what the coasts to the south of Greenland were like.

Leif Erics-son's voyage, 1000 He sailed from Brattahlid — probably in the summer or early autumn of the year 1000[1] — with a crew of five and thirty men. Some distance to the southward they came upon a barren country covered with big flat stones, so that they called it Helluland, or " slate-land." There is little

Helluland room for doubt that this was the coast opposite Greenland, either west or east of the Strait of Belle Isle ; in other words, it was either Labrador or the northern coast of Newfoundland. Thence, keeping generally to the southward, our explorers came after some days to

[1] The year seems to have been that in which Christianity was definitely established by law in Iceland, viz., A. D. 1000. The chronicle *Thattr Eireks Raudha* is careful about verifying its dates by checking one against another. See Rafn, p. 15. The most masterly work on the conversion of the Scandinavian people is Maurer's *Die Bekehrung des Norwegischen Stammes zum Christenthume*, Munich, 1855 ; for an account of the missionary work in Iceland and Greenland, see vol. i. pp. 191–242, 443–452.

a thickly wooded coast, where they landed and inspected the country. What chiefly impressed them was the extent of the forest, so that they called the place Markland, or " wood-land." Some critics have supposed that this spot was somewhere upon the eastern Markland or southern coast of Newfoundland, but the more general opinion places it somewhere upon the coast of Cape Breton Island or Nova Scotia. From this Markland our voyagers stood out to sea, and running briskly before a stiff northeaster it was more than two days before they came in sight of land. Then, after following the coast for a while, they went ashore at a place where a river, issuing from a lake, fell into the sea. They brought their ship up into the lake and cast anchor. The water abounded in excellent fish, and the country seemed so pleasant that Leif decided to pass the winter there, and accordingly his men put up some comfortable wooden huts or booths. One day one of the party, a " south country " man, whose name was Tyrker,[1] came in from a ramble in the neigh-

---

[1] The name means " Turk," and has served as a touchstone for the dulness of commentators. To the Northmen a " Southman " would naturally be a German, and why should a German be called a Turk ? or how should these Northmen happen to have had a Turk in their company ? Mr. Laing suggests that he may have been a Magyar. Yes ; or he may have visited the Eastern Empire and taken part in a fight

bourhood making grimaces and talking to himself in his own language (probably German), which his comrades did not understand. On being interrogated as to the cause of his excitement, he replied that he had discovered vines loaded with grapes, and was much pleased at the sight inasmuch as he had been brought up in a vine country. Wild grapes, indeed, abounded in this autumn season, and Leif accordingly called the country Vinland. The winter seems to have passed off very comfortably. Even the weather seemed mild to these visitors from high latitudes, and they did not fail to comment on the unusual length of the winter day. Their language on this point has been so construed as to make the length of the shortest winter day exactly nine hours, which would place their Vinland in about the latitude of Boston. But their expressions do not admit of any such precise construction ; and when we

Vinland

against Turks, and so have got a sobriquet, just as Thorhall Gamlason, after returning from Vinland to Iceland, was ever afterward known as " the Vinlander." That did not mean that he was an American redskin. See below, p. 235. From Tyrker's grimaces one commentator sagely infers that he had been eating grapes and got drunk ; and another (even Mr. Laing !) thinks it necessary to remind us that all the grape-juice in Vinland would not fuddle a man unless it had been fermented, — and then goes on to ascribe the absurdity to our innocent chronicle, instead of the stupid annotator. See *Heimskringla*, vol. i. p. 168.

remember that they had no accurate instruments for measuring time, and that a difference of about fourteen minutes between sunrise and sunset on the shortest winter day would make all the difference between Boston and Halifax, we see how idle it is to look for the requisite precision in narratives of this sort, and to treat them as one would treat the reports of a modern scientific exploring expedition.

In the spring of 1001 Leif returned to Greenland with a cargo of timber.[1] The voyage made much talk. Leif's brother Thorvald caught the inspiration,[2] and, borrowing Leif's ship, sailed in 1002, and succeeded in finding Vinland and Leif's huts, where his men spent two winters. In the intervening summer they went on an exploring expedition along the coast, fell in with some savages in ca- noes, and got into a fight in which Thorvald was killed by an arrow. In the spring of 1004 the ship returned to Brattahlid. Next year the third brother, Thorstein Ericsson, set out in the

Voyages of
Thorvald and
Thorstein,
1002–05

---

[1] On the homeward voyage he rescued some shipwrecked sailors near the coast of Greenland, and was thenceforward called Leif the Lucky (et postea cognominatus est Leivus Fortunatus). The pleasant reports from the newly found country gave it the name of " Vinland the Good." In the course of the winter following Leif's return his father died.

[2] " Jam crebri de Leivi in Vinlandiam profectione sermones serebantur, Thorvaldus vero, frater ejus, nimis pauca terræ loca explorata fuisse judicavit." Rafn, p. 39.

same ship, with his wife Gudrid and a crew of thirty-five men ; but they were sore bestead with foul weather, got nowhere, and accomplished nothing. Thorstein died on the voyage, and his widow returned to Greenland.

In the course of the next summer, 1006, there came to Brattahlid from Iceland a notable personage, a man of craft and resource, wealthy withal and well born, with the blood of many kinglets or jarls flowing in his veins. This man, Thorfinn Karlsefni, straightway fell in love with the young and beautiful widow Gudrid, and in the course of the winter there was a merry wedding at Brattahlid. Persuaded by his adventurous

Thorfinn Karlsefni, and his unsuccessful attempt to found a colony in Vinland, 1007–10

bride, whose spirit had been roused by the reports from Vinland and by her former unsuccessful attempt to find it, Thorfinn now undertook to visit that country in force sufficient for founding a colony there. Accordingly in the spring of 1007 he started with three or four ships,[1] carrying one hundred and

---

[1] Three is the number usually given, but at least four of their ships would be needed for so large a company ; and besides Thorfinn himself, three other captains are mentioned, — Snorro Thorbrandsson, Bjarni Grimolfsson, and Thorhall Gamlason. The narrative gives a picturesque account of this Thorhall, who was a pagan and fond of deriding his comrades for their belief in the new-fangled Christian notions. He seems to have left his comrades and returned to Europe before they

sixty men, several women, and quite a cargo
of cattle. In the course of that year his son
Snorro was born in Vinland,[1] and our chronicle
tells us that this child was three years old before
the disappointed company turned their backs
upon that land of promise and were fain to make
their way homeward to the fiords of Greenland.
It was the hostility of the natives that compelled
Thorfinn to abandon his enterprise. At first
they traded with him, bartering valuable furs for
little strips of scarlet cloth which they sought
most eagerly ; and they were as terribly frightened by his cattle as the Aztecs were in later
days by the Spanish horses.[2] The chance bellowing of a bull sent them squalling to the
woods, and they did not show themselves again
for three weeks. After a while quarrels arose,
the natives attacked in great numbers, many
Northmen were killed, and in 1010 the survivors returned to Greenland with a cargo of timber

had abandoned their enterprise.   A further reference to him
will be made below, p. 235.

[1] To this boy Snorro many eminent men have traced their
ancestry, — bishops, university professors, governors of Iceland, and ministers of state in Norway and Denmark. The
learned antiquarian Finn Magnusson and the celebrated sculptor
Thorwaldsen regarded themselves as thus descended from
Thorfinn Karlsefni.

[2] Compare the alarm of the Wampanoag Indians in 1603
at the sight of Martin Pring's mastiff.   Winsor, *Narr. and
Crit. Hist.*, iii. 174.

and peltries. On the way thither the ships seem
to have separated, and one of them, commanded
by Bjarni Grimolfsson, found itself bored by
worms (the *teredo*) and sank, with its commander
and half the crew.[1]

Among Karlsefni's companions on this memorable expedition was one Thorvard, with his
wife Freydis, a natural daughter of Eric the Red.

---

[1] The fate of Bjarni was pathetic and noble. It was decided that as many as possible should save themselves in the
stern boat. "Then Bjarni ordered that the men should go in
the boat by lot, and not according to rank. As it would not
hold all, they accepted the saying, and when the lots were
drawn, the men went out of the ship into the boat. The lot
was that Bjarni should go down from the ship to the boat with
one half of the men. Then those to whom the lot fell went
down from the ship to the boat. When they had come into
the boat, a young Icelander, who was the companion of Bjarni,
said : ' Now thus do you intend to leave me, Bjarni ? ' Bjarni
replied, ' That now seems necessary.' He replied with these
words : ' Thou art not true to the promise made when I left
my father's house in Iceland.' Bjarni replied : ' In this thing
I do not see any other way ; ' continuing, ' What course can
you suggest ? ' He said : ' I see this, that we change places
and thou come up here and I go down there.' Bjarni replied :
' Let it be so, since I see that you are so anxious to live, and
are frightened by the prospect of death.' Then they changed
places, and he descended into the boat with the men, and
Bjarni went up into the ship. It is related that Bjarni and the
sailors with him in the ship perished in the worm sea. Those
who went in the boat went on their course until they came to
land, where they told all these things." De Costa's version
from *Saga Thorfinns Karlsefnis*, Rafn, pp. 184–186.

About the time of their return to Greenland in the summer of 1010, a ship arrived from Norway, commanded by two brothers, Helgi and Finnbogi. During the winter a new expedition was planned, and in the summer of 1011 two ships set sail for Vinland, one with Freydis, Thorvard, and a crew of 30 men, the other with Helgi and Finnbogi, and a crew of 35 men. There were also a number of women. The purpose was not to found a colony but to cut timber. The brothers arrived first at Leif's huts and had begun carrying in their provisions and tools, when Freydis, arriving soon afterward, ordered them off the premises. They had no right, she said, to occupy her brother's houses. So they went out and built other huts for their party a little farther from the shore. Before their business was accomplished "winter set in, and the brothers proposed to have some games for amusement to pass the time. So it was done for a time, till discord came among them, and the games were given up, and none went from one house to the other; and things went on so during a great part of the winter." At length came the catastrophe. Freydis one night complained to her husband that the brothers had given her evil words and struck her, and insisted that he should forthwith avenge the affront. Presently Thorvard, unable to bear her taunts, was aroused to a deed of

Freydis, and
her evil deeds
in Vinland,
1011–12

195

blood. With his followers he made a night attack upon the huts of Helgi and Finnbogi, seized and bound all the occupants, and killed the men one after another in cold blood. Five women were left whom Thorvard would have spared ; as none of his men would raise a hand against them, Freydis herself took an axe and brained them one and all. In the spring of 1012 the party sailed for Brattahlid in the ship of the murdered brothers, which was the larger and better of the two. Freydis pretended that they had exchanged ships and left the other party in Vinland. With gifts to her men, and dire threats for any who should dare tell what had been done, she hoped to keep them silent. Words were let drop, however, which came to Leif's ears, and led him to arrest three of the men and put them to the torture until they told the whole story. " ' I have not the heart,' said Leif, ' to treat my wicked sister as she deserves ; but this I will foretell them [Freydis and Thorvard] that their posterity will never thrive.' So it went that nobody thought anything of them save evil from that time."

With this gruesome tale ends all account of Norse attempts at exploring or colonizing Vinland, though references to Vinland by no means end here.[1] Taking the narrative as a whole, it

[1] The stories of Gudleif Gudlaugsson and Ari Marsson, with the fanciful speculations about " Hvitramannaland "

seems to me a sober, straightforward, and eminently probable story. We may not be able
to say with confidence exactly where The whole
such places as Markland and Vin- story is emi-
nently prob-
land were, but it is clear that the able
coasts visited on these southerly and southwesterly voyages from Brattahlid must have been
parts of the coast of North America, unless the
whole story is to be dismissed as a figment of
somebody's imagination. But for a figment of
the imagination, and of European imagination
withal, it has far too many points of verisimilitude, as I shall presently show.

In the first place, it is an extremely probable
story from the time that Eric once gets settled in
Brattahlid. The founding of the Greenland colony is the only strange or improbable part of the
narrative, but that is corroborated in so many
other ways that we know it to be true ; as already
observed, no fact in mediæval history is better
established. When I speak of the settlement of
Greenland as strange, I do not mean that there
is anything strange in the Northmen's accom-
plishing the voyage thither from Iceland. That
island is nearer to Greenland than to Norway,
and we know, moreover, that Norse sailors

and " Irland it Mikla," do not seem worthy of notice in
this connection. They may be found in De Costa, *op. cit.*
pp. 159–177 ; and see Reeves, *The Finding of Wineland the
Good,* chap. v.

achieved more difficult things than penetrating the fiords of southern Greenland. Upon the island of Kingitorsook in Baffin's Bay (72° 55′ N., 56° 5′ W.) near Upernavik, in a region supposed to have been unvisited by man before the modern age of Arctic exploration, there were found in 1824 some small artificial mounds with an inscription upon stone: "Erling Sighvatson and Bjarni Thordharson and Eindrid Oddson raised these marks and cleared ground on Saturday before Ascension Week, 1135." That is to say, they took symbolic possession of the land.[1]

Voyage into Baffin's Bay, 1135

In order to appreciate how such daring voyages were practicable, we must bear in mind that the Viking "ships" were probably stronger and more seaworthy, and certainly much swifter, than the Spanish vessels of the time of Columbus. One was unearthed a few years ago at Sandefiord in Norway, and may be seen at the museum in Christiania. Its pagan owner had been buried in it, and his bones were found amidships, along with the bones of a dog and a peacock, a few iron fish-hooks and other articles. Bones of horses and dogs, probably sacrificed at the funeral according to the ancient Norse custom, lay scattered about. This craft has been so well

A Viking ship discovered at Sandefiord, in Norway

[1] Laing, *Heimskringla*, i. 152.

described by Colonel Higginson,[1] that I may as well quote the passage in full : —

She " was seventy-seven feet eleven inches at the greatest length, and sixteen feet eleven inches at the greatest width, and from the top of the keel to the gunwale amidships she was five feet nine inches deep. She had twenty ribs, and would draw less than four feet of water. She was clinker-built ; that is, had plates slightly overlapped, like the shingles on the side of a house. The planks and timbers of the frame were fastened together with withes made of roots, but the oaken boards of the side were united by iron rivets firmly clinched. The bow and stern were similar in shape, and must have risen high out of water, but were so broken that it was impossible to tell how they originally ended. The keel was deep and made Description of thick oak beams, and there was no of the ship trace of any metallic sheathing ; but an iron anchor was found almost rusted to pieces. There was no deck and the seats for rowers had been taken out. The oars were twenty feet long, and the oar-holes, sixteen on each side, had slits sloping toward the stern to allow the blades of the oars to be put through from inside. The most peculiar thing about the ship was the rudder, which was on the starboard or right side,

[1] See his *Larger History of the United States,* pp. 32–34.

this side being originally called ' steerboard' from this circumstance. The rudder was like a large oar, with long blade and short handle, and was attached, not to the side of the boat, but to the end of a conical piece of wood which projected almost a foot from the side of the vessel, and almost two feet from the stern. This piece of wood was bored down its length, and no doubt a rope passing through it secured the rudder to the ship's side. It was steered by a tiller attached to the handle, and perhaps also by a rope fastened to the blade. As a whole, this disinterred vessel proved to be anything but the rude and primitive craft which might have been expected; it was neatly built and well preserved, constructed on what a sailor would call beautiful lines, and eminently fitted for sea service. Many such vessels may be found depicted on the celebrated Bayeux tapestry; and the peculiar position of the rudder explains the treaty mentioned in the ' Heimskringla,' giving to Norway all lands lying west of Scotland between which and the mainland a vessel could pass with her rudder shipped. . . . This was not one of the very largest ships, for some of them had thirty oars on each side, and vessels carrying from twenty to twenty-five were not uncommon. The largest of these were called Dragons, and other sizes were known as Serpents or Cranes. The ship itself was often so

built as to represent the name it bore: the
dragon, for instance, was a long low vessel, with
the gilded head of a dragon at the bow, and the
gilded tail at the stern; the moving oars at the
side might represent the legs of the imaginary
creature, the row of shining red and white
shields that were hung over the gunwale looked
like the monster's scales, and the sails striped
with red and blue might suggest his wings. The
ship preserved at Christiania is described as
having had but a single mast, set into a block
of wood so large that it is said no such block
could now be cut in Norway. Probably the sail
was much like those still carried by large open
boats in that country, — a single square on a
mast forty feet long.[1] These masts have no
standing rigging, and are taken down when not
in use; and this was probably the practice of
the Vikings."

In such vessels, well stocked with food and
weapons, the Northmen were accustomed to
spend many weeks together on the sea, now and
then touching land. In such vessels they made
their way to Algiers and Constantinople, to the
White Sea, to Baffin's Bay. It is not, therefore,
their voyage to Greenland that seems strange,

[1] Perhaps it may have been a square-headed lug, like those
of the Deal galley-punts ; see Leslie's *Old Sea Wings, Ways,
and Words, in the Days of Oak and Hemp*, London, 1890,
p. 21.

but it is their success in founding a colony which could last for more than four centuries in that inhospitable climate. The question is some-
The climate of Greenland times asked whether the climate of Greenland may not have undergone some change within the last thousand years.[1] If there has been any change, it must have been very slight; such as, perhaps, a small variation in the flow of ocean currents might occasion. I am inclined to believe that there may have been such a change, from the testimony of Ivar Bardsen, steward of the Gardar bishopric in the latter half of the fourteenth century, or about halfway between the time of Eric the Red and our own time. According to Bardsen there had long been a downward drifting of ice from the north and a consequent accumulation of bergs and floes upon the eastern coast of Greenland, insomuch that the customary route formerly followed by ships coming from Iceland was no longer safe, and a more southerly route had been generally adopted.[2] This slow southward

[1] Some people must have queer notions about the lapse of past time. I have more than once had this question put to me in such a way as to show that what the querist really had in mind was some vague impression of the time when oaks and chestnuts, vines and magnolias, grew luxuriantly over a great part of Greenland ! But that was in the Miocene period, probably not less than a million years ago, and has no obvious bearing upon the deeds of Eric the Red.

[2] Bardsen, *Descriptio Grœnlandiæ*, appended to Major's

extension of the polar ice-sheet upon the east of Greenland seems still to be going on at the present day.[1] It is therefore not at all improbable, but on the contrary quite probable, that a thousand years ago the mean annual temperature of the tip end of Greenland, at Cape Farewell, was a few degrees higher than now.[2] But a slight difference of this sort might have an important bearing upon the fortunes of a colony planted there. For example, it would directly affect the extent of the hay crop. Grass grows very well now in the neighbourhood of Julianeshaab. In summer it is still a " green land," with good pasturage for cattle, but there is difficulty in getting hay enough to last through the nine

Voyages of the Venetian Brothers, etc., pp. 40, 41 ; and see below, p. 278.

[1] Zahrtmann, *Journal of Royal Geographical Society,* London, 1836, vol. v. p. 102. On this general subject see J. D. Whitney, " The Climate Changes of Later Geological Times," in *Memoirs of the Museum of Comparative Zoölogy at Harvard College,* Cambridge, 1882, vol. vii. According to Professor Whitney there has also been a deterioration in the climate of Iceland.

[2] One must not too hastily infer that the mean temperature of points on the American coast south of Davis Strait would be affected in the same way. The relation between the phenomena is not quite so simple. For example, a warm early spring on the coast of Greenland increases the discharge of icebergs from its fiords to wander down the Atlantic Ocean ; and this increase of floating ice tends to chill and dampen the summers at least as far south as Long Island, if not farther.

months of winter. In 1855 " there were in Greenland 30 to 40 head of horned cattle, about 100 goats, and 20 sheep ; " but in the ancient colony, with a population not exceeding 6000 persons, " herds of cattle were kept which even yielded produce for exportation to Europe." [1] So strong a contrast seems to indicate a much more plentiful grass crop than to-day, although some hay might perhaps have been imported from Iceland in exchange for Greenland exports, which were chiefly whale oil, eider down, and skins of seals, foxes, and white bears.

When once the Northmen had found their way to Cape Farewell, it would have been marvellous if such active sailors could long have avoided stumbling upon the continent of North America. Without compass or astrolabe these daring men were accustomed to traverse long stretches of open sea, trusting to the stars ; and

With the Northmen once in Greenland, the discovery of the American continent was almost inevitable

it needed only a stiff northeasterly breeze, with persistent clouds and fog, to land a westward bound " dragon " anywhere from Cape Race to Cape Cod. This is what appears to have happened to Bjarni Herjulfsson in 986, and something quite like it happened to Henry Hudson in 1609.[2] Curiosity is a motive

[1] Rink's *Danish Greenland*, pp. 27, 96, 97.
[2] See Read's *Historical Inquiry concerning Henry Hudson*, Albany, 1866, p. 160.

quite sufficient to explain Leif's making the
easy summer voyage to find out what sort of
country Bjarni had seen. He found it thickly
wooded, and as there was a dearth of good timber both in Greenland and in Iceland, it would
naturally occur to Leif's friends that voyages
for timber, to be used at home and also to be
exported to Iceland, might turn out to be profitable.[1] As Laing says, "to go in Voyages for
quest of the wooded countries to the timber
southwest, from whence driftwood came to their
shores, was a reasonable, intelligible motive for
making a voyage in search of the lands from
whence it came, and where this valuable material
could be got for nothing."[2]

If now we look at the details of the story we
shall find many ear-marks of truth in it. We
must not look for absolute accuracy in a narrative which — as we have it — is not the work
of Leif or Thorfinn or any of their comrades,
but of compilers or copyists, honest and careful
as it seems to me, but liable to misplace details
and to call by wrong names things which they
had never seen. Starting with these modest ex-
pectations we shall find the points of verisimili-

---

[1] "Nú tekst umrædha at nýju um Vínlandsferdh, thviat sú
ferdh thikir bædhi gódh til fjár ok virdhíngar," *i. e.* "Now
they began to talk again about a voyage to Vinland, for the
voyage thither was both gainful and honourable." Rafn, p. 65.

[2] *Heimskringla,* i. 168.

tude numerous. To begin with the least significant, somewhere on our northeastern coast

Ear-marks
of truth in
the narrative the voyagers found many foxes.[1]
These animals, to be sure, are found
in a great many countries, but the point
for us is that in a southerly and southwesterly
course from Cape Farewell these sailors are said
to have found them. If our narrators had been
drawing upon their imaginations or dealing with
semi-mythical materials, they would as likely as
not have lugged into the story elephants from
Africa or hippogriffs from Dreamland ; mediæval writers were blissfully ignorant of all canons
of probability in such matters.[2] But our narrators simply mention an animal which has for
ages abounded on our northeastern coasts. One
such instance is enough to suggest that they
were following reports or documents which
emanated ultimately from eye-witnesses and told
the plain truth. A dozen such instances, if not
neutralized by counter-instances, are enough to
make this view extremely probable ; and then
one or two instances which could not have origi-

[1] " Fjöldi var thar melrakka," *i. e.* " ibi vulpium magnus
numerus erat." Rafn, p. 138.

[2] It is extremely difficult for an impostor to concoct a narrative without making blunders that can easily be detected by
a critical scholar. For example, *The Book of Mormon*, in the
passage cited (see above, p. 4), in supremely blissful ignorance introduces oxen, sheep, and silk-worms, as well as the
knowledge of smelting iron, into pre-Columbian America.

nated in the imagination of a European writer will suffice to prove it.

Let us observe, then, that on coming to Markland they " slew a bear ; " [1] the river and lake (or bay) in Vinland abounded with salmon bigger than Leif's people had ever seen ; [2] on the coast they caught halibut ; [3] they came to an island where there were so many eider ducks breeding that they could hardly avoid treading on their eggs ; [4] and, as already observed, it was

[1] " Thar í drápu their einn björn," *i. e.* " in qua ursum interfecerunt," id. p. 138.

[2] " Hvorki skorti thar lax í ánni nè í vatninu, ok stærra lax enn their hefdhi fyrr sèdh," *i. e.* " ibi neque in fluvio neque in lacu deerat salmonum copia, et quidem majoris corporis quam antea vidissent," id. p. 32.

[3] " Helgir fiskar," *i. e.* " sacri pisces," id. p. 148. The Danish phrase is " helleflyndre," *i. e.* " holy flounder." The English *halibut* is *hali* = *holy* + *but* = *flounder*. This word *but* is classed as Middle English, but may still be heard in the north of England. The fish may have been so called " from being eaten particularly on holy days " (*Century Dict.* s. v.) ; or possibly from a pagan superstition that water abounding in flat fishes is especially safe for mariners (Pliny, *Hist. Nat.*, ix. 70) ; or possibly from some lost folk-tale about St. Peter (Maurer, *Isländische Volkssagen der Gegenwart*, Leipsic, 1860, p. 195).

[4] " Svâ var mörg ædhr í eynni, at varla mátti gánga fyri eggjum," *i. e.* " tantus in insula anatum mollissimarum numerus erat, ut præ ovis transiri fere non posset," id. p. 141. Eider ducks breed on our northeastern coasts as far south as Portland, and are sometimes in winter seen as far south as Delaware. They also abound in Greenland and Iceland,

because of the abundance of wild grapes that Leif named the southernmost country he visited Vinland.

From the profusion of grapes — such that the ship's stern boat is said on one occasion to have been filled with them [1] — we get a clue, though less decisive than could be wished, to the location of Vinland. The extreme northern limit of the vine in Canada is 47°, the parallel which cuts across the tops of Prince Edward and Cape Breton islands on the map.[2] Near this northern limit, however, wild grapes are by no means plenty ; so that the coast upon which Leif wintered must apparently have been south of Cape Breton. Dr. Storm, who holds that Vinland was on the southern coast of Nova Scotia, has collected

Northern limit of the vine

and, as Wilson observes, "their nests are crowded so close together that a person can scarcely walk without treading on them. . . .The Icelanders have for ages known the value of eider down, and have done an extensive business in it." See Wilson's *American Ornithology*, vol. iii. p. 50.

[1] { "Svâ er sagt at eptirbátr theirra var fylldr af vín-
      So it-is-said that afterboat their was filled of vine-

berjum." }
berries. } Rafn, p. 36.

[2] Storm, "Studies on the Vinland Voyages," *Mémoires de la société royale des antiquaires du Nord*, Copenhagen, 1888, p. 351. The limit of the vine at this latitude is some distance inland ; near the shore the limit is a little farther south, and in Newfoundland it does not grow at all. Id. p. 308.

some interesting testimony as to the growth of
wild grapes in that region, but on the whole the
abundance of this fruit seems rather to point
to the shores of Massachusetts Bay.[1]

We may now observe that, while it is idle to
attempt to determine accurately the length of the
winter day, as given in our chronicles, Length of the
nevertheless since that length attracted winter day
the attention of the voyagers, as something remarkable, it may fairly be supposed to indicate
a latitude lower than they were accustomed to
reach in their trading voyages in Europe. Such
a latitude as that of Dublin, which lies opposite
Labrador, would have presented no novelty to
them, for voyages of Icelanders to their kinsmen in Dublin, and in Rouen as well, were
common enough. Halifax lies about opposite
Bordeaux, and Boston a little south of opposite
Cape Finisterre, in Spain, so that either of these
latitudes would satisfy the conditions of the
case; either would show a longer winter day
than Rouen, which was about the southern limit
of ordinary trading voyages from Iceland. At
all events, the length of day indicates for Vinland a latitude south of Cape Breton.

The next point to be observed is the mention

---

[1] The attempt of Dr. Kohl (*Maine Hist. Soc.*, New
Series, vol. i.) to connect the voyage of Thorfinn with the
coast of Maine seems to be successfully refuted by De Costa,
Northmen in Maine, etc., Albany, 1870.

of " self-sown wheat-fields." [1] This is not only an important ear-mark of truth in the narrative, but it helps us somewhat further in determining the position of Vinland. The " self-sown " cereal, which these Icelanders called " wheat," was in all probability what the English settlers six hundred years afterward called Indian corn " corn," in each case applying to a new and nameless thing the most serviceable name at hand. In England " corn " means either wheat, barley, rye, and oats collectively, or more specifically wheat; in Scotland it generally means oats; in America it means maize, the " Indian corn," the cereal peculiar to the western hemisphere. The beautiful waving plant, with its exquisitely tasselled ears, which was one of the first things to attract Champlain's attention, could not have escaped the notice of such keen observers as we are beginning to find Leif and Thorfinn to have been. A cereal like this, requiring so little cultivation that without much latitude of speech it might be described as growing wild, would be interesting to Europeans visiting the American coast; but it would hardly occur to European fancy to invent such a thing. The mention of it is therefore a very significant ear-mark of the truth of the narrative. As regards the position of Vinland, the presence of

[1] { " Sjálfsána hveitiakra." } Rafn, p. 147.
{ Self-sown wheat-acres. }

maize seems to indicate a somewhat lower latitude than Nova Scotia. Maize requires intensely
hot summers, and even under the most careful
European cultivation does not flourish north of
the Alps. In the sixteenth century its northern-
most limit on the American coast seems to have
been at the mouth of the Kennebec (44°), though
farther inland it was found by Cartier at Hoche-
laga, on the site of Montreal (45° 30′). A presumption is thus raised in favour of the opinion
that Vinland was not farther north than Massachusetts Bay.[1]

This presumption is supported by what is
said about the climate of Vinland, though it
must be borne in mind that general statements
about climate are apt to be very loose and misleading. We are told that it seemed to Leif's
people that cattle would be able to   Winter
pass the winter out of doors there, for weather in
there was no frost and the grass was   Vinland
not much withered.[2] On the other hand, Thor-

---

[1] Dr. Storm makes perhaps too much of this presumption.
He treats it as decisive against his own opinion that Vinland
was the southern coast of Nova Scotia, and accordingly he
tries to prove that the self-sown corn was not maize, but
"wild rice" (*Zizania aquatica*). *Mémoires*, etc., p. 356.
But his argument is weakened by excess of ingenuity.

[2] "Thar var svâ gódhr landskostr at thví er theim sýndist,
at thar mundi eingi fènadhr fódhr thurfa á vetrum ; thar kvomu
eingi frost á vetrum, ok lítt rènudhu thar grös," *i. e.* "tanta
autem erat terræ bonitas, ut inde intelligere esset, pecora hieme

finn's people found the winter severe, and suffered from cold and hunger.[1] Taken in connection with each other, these two statements would apply very well to-day to our variable winters on the coast southward from Cape Ann. The winter of 1889–90 in Cambridge, for example, might very naturally have been described by visitors from higher latitudes as a winter without frost and with grass scarcely withered. Indeed, we might have described it so ourselves. On Narragansett and Buzzard's bays such soft winter weather is still more common; north of Cape Ann it is much less common. The severe winter (*magna hiems*) is of course familiar enough anywhere along the northeastern coast of America.

On the whole, we may say with some confidence that the place described by our chroniclers as Vinland was situated somewhere between Point Judith and Cape Breton; possibly we may narrow our limits and say that it was somewhere between Cape Cod and Cape Ann. But the latter conclusion

Probable situation of Vinland

pabulo non indigere posse, nullis incidentibus algoribus hiemalibus, et graminibus parum flaccescentibus." Rafn, p. 32.

[1] "Thar voru their um vetrinn; ok gjördhist vetr mikill, en ekki fyri unnit ok gjördhist íllt til matarins, ok tókust af veidhirnar," *i. e.* "hic hiemarunt; cum vero magna incideret hiems, nullumque provisum esset alimentum, cibus cœpit deficere capturaque cessabat." Id. p. 174.

is much less secure than the former. In such a case as this, the more we narrow our limits the greater our liability to error.[1] While by such narrowing, moreover, the question may acquire more interest as a bone of contention among local antiquarians, its value for the general historian is not increased.

But we have not yet done with the points of verisimilitude in our story. We have now to cite two or three details that are far more striking than any as yet mentioned, — details that could never have been conjured up by the fancy of any mediæval European. We must bear in mind that "savages," whether true savages or people in the lower status of barbarism, were practically unknown to Europeans before the fifteenth century. There were no such people in Europe or in any part of Asia or Africa visited by Europeans before the great voyages of the Portuguese. Mediæval

"Savages" unknown to mediæval Europeans

---

[1] A favourite method of determining the exact spots visited by the Northmen has been to compare their statements regarding the shape and trend of the coasts, their bays, headlands, etc., with various well-known points on the New England coast. It is a tempting method, but unfortunately treacherous, because the same general description will often apply well enough to several different places. It is like summer boarders in the country struggling to tell one another where they have been to drive, — past a school-house, down a steep hill, through some woods, and by a saw-mill, etc.

Europeans knew nothing whatever about people who would show surprise at the sight of an iron tool [1] or frantic terror at the voice of a bull, or who would eagerly trade off valuable property for worthless trinkets. Their imagination might be up to inventing hobgoblins and people with heads under their shoulders,[2] but it

---

[1] It is not meant that stone implements did not continue to be used in some parts of Europe far into the Middle Ages. But this was not because iron was not perfectly well known, but because in many backward regions it was difficult to obtain or to work, so that stone continued in use. As my friend, Mr. T. S. Perry, reminds me, Helbig says that stone-pointed spears were used by some of the English at the battle of Hastings, and stone battle-axes by some of the Scots under William Wallace at the end of the thirteenth century. *Die Italiker in der Poebene*, Leipsic, 1879, p. 42. Helbig's statement as to Hastings is confirmed by Freeman, *Norman Conquest of England*, vol. iii. p. 473.

[2] My use of the word " inventing " is, in this connection, a slip of the pen. Of course the tales of " men whose heads do grow beneath their shoulders," the Sciopedæ, etc., as told by Sir John Mandeville, were not invented by the mediæval imagination, but copied from ancient authors. They may be found in Pliny, *Hist. Nat.*, lib. vii., and were mentioned before his time by Ktesias, as well as by Hecatæus, according to Stephanus of Byzantium. Cf. Aristophanes, *Aves*, 1553; Julius Solinus, *Polyhistor*, ed. Salmasius, cap. 240. Just as these sheets are going to press there comes to me Mr. Perry's acute and learned *History of Greek Literature*, New York, 1890, in which this subject is mentioned in connection with the mendacious and medical Ktesias : These stories have probably acquired a literary currency " by

was not up to inventing such simple touches of nature as these. Bearing this in mind, let us observe that Thorfinn found the natives of Vinland eager to give valuable furs[1] in exchange for little strips of scarlet cloth to bind about their heads. When the Northmen found the cloth growing scarce they cut it into extremely narrow strips, but the desire of the natives was so great that they would still give a whole skin for the smallest strip. They wanted also to buy weapons, but Thorfinn forbade his men to sell them. One of the natives picked up an iron hatchet and cut wood with it; one after another tried and admired it; at length one tried it on a stone and broke its edge, and then they scornfully threw it down.[2]

The natives of Vinland

exercise of the habit, not unknown even to students of science, of indiscriminate copying from one's predecessors, so that in reading Mandeville we have the ghosts of the lies of Ktesias, almost sanctified by the authority of Pliny, who quoted them and thereby made them a part of mediæval folklore — and from folk-lore, probably, they took their remote start" (p. 522).

[1] "En that var grávara ok safvali ok allskonar skinnavara" (Rafn, p. 59), — i. e. gray fur and sable and all sorts of skinwares; in another account, "skinnavöru ok algrá skinn," which in the Danish version is "skindvarer og ægte graaskind" (id. p. 150), — i. e. skinwares and genuine gray furs. Cartier in Canada and the Puritans in Massachusetts were not long in finding that the natives had good furs to sell.

[2] Rafn, p. 156.

One day while they were trading, Thorfinn's bull ran out before them and bellowed, whereupon the whole company was instantly scattered in headlong flight. After this, when threatened with an attack by the natives, Thorfinn drew up his men for a fight and put the bull in front, very much as Pyrrhus used elephants — at first with success — to frighten the Romans and their horses.[1]

These incidents are of surpassing interest, for they were attendant upon the first meeting (in all probability) that ever took place between civilized Europeans and any people below the

---

[1] Much curious information respecting the use of elephants in war may be found in the learned work of the Chevalier Armandi, *Histoire militaire des éléphants*, Paris, 1843. As regards Thorfinn's bull, Mr. Laing makes the kind of blunder that our British cousins are sometimes known to make when they get the Rocky Mountains within sight of Bunker Hill Monument. " A continental people in that part of America," says Mr. Laing, " could not be strangers to the much more formidable bison." *Heimskringla*, p. 169. Bisons on the Atlantic coast, Mr. Laing ? ! And then his comparison quite misses the point ; a bison, if the natives had been familiar with him, would not have been at all formidable as compared to the bull which they had never before seen. A horse is much less formidable than a cougar, but Aztec warriors who did not mind a cougar were paralyzed with terror at the sight of men on horseback. It is the unknown that frightens in such cases. Thorfinn's natives were probably familiar with such large animals as moose and deer, but a deer is n't a bull.

upper status of barbarism.[1] Who were these
natives encountered by Thorfinn ? The Northmen called them "Skrælings," a name which
one is at first sight strongly tempted to derive
from the Icelandic verb *skrækja*, identical with
the English *screech*. A crowd of excited Indians
might most appropriately be termed Screechers.[2]
This derivation, however, is not correct. The
word *skræling* survives in modern Norwegian,
and means a feeble or puny or *insignificant* person. Dr. Storm's suggestion is in all
probability correct, that the name
"Skrælings," as applied to the natives of America, had no ethnological significance, but simply meant " inferior people ; " it
gave concise expression to the white man's
opinion that they were " a bad lot." In Icelandic literature the name is usually applied to
the Eskimos, and hence it has been rashly inferred that Thorfinn found Eskimos in Vinland. Such was Rafn's opinion, and since his
time the commentators have gone off upon a
wrong trail and much ingenuity has been

Meaning of the epithet "Skrælings"

---

[1] The Phœnicians, however (who in this connection may
be classed with Europeans), must have met with some such
people in the course of their voyages upon the coasts of Africa.
I shall treat of this more fully below, p. 375.

[2] As for Indians, says Cieza de Leon, they are all noisy
(alharaquientos). *Segunda Parte de la Crónica del Peru,*
cap. xxiii.

wasted.[1] It would be well to remember, however, that the Europeans of the eleventh century were not ethnologists ; in meeting these
inferior peoples for the first time they were more
likely to be impressed with the broad fact of
their inferiority than to be nice in making dis-
tinctions. When we call both Australians and
Fuegians " savages," we do not assert identity
or relationship between them ; and so when the
Northmen called Eskimos and Indians by the
same disparaging epithet, they doubtless simply
meant to call them savages.

Our chronicle describes the Skrælings of Vinland as swarthy in hue, ferocious in aspect, with
ugly hair, big eyes, and broad cheeks.[2] This

---

[1] For example, Dr. De Costa refers to Dr. Abbott's discoveries as indicating " that the Indian was preceded by a
people like the Eskimos, whose stone implements are found in
the Trenton gravel." *Pre-Columbian Discovery*, p. 132.
Quite so ; but that was in the Glacial period (! !) and when
the edge of the ice-sheet slowly retreated northward, the
Eskimo, who is emphatically an Arctic creature, doubtless retreated with it, just as he retreated from Europe. See above,
p. 21. There is not the slightest reason for supposing that
there were any Eskimos south of Labrador so lately as nine
hundred years ago.

[2] " Their voru svartir menn ok illiligir, ok havdhu íllt hár
á höfdhi. Their voru mjök eygdhir ok breidhir í kinnum,"
i. e. " Hi homines erant nigri, truculenti specie, fœdam in
capite comam habentes, oculis magnis et genis latis." Rafn,
p. 149. The Icelandic *svartr* is more precisely rendered by
the identical English *swarthy* than by the Latin *niger*.

will do very well for Indians, except as to the eyes. We are accustomed to think of Indian eyes as small ; but in this connection it is worthy of note that a very keen ob-server, Marc Lescarbot, in his minute and elaborate description of the physical ap-pearance of the Micmacs of Acadia, speaks with some emphasis of their large eyes.[1] Dr. Storm quite reasonably suggests that the Norse ex-pression may refer to the size not of the eye-ball, but of the eye-socket, which in the Indian face is apt to be large ; and very likely this is what the Frenchman also had in mind.

Personal appearance of the Skrælings

These Skrælings were clad in skins, and their weapons were bows and arrows, slings, and stone hatchets. In the latter we may now, I think, be allowed to recognize the familiar tomahawk ; and when we read that, in a sharp fight with the natives, Thorbrand, son of the commander Snorro, was slain, and the woman Freydis after-ward found his corpse in the woods, with a flat stone sticking in the head, and his naked sword lying on the ground beside him, we seem to see

---

[1] " Mais quãt à noz Sauvages, pour ce qui regarde les ïeux ilz ne les ont ni bleuz, ni verds, mais noirs pour la pluspart, ainsi que les cheveux ; & neantmoins ne sont petits, cõme ceux des anciens Scythes, mais d'une grandeur bien agreable." Lescarbot, *Histoire de la Nouvelle France,* Paris, 1612, tom. ii. p. 714.

how it all happened.[1] We seem to see the
stethly Indian suddenly dealing the death-blow,
and then obliged for his own safety to
dart away among the trees without recovering his tomahawk or seizing the
sword. The Skrælings came up the
river or lake in a swarm of canoes,
all yelling at the top of their voices (*et illi omnes
valde acutum ululabant*), and, leaping ashore,
began a formidable attack with slings and arrows. The narrative calls these canoes " skin-
boats " (*hudhkeipar*), whence it has been inferred
that the writer had in mind the *kayaks* and *umiaks*
of the Eskimos.[2] I suspect that the writer did
have such boats in mind, and accordingly used
a word not strictly accurate. Very likely his
authorities failed to specify a distinction between
bark-boats and skin-boats, and simply used the
handiest word for designating canoes as contrasted with their own keeled boats.[3]

*The Skræ-
lings of Vin-
land were In-
dians, — very
likely Algon-
quins*

One other point which must be noticed here
in connection with the Skrælings is a singular
manœuvre which they are said to have practised

[1] " Hún fann fyrir sèr mann daudhan, thar var Thorbrandr
Snorrason, ok stódh hellusteinn í höfdhi honum ; sverdhit lá
bert í hjá honum," *i. e.* " Illa incidit in mortuum hominem,
Thorbrandum Snorrii filium, cujus capiti lapis planus impactus
stetit ; nudus juxta eum gladius jacuit." Rafn, p. 154.

[2] These Eskimo skin-boats are described in Rink's *Danish
Greenland*, pp. 113, 179.

[3] Cf. Storm, *op. cit.* pp. 366, 367.

torical Society, — "that there is the same sort of reason for believing in the existence of Leif Ericsson that there is for believing in the existence of Agamemnon. They are both traditions accepted by later writers, and there is no more reason for regarding as true the details related about the discoveries of the former than there is for accepting as historic truth the narrative contained in the Homeric poems." The report goes on to observe that "it is antecedently probable that the Northmen discovered America in the early part of the eleventh century; and this discovery is confirmed by the same sort of historical tradition, not strong enough to be called evidence, upon which our belief in many of the accepted facts of history rests."[1] The second of these statements is characterized by critical moderation, and expresses the inevitable and wholesome reaction against the rash enthusiasm of Professor Rafn half a century ago, and the vagaries of many an uninstructed or uncritical writer since his time. But the first statement is singularly unfortunate. It would be difficult to find a comparison more inappropriate than that between Agamemnon and Leif, between the Iliad and the Saga of Eric the Red. The story of the Trojan War and its heroes, as we have it in Homer and the Athenian

Unfortunate comparison between Leif Ericsson and Agamemnon

[1] *Proceedings Mass. Hist. Soc.*, December, 1887.

dramatists, is pure folk-lore as regards form, and chiefly folk-lore as regards contents. It is in a high degree probable that this mass of folk-lore surrounds a kernel of plain fact, that in times long before the first Olympiad an actual " king of men " at Mycenæ conducted an expedition against the great city by the Simois, that the Agamemnon of the poet stands in some such relation toward this chieftain as that in which the Charlemagne of mediæval romance stands toward the mighty Emperor of the West.[1] Nevertheless the story, as we have it, is simply folk-lore. If the Iliad and Odyssey contain faint reminiscences of actual events, these events are so inextricably wrapped up with mythical phraseology that by no cunning of the scholar can they be construed into history. The motives and capabilities of the actors and the conditions under which they accomplish their destinies are such as exist only in fairy-tales. Their world is as remote from that in which we live as the world of Sindbad and Camaralzaman ; and this is not essentially altered by the fact that Homer introduces us to definite localities and familiar

The story of the Trojan War, as we have it, is pure folk-lore

---

[1] I used this argument twenty years ago in qualification of the over-zealous solarizing views of Sir G. W. Cox and others. See my *Myths and Myth-Makers*, vii., and cf. Freeman on " The Mythical and Romantic Elements in Early English History," in his *Historical Essays*, i. 1–39.

customs as often as the Irish legends of Finn M'Cumhail.[1]

It would be hard to find anything more unlike such writings than the class of Icelandic sagas to which that of Eric the Red belongs.   Here we have quiet and sober narrative, not in the least like a fairy-tale, but often much like a ship's log.   What-ever such narrative may be, it is not folk-lore. In act and motive, in its conditions and laws, its world is the every-day world in which we live.   If now and then a " uniped " happens to stray into it, the incongruity is as conspicuous as in the case of Hudson's mermaid, or a ghost in a modern country inn ; whereas in the Ho-meric fabric the supernatural is warp and woof. To assert a likeness between two kinds of lit-erature so utterly different is to go very far astray.

The Saga of Eric the Red is not folk-lore

As already observed, I suspect that mislead-ing associations with the word " saga " may have exerted an unconscious influence in pro-ducing this particular kind of blunder, — for it is nothing less than a blunder.   Resemblance is tacitly assumed between the Iliad and an Ice-landic saga.   Well, between the Iliad and *some* Icelandic sagas there is a real and strong resem-

[1] Curtin, *Myths and Folk-Lore of Ireland*, pp. 12, 204, 303 ; Kennedy, *Legendary Fictions of the Irish Celts*, pp. 203–311.

blance. In truth these sagas are divisible into two well-marked and sharply contrasted classes. In the one class belong the Eddic Lays, and the *mythical sagas*, such as the Volsunga, the stories of Ragnar, Frithiof, and others ; and along with these, though totally different in source, we may for our present purpose group the *romantic sagas*, such as Parceval, Remund, Karlamagnus, and others brought from southern Europe. These are alike in being composed of legendary and mythical materials ; they belong essentially to the literature of folk-lore. In the other class come the *historical sagas*, such as those of Njal and Egil, the Sturlunga, and many others, with the numerous biographies and annals.[1] These writings give us history, and often very good history indeed. " Saga " meant simply any kind of literature in narrative form ; the good people of Iceland did not happen to have such a handy word as " history," which they could keep entire when they meant it in sober earnest and chop down into " story " when they meant it otherwise. It is very much as if we were to apply the same

Mythical and historical sagas

---

[1] Nowhere can you find a more masterly critical account of Icelandic literature than in Vigfusson's " Prolegomena " to his edition of *Sturlunga Saga*, Oxford, 1878, vol. i. pp. ix–ccxiv. There is a good but very brief account in Horn's *History of the Literature of the Scandinavian North*, transl. by R. B. Anderson, Chicago, 1884, pp. 50–70.

word to the Arthur legends and to William of Malmesbury's judicious and accurate chronicles, and call them alike " stories."

The narrative upon which our account of the Vinland voyages is chiefly based belongs to the class of historical sagas. It is the Saga of Eric the Red, and it exists in two different versions, of which one seems to have been made in the north, the other in the west, of Iceland. The western version is the earlier and in some respects the better. It is found in two vellums, that of the great collection known as *Hauks-bók* (AM. 544), and that which is simply known as AM. 557 from its catalogue number in Arni Magnusson's collection. Of these the former, which is the best preserved, was written in a beautiful hand by Hauk Erlendsson, between 1305 and 1334, the year of his death. This western version is the one which has generally been printed under the title, " Saga of Thorfinn Karlsefni." It is the one to which I have most frequently referred in the present chapter.[1]

The western or Hauks-bók version of Eric the Red's Saga

The northern version is that which was made about the year 1387 by the priest Jón Thórdharson, and contained in the famous compilation

[1] It is printed in Rafn, pp. 84–187, and in *Grönlands historiske Mindesmærker*, i. 352–443. The most essential part of it may now be found, under its own name, in Vigfusson's *Icelandic Prose Reader*, pp. 123–140.

known as the *Flateyar-bók*, or "Flat Island Book."[1] This priest was editing the saga of King Olaf Tryggvesson, which is con-tained in that compilation, and inas-much as Leif Ericsson's presence at King Olaf's court was connected both with the introduction of Christianity into Greenland and with the discovery of Vinland, Jón paused, after the manner of mediæval chroniclers, and in-serted then and there what he knew about Eric and Leif and Thorfinn. In doing this, he used parts of the original saga of Eric the Red (as we find it reproduced in the western version), and added thereunto a considerable amount of material concerning the Vinland voyages derived from other sources. Jón's version thus made has generally been printed under the title, "Saga of Eric the Red."[2]

The northern or Flateyar-bók version

Now the older version, written at the begin-ning of the fourteenth century, gives an account of things which happened three centuries before it was written. A cautious scholar will, as a rule, be slow to consider any historical narrative as quite satisfactory authority, even when it con-

---

[1] It belonged to a man who lived on Flat Island, in one of the Iceland fiords.

[2] It is printed in Rafn, pp. 1–76, under the title "Thættir af Eireki Rauda ok Grænlendíngum." For a critical account of these versions, see Storm, *op. cit.* pp. 319–325 ; I do not, in all respects, follow him in his depreciation of the Flateyar-bók version.

tains no improbable statements, unless it is nearly contemporary with the events which it records. Such was the rule laid down by the late Sir George Cornewall Lewis, and it is a very good rule ; the proper application of it has disencumbered history of much rubbish. At the same time, like all rules, it should be used with judicious caution and not allowed to run away with us. As applied by Lewis to Roman history it would have swept away in one great cataclysm not only kings and decemvirs, but Brennus and his Gauls to boot, and left us with nothing to swear by until the invasion of Pyrrhus.[1] Subsequent research has shown that this was going altogether too far. The mere fact of distance in time between a document and the events which it records is only negative testimony against its value, for it may be a faithful transcript of some earlier document or documents since lost. It is so difficult to prove a negative that the mere lapse of time simply raises a presumption the weight of which should be estimated by a careful survey of all the probabilities in the case. Among the many Icelandic vellums that are known to have perished[2] there may well have been earlier copies of Eric the Red's Saga.

Presumption against sources not contemporary

[1] Lewis's *Inquiry into the Credibility of the Early Roman History*, 2 vols., London, 1855.

[2] And notably in that terrible fire of October, 1728, which

Hauk Erlendsson reckoned himself a direct descendant, in the eighth generation, from Snorro, son of Thorfinn and Gudrid, born in Vinland. He was an important personage in Iceland, a man of erudition, author of a brief book of contemporary annals and a treatise on arithmetic in which he introduced the Arabic numerals into Iceland. In those days the lover of books, if he would add them to his library, might now and then obtain an original manuscript, but usually he had to copy them or have them copied by hand. The Hauks-bók, with its 200 skins, one of the most extensive Icelandic vellums now in existence, is really Hauk's private library, or what there is left of it, and it shows that he was a man who knew how to make a good choice of books. He did a good deal of his copying himself, and also employed two clerks in the same kind of work.[1]

Hauk Er-lendsson and his manu-scripts

consumed the University Library at Copenhagen, and broke the heart of the noble collector of manuscripts, Arni Magnusson. The great eruption of Hecla in 1390 overwhelmed two famous homesteads in the immediate neighbourhood. From the local history of these homesteads and their inmates, Vigfusson thinks it not unlikely that some records may still be there " awaiting the spade and pickaxe of a new Schliemann." *Sturlunga Saga*, p. cliv.

[1] An excellent facsimile of Hauk's handwriting is given in Rafn, tab. iii., lower part ; tab. iv. and the upper part of tab. iii. are in the hands of his two amanuenses. See Vigfusson, *op. cit.* p. clxi.

Now I do not suppose it will occur to any rational being to suggest that Hauk may have written down his version of Eric the Red's Saga from an oral tradition nearly three centuries old. The narrative could not have been so long preserved in its integrity, with so little extravagance of statement and so many marks of truthfulness in details foreign to ordinary Icelandic experience, if it had been entrusted to oral tradition alone. One might as well try to imagine Drake's " World Encompassed " handed down by oral tradition from the days of Queen Elizabeth to the days of Queen Victoria. Such transmission is possible enough with heroic poems and folk-tales, which deal with a few dramatic situations and a stock of mythical conceptions familiar at every fireside ; but in a simple matter of fact record of sailors' observations and experiences on a strange coast, oral tradition would not be long in distorting and jumbling the details into a result quite undecipherable. The story of the Zeno brothers, presently to be cited, shows what strange perversions occur, even in written tradition, when the copyist, instead of faithfully copying records of unfamiliar events, tries to edit and amend them. One cannot reasonably doubt that Hauk's vellum of Eric the Red's Saga, with its many ear-marks of truth above mentioned, was copied by him

The story is not likely to have been preserved to Hauk's time by oral tradition only

— and quite carefully and faithfully withal — from some older vellum not now forthcoming.

As we have no clue, however, beyond the internal evidence, to the age or character of the sources from which Hauk copied, there is nothing left for us to do but to look into other Icelandic documents, to see if anywhere they betray a knowledge of Vinland and the voyages thither. Incidental references to Vinland, in narratives concerned with other matters, are of great significance in this connection; for they imply on the part of the narrator a presumption that his readers understand such references, and that it is not necessary to interrupt his story in order to explain them. Such incidental references imply the existence, during the interval between the Vinland voyages and Hauk's manuscript, of many intermediate links of sound testimony that have since dropped out of sight; and therefore they go far toward removing whatever presumption may be alleged against Hauk's manuscript because of its distance from the events.

Allusions to Vinland in other documents

Now the Eyrbyggja Saga, written between 1230 and 1260, is largely devoted to the settlement of Iceland, and is full of valuable notices of the heathen institutions and customs of the tenth century. The Eyrbyggja, having occasion to speak of Thorbrand Snorrason, observes incidentally that he went from Greenland to Vinland with Karlsefni and was killed in a battle with the Skrælings.[1] We have already mentioned the death of this Thorbrand, and how Freydis found his body in the woods. *Eyrbyggja Saga*

Three Icelandic tracts on geography, between the twelfth and fourteenth centuries, mention Helluland and Vinland, and in two of these accounts Markland is interposed between Helluland and Vinland.[2] One of these tracts mentions the voyages of Leif and Thorfinn. It forms part of an essay called "Guide to the Holy Land," by Nikulas Sæmundsson, abbot of Thvera, in the north of Iceland, who died 1159. This Nikulas was curious in matters of geography, and had travelled extensively. *The abbot Nikulas, etc.*

With the celebrated Ari Thorgilsson, usually known as Fródhi, "the learned," we come to testimony nearly contemporaneous in time and extremely valuable in character. This erudite

[1] Vigfusson, *Eyrbyggja Saga*, pp. 91, 92. Another of Karlsefni's comrades, Thorhall Gamlason, is mentioned in *Grettis Saga*, Copenhagen, 1859, pp. 22, 70; he went back to Iceland, settled on a farm there, and was known for the rest of his life as "the Vinlander." See above, pp. 190, 192.

[2] Werlauf, *Symbolæ ad Geogr. Medii Ævi*, Copenhagen, 1820.

priest, born in 1067, was the founder of historical writing in Iceland. He was the principal
author of the " Landnáma-bók," already men-
Ari Fródhi   tioned as a work of thorough and
painstaking research unequalled in
mediæval literature. His other principal works
were the " Konunga-bók," or chronicle of the
kings of Norway, and the "Islendinga-bók," or
description of Iceland.[1] Ari's books, written
not in monkish Latin, but in a good vigorous
vernacular, were a mine of information from
which all subsequent Icelandic historians were
accustomed to draw such treasures as they
needed. To his diligence and acumen they were
all, from Snorro Sturlason down, very much
indebted. He may be said to have given the
tone to history-writing in Iceland, and it was a
high tone.

Unfortunately Ari's Islendinga-bók has perished. One cannot help suspecting that it may
have contained the contemporary materials from
which Eric the Red's Saga in the Hauks-bók
was ultimately drawn. For Ari made an abridg-
ment or epitome of his great book, and this
epitome, commonly known as " Libellus Islan-

[1] For a critical estimate of Ari's literary activity and the
extent of his work, the reader is referred to Möbius, *Are's
Isländerbuch*, Leipsic, 1869 ; Maurer, " Über Ari Thorgilsson und sein Isländerbuch," in *Germania*, xv.; Olsen, *Ari
Thorgilsson hinn Fródhi*, Reykjavik, 1889, pp. 214–240.

dorum," still survives. In it Ari makes brief mention of Greenland, and refers to his paternal uncle, Thorkell Gellison, as authority for his statements. This Thorkell Gellison, of Helgafell, a man of high consideration who flourished about the middle of the eleventh century, had visited Greenland and talked with one of the men Ari's significant allusion to Vinland who accompanied Eric when he went to settle in Brattahlid in 986. From this source Ari gives us the interesting information that Eric's party found in Greenland "traces of human habitations, fragments of boats, and stone implements ; so from this one might conclude that people of the kind who inhabited Vinland and were known by the (Norse) Greenlanders as Skrælings must have roamed about there." [1] Observe the force of this allusion. The settlers in Greenland did not at first (nor for a long time) meet with barbarous or savage natives there, but only with the vestiges of their former presence. But when Ari wrote the above passage,

---

[1] " Their fundo thar manna vister bæthi austr ok vestr á landi ok kæiplabrot ok steinsmíthi, that es af thví má scilja, at thar hafdhi thessconar thjóth farith es Vínland hefer bygt, ok Grænlendínger calla Skrelínga," *i. e.* "invenerunt ibi, tam in orientali quam occidentali terræ parte, humanæ habitationis vestigia, navicularum fragmenta et opera fabrilia ex lapide, ex quo intelligi potest, ibi versatum esse nationem quæ Vinlandiam incoluit quamque Grænlandi Skrælingos appellant." Rafn, p. 207.

the memory of Vinland and its fierce Skrælings was still fresh, and Ari very properly inferred from the archæological remains in Greenland that a people similar (in point of barbarism) to the Skrælings must have been there. Unless Ari and his readers had a distinct recollection of the accounts of Vinland, such a reference would have been only an attempt to explain the less obscure by the more obscure. It is to be regretted that we have in this book no more allusions to Vinland; but if Ari could only leave us one such allusion, he surely could not have made that one more pointed.

But this is not quite the only reference that Ari makes to Vinland. There are three others that must in all probability be assigned to him. Two occur in the Landnáma-bók, the first in a passage where mention is made of Ari Marsson's voyage to a place in the western ocean near Vinland;[1] the only point in this allusion which need here concern us is that Vinland is tacitly assumed to be a known geographical sit-

Other references uation to which others may be referred. The second reference occurs in one of those elaborate and minutely specific genealogies in the Landnáma-bók : " Their son was Thordhr Hest-höfdhi, father of Karlsefni, who found Vinland the Good, Snorri's father," etc.[2] The third reference occurs in the Kristni

[1] *Landnáma-bók*, pt. ii. ch. xxii.   [2] Id. pt. iii. ch. x.

Saga, a kind of supplement to the Landnáma-
bók, giving an account of the introduction of
Christianity into Iceland ; here it is related how
Leif Ericsson came to be called " Leif the
Lucky," 1. from having rescued a shipwrecked
crew off the coast of Greenland, 2. from having
discovered " Vinland the Good." [1] From these
brief allusions, and from the general relation in
which Ari Fródhi stood to later writers, I suspect that if the greater Islendinga-bók had survived to our time we should have found in it
more about Vinland and its discoverers. At
any rate, as to the existence of a definite and
continuous tradition all the way from Ari down
to Hauk Erlendsson, there can be no question
whatever.[2]

[1] *Kristni Saga,* apud *Biskupa Sögur,* Copenhagen, 1858,
vol. i. p. 20.

[2] Indeed, the parallel existence of the Flateyar-bók version
of Eric the Red's Saga, alongside of the Hauks-bók version, is
pretty good proof of the existence of a written account older
than Hauk's time. The discrepancies between the two versions are such as to show that Jón Thórdharson did not copy
from Hauk, but followed some other version not now forthcoming. Jón mentions six voyages in connection with
Vinland : 1. Bjarni Herjulfsson ; 2. Leif ; 3. Thorvald ;
4. Thorstein and Gudrid ; 5. Thorfinn Karlsefni ; 6. Freydis. Hauk, on the other hand, mentions only the two principal voyages, those of Leif and Thorfinn ; ignoring Bjarni, he
accredits his adventures to Leif on his return voyage from
Norway in 999, and he makes Thorvald a comrade of Thorfinn, and mixes his adventures with the events of Thorfinn's

The testimony of Adam of Bremen brings us yet one generation nearer to the Vinland voyages, and is very significant. Adam was much interested in the missionary work in the north of Europe, and in 1073, the same year that Hildebrand was elected to the papacy, he published his famous " Historia Ecclesiastica," in which he gave an account of the conversion of the northern nations from the time of Leo III. to that of Hildebrand's predecessor. In prosecuting his studies, Adam

Adam of Bremen

voyage. Dr. Storm considers Hauk's account intrinsically the more probable, and thinks that in the Flateyar-bók we have a later amplification of the tradition. But while I agree with Dr. Storm as to the general superiority of the Hauk version, I am not convinced by his arguments on this point. It seems to me likely that the Flateyar-bók here preserves more faithfully the details of an older tradition too summarily epitomized in the Hauks-bók. As the point in no way affects the general conclusions of the present chapter, it is hardly worth arguing here. The main thing for us is that the divergencies between the two versions, when coupled with their agreement in the most important features, indicate that both writers were working upon the basis of an antecedent written tradition, like the authors of the first and third synoptic gospels. Only here, of course, there are in the divergencies no symptoms of what the Tübingen school would call " *tendenz,*" impairing and obscuring to an indeterminate extent the general trustworthiness of the narratives. On the whole, it is pretty clear that Hauks-bók and Flateyar-bók were independent of each other, and collated, each in its own way, earlier documents that have probably since perished.

made a visit to the court of Swend Estridhsen, king of Denmark, nephew of Cnut the Great, king of Denmark and England. Swend's reign began in 1047, so that Adam's visit must have occurred between that date and 1073. The voyage of Leif and Thorfinn would at that time have been within the memory of living men, and would be likely to be known in Denmark, because the intercourse between the several parts of the Scandinavian world was incessant; there was continual coming and going. Adam learned what he could of Scandinavian geography, and when he published his history, he did just what a modern writer would do under similar circumstances; he appended to his book some notes on the geography of those remote countries, then so little known to his readers in central and southern Europe. After giving some account of Denmark, Sweden, and Norway, he describes the colony in Iceland, and then the further colony in Greenland, and concludes by saying that out in that ocean there is another country, or island, which has been visited by many persons, and is called Vinland because of wild grapes that grow there, out of which a very good wine can be made. Either rumour had exaggerated the virtues of fox-grape juice, or the Northmen were not such good judges of wine as of ale. Adam goes on to say that corn, likewise, grows in Vinland without cultivation ; and as such a statement to European readers must needs have a smack of falsehood, he adds that it is based not upon fable and guesswork, but upon " trustworthy reports (*certa relatione*) of the Danes."

Scanty as it is, this single item of strictly contemporary testimony is very important, because quite incidentally it gives to the later accounts such confirmation as to show that they rest upon a solid basis of continuous tradition and not upon mere unintelligent hearsay.[1] The unvarying character of the tradition, in its essential details, indicates that it must have been committed to writing at a very early period, probably not later than the time of Ari's uncle Thorkell, who was contemporary with Adam of Bremen. If, however, we read the whole passage in which Adam's mention of Vinland occurs, it is clear from the context that his own information was

---

[1] It is further interesting as the only undoubted reference to Vinland in a mediæval book written beyond the limits of the Scandinavian world. There is also, however, a passage in Ordericus Vitalis (*Historia Ecclesiastica*, iv. 29), in which *Finland* and the Orkneys, along with Greenland and Iceland, are loosely described as forming part of the dominions of the kings of Norway. This Finland does not appear to refer to the country of the Finns, east of the Baltic, and it has been supposed that it may have been meant for Vinland. The book of Ordericus was written about 1140.

not derived from an inspection of Icelandic documents. He got it, as he tells us, by talking with King Swend ; and all that he got, or all that he thought worth telling, was this curious fact about vines and self-sown corn growing so near to Greenland ; for Adam quite misconceived the situation of Vinland, and imagined it far up in the frozen North. After his mention of Vinland, the continental character of which he evidently did not suspect, he goes on immediately to say, " After this island nothing inhabitable is to be found in that ocean, all being covered with unendurable ice and boundless darkness." That most accomplished king, Harold Hardrada, says Adam, tried not long since to ascertain how far the northern ocean extended, and plunged along through this darkness until he actually reached the end of the world, and came near tumbling off ! [1] Thus the worthy Adam, while telling the

Adam's misconception of the situation

---

[1] The passage from Adam of Bremen deserves to be quoted in full : " Præterea unam adhuc insulam [regionam] recitavit [*i. e.* Svendus rex] a multis in eo repertam oceano, quæ dicitur Vinland, eo quod ibi vites sponte nascantur, vinum bonum gerentes [ferentes] ; nam et fruges ibi non seminatas abundare, non fabulosa opinione, sed certa comperimus relatione Danorum. Post quam insulam terra nulla invenitur habitabilis in illo oceano, sed omnia quæ ultra sunt glacie intolerabili ac caligine immensa plena sunt ; cujus rei Marcianus ita meminit : ultra Thyle, inquiens, navigare unius diei mare concretum est.

truth about fox-grapes and maize as well as he knew how, spoiled the effect of his story by putting Vinland in the Arctic regions. The juxtaposition of icebergs and vines was a little too close even for the mediæval mind so hospitable to strange yarns. Adam's readers generally disbelieved the " trustworthy reports of the Danes," and when they thought of Vinland at all, doubtless thought of it as somewhere near the North Pole.[1] We shall do well to bear

Tentavit hoc nuper experientissimus Nordmannorum princeps Haroldus, qui latitudinem septentrionalis oceani perscrutatus navibus, tandem caligantibus ante ora deficientis mundi finibus, immane abyssi baratrum, retroactis vestigiis, vix salvus evasit."
Descriptio insularum aquilonis, cap. 38, apud *Hist. Ecclesiastica,* iv. ed. Lindenbrog, Leyden, 1595. No such voyage is known to have been undertaken by Harold of Norway, nor is it likely. Adam was probably thinking of an Arctic voyage undertaken by one Thorir under the auspices of King Harold ; one of the company brought back a polar bear and gave it to King Swend, who was much pleased with it. See Rafn, p. 339. " Regionam " and " ferentes " in the above extract are variant readings found in some editions.

[1] " Det har imidlertid ikke forhindret de senere forfattere, der benyttede Adam, fra at blive mistænksomme, og saalænge Adams beretning stod alene, har man i regelen vægret sig for at tro den. Endog den norske forfatter, der skrev ' Historia Norvegiæ ' og som foruden Adam vel ogsaa har kjendt de hjemlige sagn om Vinland, maa have anseet beretningen for fabelagtig og derfor forbigaaet den ; han kjendte altfor godt Grønland som et nordligt isfyldt Poꞏarland til at ville tro paa, at i nærheden fandtes et Vinland." Storm, in *Aarbøger*

this in mind when we come to consider the possibility of Columbus having obtained from Adam of Bremen any hint in the least likely to be of use in his own enterprise.[1]

To sum up the argument : we have in Eric the Red's Saga, as copied by Hauk Erlendsson, a document for the existence of which Summary of we are required to account. That the argument document contains unmistakable knowledge of some things which mediæval Europeans could by no human possibility have learned, except through a visit to some part of the coast of North America further south than Labrador or Newfoundland. It tells an eminently probable story in a simple, straightforward way, agreeing in its details with what we know of the North American coast between Point Judith and Cape Breton. Its general accuracy in the statement and grouping of so many remote details is proof that its statements were controlled by an exceedingly strong and steady tradition, — altogether too strong and steady, in my opinion, to have been maintained simply by word of mouth. These Icelanders were people so much given to writing that their historic records during the Middle Ages were, as the late Sir Richard Burton truly

for Nordisk Oldkyndighed, etc., Copenhagen, 1887, p. 300.

[1] See below, vol. ii. p. 61.

observed, more complete than those of any other country in Europe.[1] It is probable that the facts mentioned in Hauk's document rested upon some kind of a written basis as early as the eleventh century ; and it seems quite clear that the constant tradition, by which all the allusions to Vinland and the Skrælings are controlled, had become established by that time. The data are more scanty than we could wish, but they all point in the same direction as surely as straws blown by a steady wind, and their cumulative force is so great as to fall but little short of demonstration. For these reasons it seems to me that the Saga of Eric the Red should be accepted as history ; and there is another reason which might not have counted for much at the beginning of this discussion, but at the end seems quite solid and worthy of respect. The narrative begins with the colonization of Greenland and goes on with the visits to Vinland. It is unquestionably sound history for the first part ; why should it be anything else for the second part ? What shall be said of a style of criticism which, in dealing with one and the same document, arbitrarily cuts it in two in the middle and calls the first half history and the last half legend ? which accepts its statements as serious so long as they keep to the north of the sixtieth parallel, and dismisses them as idle as soon as they pass

[1] Burton, *Ultima Thule*, London, 1875, i. 237.

to the south of it? Quite contrary to common sense, I should say.

The only discredit which has been thrown upon the story of the Vinland voyages, in the eyes either of scholars or of the general public, has arisen from the eager credulity with which ingenious antiquarians have now and then tried to prove more than facts will warrant. It is peculiarly a case in which the judicious historian has had frequent occasion to exclaim, Save me from my friends! The only fit criticism upon the wonderful argument from the Dighton inscription is a reference to the equally wonderful discovery made by Mr. Pickwick at Cobham ;[1] and when it was attempted,

Absurd speculations of zealous antiquarians

[1] See *Pickwick Papers*, chap. xi. I am indebted to Mr. Tillinghast, of Harvard University Library, for calling my attention to a letter from Rev. John Lathrop, of Boston, to Hon. John Davis, August 10, 1809, containing George Washington's opinion of the Dighton inscription. When President Washington visited Cambridge in the fall of 1789, he was shown about the college buildings by the president and fellows of the university. While in the museum he was observed to " fix his eye " upon a full-size copy of the Dighton inscription made by the librarian, James Winthrop. Dr. Lathrop, who happened to be standing near Washington, " ventured to give the opinion which several learned men had entertained with respect to the origin of the inscription." Inasmuch as some of the characters were thought to resemble " oriental " characters, and inasmuch as the ancient Phœnicians had sailed outside of the Pillars of Hercules, it was " conjectured " that

some sixty years ago, to prove that Governor
Arnold's old stone windmill at Newport was a

some Phœnician vessels had sailed into Narragansett Bay and
up the Taunton River. "While detained by winds, or other
causes now unknown, the people, it has been conjectured,
made the inscription, now to be seen on the face of the rock,
and which we may suppose to be a record of their fortunes or
of their fate."

"After I had given the above account, the President smiled
and said he believed the learned gentlemen whom I had mentioned were mistaken ; and added that in the younger part of his
life his business called him to be very much in the wilderness of
Virginia, which gave him an opportunity to become acquainted
with many of the customs and practices of the Indians. The
Indians, he said, had a way of writing and recording their transactions, either in war or hunting. When they wished to make
any such record, or leave an account of their exploits to any who
might come after them, they scraped off the outer bark of a
tree, and with a vegetable ink, or a little paint which they carried with them, on the smooth surface they wrote in a way that
was generally understood by the people of their respective tribes.
As he had so often examined the rude way of writing practised
by the Indians of Virginia, and observed many of the characters
on the inscription then before him so nearly resembled the characters used by the Indians, he had no doubt the inscription was
made long ago by some natives of America." *Proceedings of
Massachusetts Historical Society*, vol. x. p. 115. This pleasant
anecdote shows in a new light Washington's accuracy of observation and unfailing common-sense. Such inscriptions have
been found by the thousand, scattered over all parts of the
United States ; for a learned study of them see Garrick Mallery,
"Pictographs of the North American Indians," *Reports of
Bureau of Ethnology*, iv. 13–256. "The voluminous discussion upon the Dighton rock inscription," says Colonel Mallery,

tower built by the Northmen,[1] no wonder if the
exposure of this rather laughable notion should
have led many people to suppose that the story

" renders it impossible wholly to neglect it. . . . It is merely
a type of Algonquin rock-carving, not so interesting as many
others. . . . It is of purely Indian origin, and is executed in
the peculiar symbolic character of the Kekeewin," p. 20.
The characters observed by Washington in the Virginia forests
would very probably have been of the same type. Judge Davis,
to whom Dr. Lathrop's letter was addressed, published in 1809
a paper maintaining the Indian origin of the Dighton inscription.

A popular error, once started on its career, is as hard to kill
as a cat. Otherwise it would be surprising to find, in so
meritorious a book as Oscar Peschel's *Geschichte des Zeitalters
der Entdeckungen*, Stuttgart, 1877, p. 82, an unsuspecting
reliance upon Rafn's ridiculous interpretation of this Algonquin
pictograph. In an American writer as well equipped as
Peschel, this particular kind of blunder would of course be
impossible ; and one is reminded of Humboldt's remark, " Il
est des recherches qui ne peuvent s'exécuter que près des
sources mêmes." *Examen critique*, etc., tom. ii. p. 102.

In old times, I may add, such vagaries were usually saddled
upon the Phœnicians, until since Rafn's time the Northmen
have taken their place as the pack-horses for all sorts of antiquarian " conjecture."

[1] See Palfrey's *History of New England*, vol. i. pp. 57–59 ;
Mason's *Reminiscences of Newport*, pp. 392–407. Laing
(*Heimskringla*, pp. 182–185) thinks the Yankees must have
intended to fool Professor Rafn and the Royal Society of An-
tiquaries at Copenhagen : " Those sly rogues of Americans,"
says he, " dearly love a quiet hoax ; " and he can almost
hear them chuckling over their joke in their club-room at
Newport. I am afraid these Yankees were less rogues and
more fools than Mr. Laing makes out.

of Leif and Thorfinn had thereby been deprived of some part of its support. But the story never rested upon any such evidence, and does not call for evidence of such sort. There is nothing in the story to indicate that the Northmen ever founded a colony in Vinland, or built durable buildings there. The distinction im-

There is no reason for supposing that the Northmen founded a colony in Vinland

plicitly drawn by Adam of Bremen, who narrates the colonization of Iceland and Greenland, and then goes on to speak of Vinland, not as colonized, but simply as discovered, is a distinction amply borne out by our chronicles. Nowhere is there the slightest hint of a colony or settlement established in Vinland. On the contrary, our plain, business-like narrative tells us that Thorfinn Karlsefni tried to found a colony and failed; and it tells us why he failed. The Indians were too many for him. The Northmen of the eleventh century, without firearms, were in much less favourable condition for withstanding the Indians than the Englishmen of the seventeenth; and at the former period there existed no cause for emigration from Norway and Iceland at all comparable to the economic, political, and religious circumstances which, in a later age, sent thousands of Englishmen to Virginia and New England. The founding of colonies in America in the sixteenth and seventeenth centuries was no pastime; it was a tale of drudgery, starvation, and bloodshed, that curdles one's blood to read ; more attempts failed than succeeded. Assuredly Thorfinn gave proof of the good sense ascribed to him when he turned his back upon Vinland. But if he or any other Northman had ever succeeded in establishing a colony there, can anybody explain why it should not have stamped the fact of its existence either upon the soil, or upon history, or both, as unmistakably as the colony of Greenland ? Archæological remains of the Northmen abound in Greenland, all the way from Immartinek to near Cape Farewell ; the existence of one such relic on the North American continent has never yet been proved. Not a single vestige of the Northmen's presence here, at all worthy of credence, has ever been found. The writers who have, from time to time, mistaken other things for such vestiges, have been led astray because they have failed to distinguish between the different conditions of proof in Greenland and in Vinland. As Mr. Laing forcibly put the case, nearly half a century ago, " Greenland was a colony with communications, trade, civil and ecclesiastical establishments, and a considerable population," for more than four centuries. " Vinland was only visited by flying parties of woodcutters, remaining at the utmost two or three winters, but never settling there perma-

No archæological remains of the Northmen have been found south of Davis Strait

251

nently. . . . To expect here, as in Greenland, material proofs to corroborate the documentary proofs, is weakening the latter by linking them to a sort of evidence which, from the very nature of the case, — the temporary visits of a ship's crew, — cannot exist in Vinland, and, as in the case of Greenland, come in to support them."[1]

The most convincing proof that the North-men never founded a colony in America, south of Davis Strait, is furnished by the total absence of horses, cattle, and other domestic animals from the soil of North America until they were brought hither by the Spanish, French, and English settlers in the sixteenth and seventeenth centuries. If the Northmen had ever settled in Vinland, they would have brought cattle with them, and if their colony had been successful, it would have introduced such cattle perma-nently into the fauna of the country. Indeed, our narrative tells us that Karlsefni's people " had with them all kinds of cattle, having the intention to settle in the land if they could."[2] Naturally the two things are coupled in the narrator's mind. So

If the Northmen had founded a successful colony, they would have introduced domestic cattle into the North American fauna;

---

[1] Laing, *Heimskringla,* vol. i. p. 181.

[2] "Their höfdhu medh sèr allskonar fènadh, thvíat their ætlödhu at byggja landit, ef their mætti that," *i. e.* "illi omne pecudum genus secum habuerunt, nam terram, si liceret, coloniis frequentare cogitarunt." Rafn, p. 57.

the Portuguese carried livestock in their earliest expeditions to the Atlantic islands ; [1] Columbus brought horses and cows, with vines and all kinds of grain, on his second voyage to the West Indies ; [2] when the French, under Baron Léry, made a disastrous attempt to found a colony on or about Cape Breton in 1518, they left behind them, upon Sable Island, a goodly stock of cows and pigs, which throve and multiplied long after their owners had gone : [3] the Pilgrims at Plymouth had cattle, goats, and swine as early as 1623. [4] In fact, it would be difficult to imagine a community of Europeans subsisting anywhere for any length of time without domestic animals. We have seen that the Northmen took pains to raise cattle in Greenland, and were quick to comment upon the climate of Vinland as favourable for pasturage. To suppose that these men ever founded a colony in North America, but did not bring domestic animals thither, would be absurd. But it would be scarcely less absurd to suppose that such animals, having been once fairly introduced into

[1] Major, *Prince Henry the Navigator*, p. 241.

[2] Irving's *Life of Columbus*, New York, 1828, i. 293.

[3] *Histoire chronologique de la Nouvelle France*, pp. 40, 58 ; this work, written in 1689 by the Recollet friar Sixte le Tac, has at length been published (Paris, 1888) with notes and other original documents by Eugène Réveillaud. See, also, Læt, *Novus Orbis*, 39.

[4] John Smith, *Generall Historie*, 247.

the fauna of North America, would afterward have vanished without leaving a vestige of their presence. As for the few cattle for which Thorfinn could find room in his three or four dragonships, we may easily believe that his people ate them up before leaving the country, especially since we are told they were threatened with famine. But that domestic cattle, after being supported on American soil during the length of time involved in the establishment of a successful colony (say, for fifty or a hundred years), should have disappeared without leaving abundant traces of themselves, is simply incredible. Horses and kine are not dependent upon man for their existence ; when left to themselves, in almost any part of the world, they run wild and flourish in what naturalists call a " feral " state. Thus we find feral horned cattle in the Falkland and in the Ladrone islands, as well as in the ancient Chillingham Park, in Northumberland ; we find feral pigs in Jamaica ; feral European dogs in La Plata ; feral horses in Turkestan, and also in Mexico, descended from Spanish horses.[1] If the Northmen had ever founded a colony in Vinland, how did it happen that the English and French in the seventeenth century, and from that day to

[1] Darwin, *Animals and Plants under Domestication*, London, 1868, vol. i. pp. 27, 77, 84.

and such animals could not have vanished and left no trace of their existence

this, have never set eyes upon a wild horse, or wild cattle, pigs, or hounds, or any such indication whatever of the former presence of civilized Europeans? I do not recollect ever seeing this argument used before, but it seems to me conclusive. It raises against the hypothesis of a Norse colonization in Vinland a presumption extremely difficult if not impossible to overcome.[1]

[1] The views of Professor Horsford as to the geographical situation of Vinland and its supposed colonization by Northmen are set forth in his four monographs, *Discovery of America by Northmen — address at the unveiling of the statue of Leif Eriksen*, etc., Boston, 1888 ; *The Problem of the Northmen*, Cambridge, 1889 ; *The Discovery of the Ancient City of Norumbega*, Boston, 1890 ; *The Defences of Norumbega*, Boston, 1891. Among Professor Horsford's conclusions the two principal are : 1. that the " river flowing through a lake into the sea " (Rafn, p. 147) is Charles River, and that Leif's booths were erected near the site of the present Cambridge Hospital ; 2. that " Norumbega " — a word loosely applied by some early explorers to some region or regions somewhere between the New Jersey coast and the Bay of Fundy — was the Indian utterance of " Norbega " or " Norway ; " and that certain stone walls and dams at and near Watertown are vestiges of an ancient " city of Norumbega," which was founded and peopled by Northmen and carried on a more or less extensive trade with Europe for more than three centuries.

With regard to the first of these conclusions, it is perhaps as likely that Leif's booths were within the present limits of Cambridge as in any of the numerous places which different writers have confidently assigned for them, all the way from Point Judith to Cape Breton. A judicious scholar will object

As for the colony in Greenland, while its population seems never to have exceeded 5000 or 6000 souls, it maintained its existence and its intercourse with Europe uninterruptedly from its settlement in 986, by Eric the Red, for more than four hundred years. Early in the fourteenth century the West Bygd, or western settlement, near Godthaab, seems to have contained ninety farmsteads and four churches ; while the East Bygd, or eastern settlement, near Julianeshaab, contained one hundred and ninety farmsteads, with one cathedral and eleven smaller churches, two villages, and three or four monasteries.[1] Between Tunnudliorbik and Igaliko fiords, and about thirty miles from the ruined stone houses of Brattahlid, there now stands, imposing in its de-

Further fortunes of the Greenland colony

not so much to the conclusion as to the character of the arguments by which it is reached. Too much weight is attached to hypothetical etymologies.

With regard to the Norse colony alleged to have flourished for three centuries, it is pertinent to ask, what became of its cattle and horses ? Why do we find no vestiges of the burial-places of these Europeans ? or of iron tools and weapons of mediæval workmanship ? Why is there no documentary mention, in Scandinavia or elsewhere in Europe, of this trans-atlantic trade ? etc., etc. Until such points as these are disposed of, any further consideration of the hypothesis may properly be postponed.

[1] Laing, *Heimskringla*, i. 141. A description of the ruins may be found in two papers in *Meddelelser om Grönland,* Copenhagen, 1883 and 1889.

cay, the simple but massive structure of Kakortok church, once the " cathedral " church of the
Gardar bishopric, where the Credo was intoned
and censers swung, while not less than ten generations lived and died. About the beginning

Ruins of the church at Kakortok

of the twelfth century there was a movement
at Rome for establishing new dioceses in " the
islands of the ocean ;" in 1106 a bishop's see
was erected in the north of Iceland, and one at
about the same time in the Færoes. In 1112,
Eric Gnupsson,[1] having been appointed by Pope
Paschal II. " bishop of Greenland and Vinland

---

[1] Sometimes called Eric Uppsi ; he is mentioned in the
Landnáma-bók as a native of Iceland.

in partibus infidelium," went from Iceland to organize his new diocese in Greenland. It is

Bishop Eric's
voyage in
search of
Vinland,
1121

mentioned in at least six different vellums that in 1121 Bishop Eric "went in search of Vinland." [1] It is nowhere mentioned that he found it, and Dr. Storm thinks it probable that he perished in the enterprise, for, within the next year or next but one, the Greenlanders asked for a new bishop, and Eric's successor, Bishop Arnold, was consecrated in 1124. [2] After Eric there was a regular succession of bishops appointed by the papal court, down at least to 1409, and seventeen of these bishops are mentioned by name. We do not learn that any of them ever repeated Eric's experiment of searching for Vinland. So far as existing Icelandic vellums know, there was no voyage to Vinland after 1121. Very likely, however, there may have been occasional voyages for timber from Greenland to the coast of the American continent, which did not attract attention or call for comment in Iceland. This is rendered somewhat probable from an entry in the " Elder Skálholt Annals," a

The ship
from Mark-
land, 1347

---

[1] Storm, *Islandske Annaler,* Christiania, 1888 ; Reeves, *The Finding of Wineland the Good,* London, 1890, pp. 79–81.

[2] Storm, in *Aarbøger for Nordisk Oldkyndighed,* 1887, p. 319.

vellum written about 1362. This informs us that in 1347 "there came a ship from Greenland, less in size than small Icelandic trading-vessels. It was without an anchor. There were seventeen men on board, and they had sailed to Markland, but had afterwards been driven hither by storms at sea."[1] This is the latest mention of any voyage to or from the countries beyond Greenland.

If the reader is inclined to wonder why a colony could be maintained in southern Greenland more easily than on the coasts of Nova Scotia or Massachusetts, or even why the Northmen did not at once abandon their fiords at Brattahlid and come in a flock to these pleasanter places, he must call to mind two important circum-

[1] Reeves, *op. cit.* p. 83. In another vellum it is mentioned that in 1347 "a ship came from Greenland, which had sailed to Markland, and there were eighteen men on board." As Mr. Reeves well observes : "The nature of the information indicates that the knowledge of the discovery had not altogether faded from the memories of the Icelanders settled in Greenland. It seems further to lend a measure of plausibility to a theory that people from the Greenland colony may from time to time have visited the coast to the southwest of their home for supplies of wood, or for some kindred purpose. The visitors in this case had evidently intended to return directly from Markland to Greenland, and had they not been driven out of their course to Iceland, the probability is that this voyage would never have found mention in Icelandic chronicles, and all knowledge of it must have vanished as completely as did the colony to which the Markland visitors belonged."

stances. First, the settlers in southern Greenland did not meet with barbarous natives, but only with vestiges of their former presence. It was not until the twelfth century that, in roaming the icy deserts of the far North in quest of seals and bearskins, the Norse hunters encountered tribes of Eskimo using stone knives and whale-bone arrow-heads;[1] and it was not until the fourteenth century that we hear of their getting into a war with these people. In 1349 the West Bygd was attacked and destroyed by Eskimos; in 1379 they invaded the East Bygd and wrought sad havoc; and it is generally believed that some time after 1409 they completed the destruction of the colony.

The Greenland colony attacked by Eskimos

Secondly, the relative proximity of Greenland to the mother country, Iceland, made it much easier to sustain a colony there than in the more distant Vinland. In colonizing, as in campaigning, distance from one's base is sometimes the supreme circumstance. This is illustrated by the fact that the very existence of the Greenland colony itself depended upon perpetual and un-trammelled exchange of commodities with Iceland; and when once the source of supply was cut off, the colony soon languished. In 1380 and 1387 the crowns of Norway and Denmark descended upon Queen Margaret, and soon she

[1] Storm, *Monumenta historica Norvegiæ,* p. 77.

made her precious contribution to the innumerable swarm of instances that show with how little wisdom the world is ruled. She made the trade to Greenland, Iceland, and the Færoe Isles " a royal monopoly which could only be carried on in ships belonging to, or licensed by, the sovereign. . . . Under the monopoly of trade the Icelanders could have no vessels, and no object for sailing to Greenland ; and the vessels fitted out by government, or its lessees, would only be ready to leave Denmark or Bergen for Iceland at the season they ought to have been ready to leave Iceland to go to Greenland. The colony gradually fell into oblivion." [1] When this prohibitory management was abandoned after 1534 by Christian III., it was altogether too late. Starved by the miserable policy of governmental interference with freedom of trade, the little Greenland colony soon became too weak to sustain itself against the natives whose hostility had, for half a century, been growing more and more dangerous. Precisely when or how it perished we do not know. The latest notice we have of

[1] Laing, *Heimskringla*, i. 147. It has been supposed that the Black Death, by which all Europe was ravaged in the middle part of the fourteenth century, may have crossed to Greenland, and fatally weakened the colony there ; but Vigfusson says that the Black Death never touched Iceland (*Sturlunga Saga*, vol. i. p. cxxix), so that it is not so likely to have reached Greenland.

the colony is of a marriage ceremony performed (probably in the Kakortok church), in 1409, by Endrede Andreasson, the last bishop.[1] When, after three centuries, the great missionary, Hans Egede, visited Greenland, in 1721, he found the ruins of farmsteads and villages, the population of which had vanished.

Our account of pre-Columbian voyages to America would be very incomplete without some mention of the latest voyage said to have been made by European vessels to the ancient settlement of the East Bygd. I refer to the famous narrative of the Zeno brothers, which has furnished so many subjects of contention for geographers that a hundred years ago John Pinkerton called it " one of the most puzzling in the whole circle of literature."[2] Nevertheless a great deal has been done, chiefly through the acute researches of Mr. Richard Henry Major and Baron Nordenskjöld, toward clearing up this mystery, so that certain points in the Zeno narrative may now be regarded as established;[3] and from these essential points we

The story of the Venetian brothers

[1] Laing, *op. cit.* i. 142.

[2] Yet this learned historian was quite correct in his own interpretation of Zeno's story, for in the same place he says, "If real, his Frisland is the Ferro Islands, and his Zichmni is Sinclair." Pinkerton's *History of Scotland*, London, 1797, vol. i. p. 261.

[3] Major, *The Voyages of the Venetian Brothers, Nicolò*

may form an opinion as to the character of sundry questionable details.

The Zeno family was one of the oldest and most distinguished in Venice. Among its members in the thirteenth and fourteenth The Zeno family centuries we find a doge, several senators and members of the Council of Ten, and military commanders of high repute. Of these, Pietro Dracone Zeno, about 1350, was captain-general of the Christian league for withstanding the Turks; and his son Carlo achieved such success in the war against Genoa that he was called the Lion of St. Mark, and his services to Venice were compared with those of Camillus to Rome. Now this Carlo had two brothers, — Nicolò, known as "the Chevalier," and Antonio. After the close of the Genoese war the Chevalier Nicolò was seized with a desire to see the world,[1] and more particularly England and Flanders. So about 1390 he fitted up a ship at his own

and Antonio Zeno, to the Northern Seas in the XIVth Century, London, 1873 (Hakluyt Society); cf. Nordenskjöld, *Om bröderna Zenos resor och de äldsta kartor öfner Norden,* Stockholm, 1883.

[1] " Or M. Nicolò il Caualiere . . . entrò in grandissimo desiderio di ueder il mondo, e peregrinare, e farsi capace di varij costumi e di lingue de gli huomini, acciò che con le occasioni poi potesse meglio far seruigio alla sua patria ed à se acquistar fama e onore." The narrative gives 1380 as the date of the voyage, but Mr. Major has shown that it must have been a mistake for 1390 (*op. cit.* xlii.–xlviii.).

expense, and, passing out from the Strait of Gibraltar, sailed northward upon the Atlantic.

Nicolò Zeno wrecked upon one of the Færoe Islands, 1390 After some days of fair weather, he was caught in a storm and blown along for many days more, until at length the ship was cast ashore on one of the Færoe Islands and wrecked, though most of the crew and goods were rescued. According to the barbarous custom of the Middle Ages, some of the natives of the island (Scandinavians) came swarming about the unfortunate strangers to kill and rob them, but a great chieftain, with a force of knights and men-at-arms, arrived upon the spot in time to prevent such an outrage. This chief was Henry Sinclair of Roslyn, who in 1379 had been invested by King Hacon VI., of Norway, with the earldom of the Orkneys and Caithness. On learning Zeno's rank and importance, Sinclair treated him with much courtesy, and presently a friendship sprang up between the two. Sinclair was then engaged with a fleet of thirteen vessels in conquering and annexing to his earldom the Færoe Islands, and on several occasions profited by the military and nautical skill of the Venetian captain. Nicolò seems to have enjoyed this stirring life, for he presently sent to his brother Antonio in Venice an account of it, which induced the latter to come and join him in the Færoe Islands. Antonio arrived in the course of 1391, and remained in the service of Sinclair fourteen years, returning to Venice in time to die there in 1406. After Antonio's arrival, his brother Nicolò was appointed to the chief command of Sinclair's little fleet, and assisted him in taking possession of the Shetland Islands, which were properly comprised within his earldom. In the course of these adventures, Nicolò seems to have had his interest aroused in reports about Greenland. It was not more than four or five years since Queen Margaret had undertaken to make a royal monopoly of the Greenland trade in furs and whale oil, and this would be a natural topic of conversation in the Færoes. In July, 1393, or 1394, Nicolò Zeno sailed to Greenland with three ships, and visited the East Bygd. Nicolò's voyage to Greenland, cir. 1394 After spending some time there, not being accustomed to such a climate, he caught cold, and died soon after his return to the Færoes, probably in 1395. His brother Antonio succeeded to his office and such emoluments as pertained to it; and after a while, at Earl Sinclair's instigation, he undertook a voyage of discovery in the Atlantic Ocean, in order to verify some fishermen's reports of the existence of land a thousand miles or more to the west. One of these fishermen was to serve as guide to the expedition, but unfortunately he died three days before the ships were ready to sail. Nevertheless, the expedition started, with Sinclair himself on board, and encountered vicissitudes of weather and fortune. In fog and storm they lost Voyage of all reckoning of position, and found Earl Sinclair and Antonio themselves at length on the western Zeno coast of a country which, in the Italian narrative, is called " Icaria," but which has been supposed, with some probability, to have been Kerry, in Ireland. Here, as they went ashore for fresh water, they were attacked by the natives and several of their number were slain. From this point they sailed out into the broad Atlantic again, and reached a place supposed to be Greenland, but which is so vaguely described that the identification is very difficult.[1] Our narrative here ends somewhat confusedly. We are told that Sinclair remained in this place, " and explored the whole of the country with great diligence, as well as the coasts on both sides of Greenland." Antonio Zeno, on the other hand, returned with part of the fleet to the Færoe Islands, where he arrived after sailing eastward for about a month, during five and twenty days of which he saw no land. After relating these

[1] It appears on the Zeno map as " Trin pmontor," about the site of Cape Farewell ; but how could six days' sail W. from Kerry, followed by four days' sail N. E., reach any such point ? and how does this short outward sail consist with the return voyage, twenty days E. and eight days S. E., to the Færoes ? The place is also said to have had " a fertile soil " and " good rivers," a description in nowise answering to Greenland.

things and paying a word of affectionate tribute to the virtues of Earl Sinclair, " a prince as worthy of immortal memory as any that ever lived for his great bravery and remarkable goodness," Antonio closes his letter abruptly : " But of this I will say no more in this letter, and hope to be with you very shortly, and to satisfy your curiosity on other subjects by word of mouth." [1]

The person thus addressed by Antonio was his brother, the illustrious Carlo Zeno. Soon after reaching home, after this long and eventful absence, Antonio died. Besides his letters he had written a more detailed account of the affairs in the northern seas. These papers remained for more than a century in the palace of the family at Venice, until one of the children, in his mischievous play, got hold of them and tore them up. This child was Antonio's great - great -great - grandson, Nicolò, born in 1515. When this young Nicolò had come to middle age, and was a member of the Council of Ten, he happened to come across some remnants of these documents, and then all at once he remembered with grief how he had, in his boyhood, pulled them to pieces.[2] In the light

[1] " Però non ui dirò altro in questa lettera, sperando tosto di essere con uoi, e di sodisfarui di molte altre cose con la uiua uoce." Major, p. 34.

[2] " All these letters were written by Messire Antonio to

of the rapid progress in geographical discovery since 1492, this story of distant voyages had now for Nicolò an interest such as it could not have had for his immediate ancestors. Searching the palace he found a few grimy old letters and a map or sailing chart, rotten with age, which had been made or at any rate brought home by his ancestor Antonio. Nicolò drew a fresh copy of this map, and pieced together the letters as best he could, with more or less explanatory text of his own, and the result was the little book which he published in 1558.[1]

Publication of the remains of the documents by the younger Nicolò Zeno

Unfortunately young Nicolò, with the laudable purpose of making it all as clear as he could, thought it necessary not simply to reproduce the old weather-beaten map, but to amend it by putting on here and there such places and Messire Carlo, his brother; and I am grieved that the book and many other writings on these subjects have, I don't know how, come sadly to ruin; for, being but a child when they fell into my hands, I, not knowing what they were, tore them in pieces, as children will do, and sent them all to ruin: a circumstance which I cannot now recall without the greatest sorrow. Nevertheless, in order that such an important memorial should not be lost, I have put the whole in order, as well as I could, in the above narrative." Major, p. 35.

[1] Nicolò Zeno, *Dello scoprimento dell' isole Frislanda, Eslanda, Engronelanda, Estotilanda, & Icaria, fatto per due fratelli Zeni, M. Nicolò il Caualiere, & M. Antonio. Libro Vno, col disegno di dette Isole.* Venice, 1558. Mr. Major's book contains the entire text, with an English translation.

ZENO

names as his diligent perusal of the manuscript led him to deem wanting to its completeness.[1]

---

[1] The map is taken from Winsor's *Narr. and Crit. Hist.*, i. 127, where it is reduced from Nordenskjöld's *Studien ok Forskningar*. A better because larger copy may be found in Major's *Voyages of the Venetian Brothers*. The original map measures 12 × 15½ inches. In the legend at the top the date is given as M CCC LXXX, but evidently one X has been omitted, for it should be 1390, and is correctly so given by Marco Barbaro, in his *Genealogie dei nobili Veneti;* of Antonio Zeno he says, " Scrisse con il fratello Nicolò Kav. li viaggi dell' Isole sotto il polo artico, e di quei scoprimente del 1390, e che per ordine di Zicno, re di Frislanda, si portò nel continente d' Estotilanda nell' America settentrionale e che si fermò 14 anni in Frislanda, cioè 4 con suo fratello Nicolò e 10 solo." (This valuable work has never been published. The original MS., in Barbaro's own handwriting, is preserved in the Biblioteca di San Marco at Venice. There is a seventeenth century copy of it among the Egerton MSS. in the British Museum.) — Nicolò did not leave Italy until after December 14, 1388 (Muratori, *Rerum Italicarum, Scriptores*, tom. xxii. p. 779). The map can hardly have been made before Antonio's voyage, about 1400. The places on the map are wildly out of position, as was common enough in old maps. Greenland is attached to Norway according to the general belief in the Middle Ages. In his confusion between the names " Estland " and " Islanda," young Nicolò has tried to reproduce the Shetland group, or something like it, and attach it to Iceland. " Icaria," probably Kerry, in Ireland, has been made into an island and carried far out into the Atlantic. The queerest of young Nicolò's mistakes was in placing the monastery of St. Olaus (" St. Thomas "). He should have placed it on the southwest coast of Greenland, near his " Af pmontor ; " but he has got it on the

Under the most favourable circumstances that is a very difficult sort of thing to do, but in this case the circumstances were far from favourable. Of course Nicolò got these names and places into absurd positions, thus perplexing the map and damaging its reputation. With regard to names, there was obscurity enough, to begin with. In the first place, they were Icelandic names falling upon the Italian ears of old Nicolò and Antonio, and spelled by them according to their own notions; in the second place, these outlandish names, blurred and defaced withal in the weather-stained manuscript, were a puzzle to the eye of young Nicolò, who could but decipher them according to *his* notions. The havoc that can be wrought upon winged words, subjected to such processes, is sometimes marvellous.[1] Perhaps the slightest sufferer, in this case, was the name of the group of islands upon one of

Queer transformations of names

extreme northeast, just above where Greenland is joined to Europe.

[1] "Combien de coquilles typographiques ou de lectures défectueuses ont créé de noms boiteux, qu'il est ensuite bien difficile, quelquefois impossible de redresser ! l'histoire et la géographie en sont pleines." Avezac, *Martin Waltzemüller*, p. 9.

It is interesting to see how thoroughly words can be disguised by an unfamiliar phonetic spelling. I have seen people hopelessly puzzled by the following bill, supposed to have

which the shipwrecked Nicolò was rescued by Sinclair. The name *Færoislander* sounded to Italian ears as *Frislanda*, and was uniformly so written.[1] Then the pronunciation of *Shetland* was helped by prefixing a vowel sound, as is common in Italian, and so it came to be *Estland* and *Esland*. This led young Nicolò's eye in two or three places to confound it with *Islanda*, or *Iceland*, and probably in one place with *Irlanda*, or *Ireland*. Where old Nicolò

been made out by an illiterate stable-keeper somewhere in England : —

Osafada	7s 6d
Takinonimome	4d
	7s 10d

Some years ago Professor Huxley told me of a letter from France which came to the London post-office thus addressed : —

> Sromfrédévi,
> Piqué du lait,
> Londres,
> Angleterre.

This letter, after exciting at first helpless bewilderment and then busy speculation, was at length delivered to the right person, *Sir Humphry Davy*, in his rooms at the Royal Institution on Albemarle Street, just off from *Piccadilly!*

[1] Columbus, on his journey to Iceland in 1477, also heard the name *Færoislander* as *Frislanda*, and so wrote it in the letter preserved for us in his biography by his son Ferdinand, hereafter to be especially noticed. See Major's remarks on this, *op. cit.* p. xix.

meant to say that the island upon which he was living with Earl Sinclair was somewhat larger than Shetland, young Nicolò understood him as saying that it was somewhat larger than Ireland ; and so upon the amended map "Frislanda" "Frislanda" appears as one great island surrounded by tiny islands.[1] After the publication of this map, in 1558, sundry details were copied from it by the new maps of that day, so that even far down into the seventeenth century it was common to depict a big "Frislanda" somewhere in mid-ocean. When at length it was proved that no such island exists, the reputation of the Zeno narrative was seriously damaged. The nadir of reaction against it was reached when it was declared to be a tissue of lies invented by the younger Nicolò,[2] apparently for the purpose of setting up a Venetian claim to the discovery of America.

[1] Perhaps in the old worn-out map the archipelago may have been blurred so as to be mistaken for one island. This would aid in misleading young Nicolò.

[2] See the elaborate paper by Admiral Zahrtmann, in *Nordisk Tidsskrift for Oldkyndighed*, Copenhagen, 1834, vol. i., and the English translation of it in *Journal of Royal Geographical Society*, London, 1836, vol. v. All that human ingenuity is ever likely to devise against the honesty of Zeno's narrative is presented in this erudite essay, which has been so completely demolished under Mr. Major's heavy strokes that there is not enough of it left to pick up. As to this part of the question, we may now safely cry, "Finis, laus Deo !"

The narrative, however, not only sets up no such claim, but nowhere betrays a consciousness that its incidents entitle it to make such a claim. It had evidently not occurred to young Nicolò to institute any comparison between his ancestors' voyages to Greenland and the voyages of Columbus to the western hemisphere, of which *we now know* Greenland to be a part. The knowledge of the North American coast, and of the bearing of one fact upon another fact in relation to it, was still, in 1558, in an extremely vague and rudimentary condition. In the mind of the Zeno brothers, as the map shows, Greenland was a European peninsula ; such was the idea common among mediæval Northmen, as is nowhere better illustrated than in this map. Neither in his references to Greenland, nor to Estotiland and Drogio, presently to be considered, does young Nicolò appear in the light of a man urging or suggesting a "claim." He appears simply as a modest and conscientious editor, interested in the deeds of his ancestors and impressed with the fact that he has got hold of important documents, but intent only upon giving his material as correctly as possible, and refraining from all sort of comment except such as now and then seems needful to explain the text as he himself understands it.

The identification of " Frislanda " with the

Fӕroe Islands was put beyond doubt by the discovery that the " Zichmni " of the narrative means Henry Sinclair ; and, in order to make this discovery, it was only necessary to know something about the history of the Orkneys ; hence old Pinkerton, as above remarked, got it right. The name " Zichmni " is, no doubt, a fearful and wonderful bejugglement; but Henry Sinclair is a personage well known to history in that corner of the world, and the deeds of " Zichmni," as recounted in the narrative, are neither more nor less than the deeds of Sinclair. Doubtless Antonio spelled the name in some queer way of his own, and then young Nicolò, unable to read his ancestor's pothooks where — as in the case of proper names — there was no clue to guide him, contrived to make it still queerer. Here we have strong proof of the genuineness of the narrative. If Nicolò had been concocting a story in which Earl Sinclair was made to figure, he would have obtained his knowledge from literary sources, and thus would have got his names right ; the earl might have appeared as Enrico de Santo Claro, but not as " Zichmni." It is not at all likely, however, that any literary knowledge of Sinclair and his doings was obtainable in Italy in the sixteenth century. The Zeno narrative, moreover, in its references to Greenland in connection with the Chevalier Nicolò's visit to the

274

Earl Sinclair

East Bygd, shows a topographical knowledge that was otherwise quite inaccessible to the younger Nicolò. Late in the fourteenth century Ivar Bardsen, steward to the Gardar bishopric, wrote a description of Greenland, with sailing directions for reaching it, which modern research has proved to have been accurate in every particular. Bardsen's details and those of the Zeno narrative mutually corroborate each other. But Bardsen's book did not make its way down into Europe until the very end of the sixteenth century,[1] and then amid the dense ignorance prevalent concerning Greenland its details were not understood until actual exploration within the last seventy years has at length revealed their meaning. The genuineness of the Zeno narrative is thus conclusively proved by its knowledge of Arctic geography, such as could have been obtained only by a visit to the far North at a time before the Greenland colony had finally lost touch with its mother country.

Bardsen's " Description of Greenland "

---

[1] It was translated into Dutch by the famous Arctic explorer, William Barentz, whose voyages are so graphically described in Motley's *United Netherlands*, vol. iii. pp. 552–576. An English translation was made for Henry Hudson. A very old Danish version may be found in Rafn's *Antiquitates Americanæ*, pp. 300–318 ; Danish, Latin, and English versions in Major's *Voyages of the Venetian Brothers*, etc., pp. 39–54 ; and an English version in De Costa's *Sailing Directions of Henry Hudson*, Albany, 1869, pp. 61–96.

The visit of the Chevalier Nicolò, therefore, about 1394, has a peculiar interest as the last distinct glimpse afforded us of the colony founded by Eric the Red before its melancholy disappearance from history. Already the West Bygd had ceased to exist. Five and forty years before that time it had been laid waste and its people massacred by Eskimos, and trusty Ivar Bardsen, tardily sent with a small force to the rescue, found nothing left alive but a few cattle and sheep running wild.[1] Nicolò Zeno, arriving

The monastery of St. Olaus and its hot spring

in the East Bygd, found there a monastery dedicated to St. Olaus, a name which in the narrative has become St. Thomas. To this monastery came friars from Norway and other countries, but for the most part from Iceland.[2] It stood "hard by a hill which vomited fire like Vesuvius and Etna." There was also in the neighbourhood a spring

---

[1] So he tells us himself: "Quo cum venissent, nullum hominem, neque christianum neque paganum, invenerunt, tantummodo fera pecora et oves deprehenderunt, ex quibus quantum naves ferre poterant in has deportato domum redierunt." *Descriptio Grœnlandiæ*, apud Major, p. 53. The glacial men had done their work of slaughter and vanished.

[2] "Ma la maggior parte sono delle Islande." Mr. Major is clearly wrong in translating it "from the Shetland Isles." The younger Nicolò was puzzled by the similarity of the names Islanda and Eslanda, and sometimes confounded Iceland with the Shetland group. But in this place Iceland is evidently meant.

of hot water which the ingenious friars conducted in pipes into their monastery and church, thereby keeping themselves comfortable in the coldest weather. This water, as it came into the kitchen, was hot enough to boil meats and vegetables. The monks even made use of it in warming covered gardens or hot-beds in which they raised sundry fruits and herbs that in milder climates grow out of doors.[1] " Hither in summer-time come many vessels from . . . the Cape above Norway, and from Trondheim, and bring the friars all sorts of comforts, taking in exchange fish . . . and skins of different kinds of animals. . . . There are continually in the harbour a number of vessels detained by the sea being frozen, and waiting for the next season to melt the ice." [2]

This mention of the volcano and the hot spring is very interesting. In the Miocene period the Atlantic ridge was one of the principal seats of volcanic activity upon the globe ; the line of volcanoes extended all the way from Greenland down into central France. But for several hundred thou-

Volcanoes of the North Atlantic ridge

---

[1] This application of the hot water to purposes of gardening reminds us of the similar covered gardens or hot-beds constructed by Albertus Magnus in the Dominican monastery at Cologne in the thirteenth century. See Humboldt's *Kosmos,* ii. 130.

[2] Major, *op. cit.* p. 16. The narrative goes on to give a description of the skin-boats of the Eskimo fishermen.

sand years this activity has been diminishing. In France, in the western parts of Great Britain and the Hebrides, the craters have long since become extinct. In the far North, however, volcanic action has been slower in dying out. Iceland, with no less than twenty active volcanoes, is still the most considerable centre of such operations in Europe. The huge volcano on Jan Mayen Island, between Greenland and Spitzbergen, is still in action. Among the submerged peaks in the northern seas explosions still now and then occur, as in 1783, when a small island was thrown up near Cape Reykianes, on the southern coast of Iceland, and sank again after a year.[1] Midway between Iceland and Greenland there appears to have stood, in the Middle Ages, a small volcanic island discovered by that Gunnbjörn who first went to Greenland. It was known as Gunnbjörn's Skerries, and was described by Ivar Bardsen.[2] This island is no longer above

Fate of Gunnbjörn's Skerries, 1456

---

[1] Daubeny, *Description of Active and Extinct Volcanoes*, London, 1848, pp. 307 ; cf. Judd, *Volcanoes*, London, 1881, p. 234.

[2] " Ab Snefelsneso Islandiæ, quâ brevissimus in Gronlandiam trajectus est, duorum dierum et duarum noctium spatio navigandum est recto cursu versus occidentem ; ibique Gunnbjœrnis scopulos invenies, inter Gronlandiam et Islandiam medio situ interjacentes. Hic cursus antiquitûs frequentabatur, nunc vero glacies ex recessu oceani euroaquilonari delata scopulos ante memoratos tam prope attigit, ut nemo sine vitæ

the surface, and its fate is recorded upon Ruysch's map of the world in the 1508 edition of Ptolemy : " Insula hæc anno Domini 1456 fuit totaliter combusta," — this island was entirely burnt (*i. e.* blown up in an eruption) in 1456 ; and in later maps Mr. Major has found the corrupted name " Gombar Scheer " applied to the dangerous reefs and shoals left behind by this explosion.[1] Where volcanic action is declining geysers and boiling springs are apt to abound, as in Iceland ; where it has become extinct at a period geologically recent, as in Auvergne and the Rhine country, its latest vestiges are left in the hundreds of thermal and mineral springs whither fashionable invalids congregate to drink or to bathe.[2] Now in Greenland, at the present day, hot springs are found, of which the most

Volcanic phenomena in Greenland

noted are those on the island of Ounartok, at the entrance to the fiord of that name. These springs seem to be the same that were described five hundred years ago by Ivar Bardsen. As to volcanoes, it has been generally assumed that those of Greenland are all extinct; but in a country as yet so imperfectly studied this only

discrimine antiquum cursum tenere possit, quemadmodum infra dicetur." *Descriptio Grœnlandiæ*, apud Major, *op. cit.* p. 40.

[1] *Op. cit.* p. lxxvi. See below, vol. ii. p. 346, note B.
[2] Judd, *op. cit.* pp. 217–220.

means that eruptions have not been recorded.[1] On the whole, it seems to me that the mention, in our Venetian narrative, of a boiling spring and an active volcano in Greenland is an instance of the peculiar sort — too strange to have been invented, but altogether probable in itself — that adds to the credit of the narrative.

Thus far, in dealing with the places actually visited by Nicolò or Antonio, or by both brothers, we have found the story consistent and intelligible. But in what relates to countries beyond Greenland, countries which were not visited by either of the brothers, but about which Antonio heard reports, it is quite a different thing. We are introduced to a jumble very unlike the clear, business-like account of Vinland voyages in the Hauks-bók. Yet in this medley there are some statements curiously suggestive of things in North America. It will be remembered that Antonio's voyage with Sinclair (somewhere about 1400) was undertaken in order to verify certain reports of the existence of land

[1] My friend, Professor Shaler, tells me that "a volcano during eruption might shed its ice mantle and afterward don it again in such a manner as to hide its true character even on a near view;" and, on the other hand, "a voyager not familiar with volcanoes might easily mistake the cloud-bonnet of a peak for the smoke of a volcano." This, however, will not account for Zeno's "hill that vomited fire," for he goes on to describe the use which the monks made of the pumice and calcareous tufa for building purposes.

more than a thousand miles west of the Færoe
Islands.

About six and twenty years ago, said Antonio
in a letter to Carlo, four small fishing craft, ven-
turing very far out upon the Atlantic, had been
blown upon a strange coast, where their crews
were well received by the people. The land
proved to be an island rather smaller
than Iceland (or Shetland?), with a   Estotiland
high mountain whence flowed four rivers. The
inhabitants were intelligent people, possessed
of all the arts, but did not understand the language of these Norse fishermen.[1] There happened, however, to be one European among
them, who had himself been cast ashore in that
country and had learned its language ; he could
speak Latin, and found some one among the
shipwrecked men who could understand him.
There was a populous city with walls, and the
king had Latin books in his library which nobody could read.[2] All kinds of metals abounded,
and especially gold.[3] The woods were of immense extent. The people traded with Green-

---

[1] They were, therefore, not Northmen.

[2] Pruning this sentence of its magniloquence, might it perhaps mean that there was a large palisaded village, and that
the chief had some books in Roman characters, a relic of
some castaway, which he kept as a fetich ?

[3] With all possible latitude of interpretation, this could not
be made to apply to any part of America north of Mexico.

land, importing thence pitch (?), brimstone, and furs. They sowed grain and made " beer." They made small boats, but were ignorant of the loadstone and the compass. For this reason, they held the newcomers in high estimation.[1] The name of the country was Estotiland.

There is nothing so far in this vague description to show that Estotiland was an American country, except its western direction and perhaps its trading with Greenland. The points of unlikeness are at least as numerous as the points of likeness. But in what follows there is a much stronger suggestion of North America.

For some reason not specified an expedition was undertaken by people from Estotiland to Drogio   a country to the southward named Drogio, and these Norse mariners, or some of them, because they understood the compass, were put in charge of it.[2] But the people of Drogio were cannibals, and the people from Estotiland on their arrival were taken prisoners and devoured, — all save the few Northmen, who were saved because of their

[1] The magnetic needle had been used by the mariners of western and northern Europe since the end of the thirteenth century.

[2] " Fanno nauigli e nauigano, ma non hanno la calamìta ne intendeno col bossolo la tramontana. Per ilche questi pescatori furono in gran pregio, si che il re li spedì con dodici nauigli uerso ostro nel paese che essi chiamano Drogio." Major, *op. cit.* p. 21.

marvellous skill in catching fish with nets. The
barbarians seemed to have set much store by
these white men, and perhaps to have regarded
them as objects of "medicine." One of the
fishermen in particular became so famous that
a neighbouring tribe made war upon the tribe
which kept him, and winning the victory took
him over into its own custody. This sort of
thing happened several times. Various tribes
fought to secure the person and services of this
Fisherman, so that he was passed about among
more than twenty chiefs, and "wandering up
and down the country without any fixed abode,
. . . he became acquainted with all those
parts."

And now comes quite an interesting passage.
The Fisherman "says that it is a very great
country, and, as it were, a new world ; Inhabitants
the people are very rude and unculti- of Drogio
vated, for they all go naked, and suf- tries beyond
fer cruelly from the cold, nor have they the
sense to clothe themselves with the skins of the
animals which they take in hunting [a gross
exaggeration]. They have no kind of metal.
They live by hunting, and carry lances of wood,
sharpened at the point. They have bows, the
strings of which are made of beasts' skins. They
are very fierce, and have deadly fights amongst
each other, and eat one another's flesh. They
have chieftains and certain laws among them-

selves, but differing in the different tribes. The farther you go southwestwards, however, the more refinement you meet with, because the climate is more temperate, and accordingly there they have cities and temples dedicated to their idols, in which they sacrifice men and afterwards eat them. In those parts they have some knowledge and use of gold and silver. Now this Fisherman, having dwelt so many years in these parts, made up his mind, if possible, to return home to his own country; but his companions, despairing of ever seeing it again, gave him God's speed, and remained themselves where they were. Accordingly, he bade them farewell, and made his escape through the woods in the direction of Drogio, where he was welcomed and very kindly received by the chief of the place, who knew him, and was a great enemy of the neighbouring chieftain; and so passing from one chief to another, being the same with whom he had been before, after a long time and with much toil, he at length reached Drogio, where he spent three years. Here, by good luck, he heard from the natives that some boats had arrived off the coast; and full of hope of being able to carry out his intention, he went down to the seaside, and to his great delight found that they had come from Estotiland. He forthwith requested that they would take him with them, which they did very willingly, and as he knew the language of the country, which none of them could speak, they employed him as their interpreter." [1]

Whither the Fisherman was first carried in these boats or vessels, Antonio's letter does not inform us. We are only told that he engaged in some prosperous voyages, and at length returned to the Færoes after these six and twenty years of strange adventures. It was apparently the Fisherman's description of Estotiland as a very rich country (*paese ricchissimo*) that led Sinclair to fit out an expedition to visit it, with Antonio as his chief captain. As we have already seen, the Fisherman died just before the ships were ready to start, and to whatever land they succeeded in reaching after they sailed without him, the narrative leaves us with the impression that it was not the mysterious Estotiland.

The Fisherman's return to "Frislanda"

To attempt to identify that country from the description of it, which reads like a parcel of ill-digested sailors' yarns, would be idle. The most common conjecture has identified it with Newfoundland, from its relations to other points mentioned in the Zeno narrative, as indicated, with fair probability, on the Zeno map. To identify it with Newfoundland is to brand the description as a "fish story," but from such a conclusion there seems anyway to be no escape.

[1] Major, *op. cit.* pp. 20–22.

With Drogio, however, it is otherwise. The description of Drogio and the vast country stretching beyond it, which was like a " new world," is the merest sketch, but it seems to contain enough characteristic details to stamp it as a description of North America, and of no other country accessible by an Atlantic voyage. It is a sketch which apparently must have had its ultimate source in somebody's personal experience of aboriginal North America. Here we are reminded that when the younger Nicolò published this narrative, in 1558, some dim knowledge of the North American tribes was beginning to make its way into the minds of people in Europe. The work of Soto and Cartier, to say nothing of other explorers, had already been done. May we suppose that Nicolò had thus obtained some idea of North America, and wove it into his reproduction of his ancestors' letters, for the sake of completeness and point, in somewhat the same uncritical mood as that in which the most worthy ancient historians did not scruple to invent speeches to put into the mouths of their heroes? It may have been so, and in such case the description of Drogio loses its point for us as a feature in the pre-Columbian voyages to America. In such case we may dismiss it at once, and pretty much all the latter part of the Zeno narrative, relating to what Antonio heard and did, becomes valueless; though the earlier part, relating to the elder Nicolò, still remains valid and trustworthy.

But suppose we take the other alternative. As in the earlier part of the story we feel sure that young Nicolò must have reproduced the ancestral documents faithfully, because it shows knowledge that he could not have got in any other way; let us now suppose that in the latter part also he added nothing of himself, but was simply a faithful editor. It will then follow that the Fisherman's account of Drogio, reduced to writing by Antonio Zeno about 1400, must probably represent personal experiences in North America; for no such happy combination of details characteristic only of North America is likely at that date to have been invented by any European. Our simplest course will be to suppose that the Fisherman really had the experiences which are narrated, that he was bandied about from tribe to tribe in North America, all the way, perhaps, from Nova Scotia to Mexico, and yet returned to the Færoe Islands to tell the tale! Could such a thing be possible? Was anything of the sort ever done before or since?

Or does it represent actual experiences in North America?

Yes: something of the sort appears to have been done about ten years after the Zeno narrative was published. In October, 1568, that

great sailor, Sir John Hawkins, by reason of
scarcity of food, was compelled to set about a
The case of
David In-
gram, 1568 hundred men ashore near the Rio de
Minas, on the Mexican coast, and
leave them to their fate. The conti-
nent was a network of rude paths or trails, as it
had doubtless been for ages, and as central Africa
is to-day. Most of these Englishmen probably
perished in the wilderness. Some who took
southwesterly trails found their way to the city
of Mexico, where, as "vile Lutheran dogges,"
they were treated with anything but kindness.
Others took northeasterly trails, and one of
these men, David Ingram, made his way from
Texas to Maine, and beyond to the St. John's
River, where he was picked up by a friendly
French ship and carried to France, and so got
home to England. The journey across North
America took him about eleven months, but
one of his comrades, Job Hortop, had no end
of adventures, and was more than twenty years
in getting back to England. Ingram told such
blessed yarns about houses of crystal and silver,
and other wonderful things, that many disbelieved his whole story, but he was subjected to
a searching examination before Sir Francis Walsingham, and as to the main fact of his journey
through the wilderness there seems to be no
doubt.[1]

[1] Ingram's narrative was first published in Hakluyt's folio

Far more important, historically, and in many ways more instructive than the wanderings of David Ingram, was the journey of Cabeza de Vaca and his ingenious comrades, in 1528–36, from the Mississippi River to their friends in Mexico. This remarkable journey will receive further consideration in another place.[1] In the course of it Cabeza de Vaca was for eight years held captive by sundry Indian tribes, and at last his escape in-

The case of Cabeza de Vaca, 1528–36

of 1589, pp. 557–562, but in his larger work, *Principal Navigations*, etc., London, 1600, it is omitted. As Purchas quaintly says, " As for David Ingram's perambulation to the north parts, Master Hakluyt in his first edition published the same ; but it seemeth some incredibilities of his reports caused him to leaue him out in the next impression, the reward of lying being not to be beleeued in truths." *Purchas his Pilgrimes*, London, 1625, vol. iv. p. 1179. The examination before Walsingham had reference to the projected voyage of Sir Humphrey Gilbert, which was made in 1583. Ingram's relation, " wch he reported vnto Sr Frauncys Walsingh$\tilde{m}$, Knight, and diuers others of good judgment and creditt, in August and Septembar, Ao D$\tilde{n}$i, 1582," is in the British Museum, Sloane MS. No. 1447, fol. 1–18 ; it was copied and privately printed in Plowden Weston's *Documents connected with the History of South Carolina*, London, 1856. There is a MS. copy in the Sparks Collection in the Harvard University Library. See the late Mr. Charles Deane's note in his edition of Hakluyt's *Discourse concerning Westerne Planting*, Cambridge, 1877, p. 229 (*Collections of Maine Hist. Soc.*, 2d series, vol. ii.) ; see, also, Winsor *Narr. and Crit. Hist.*, iii. 186.

[1] See below, vol. iii. p. 331.

volved ten months of arduous travel. On one occasion he and his friends treated some sick Indians, among other things breathing upon them and making the sign of the cross. As the Indians happened to get well, these Spaniards at once became objects of reverence, and different tribes vied with one another for access to them, in order to benefit by their supernatural gifts. In those early days, before the red men had become used to seeing Europeans, a white captive was not so likely to be put to death as to be cherished as a helper of vast and undetermined value.[1] The Indians set so much store by Cabeza de Vaca that he found it hard to tear himself away ; but at length he used his influence over them in such wise as to facilitate his moving in a direction by which he ultimately succeeded in escaping to his friends. There seems to be a real analogy between his strange experiences and those of the Fisherman in Drogio, who became an object of reverence because he could do things that the natives could not do, yet the value of which they were able to appreciate.

Now if the younger Nicolò had been in the mood for adorning his ancestor's narrative by inserting a few picturesque incidents out of his own hearsay knowledge of North America, it

[1] In the first reception of the Spaniards in Peru, we shall see a similar idea at work, vol. iii. pp. 214, 224.

does not seem likely that he would have known enough to hit so deftly upon one of the peculiarities of the barbaric mind. Here, again, we seem to have come upon one of those incidents, inherently probable, but too strange to have been invented, that tend to confirm the story. Without hazarding anything like a positive opinion, it seems to me likely enough that this voyage of Scandinavian fishermen to the coast of North America in the fourteenth century may have happened.

It was this and other unrecorded but possible instances that I had in mind at the beginning of this chapter, in saying that occasional visits of Europeans to America in pre-Columbian times may have occurred oftener than we are wont to suppose. Observe that our scanty *There may have been unrecorded instances of visits to North America* records — naturally somewhat perplexed and dim, as treating of remote and unknown places — refer us to that northern Atlantic region where the ocean is comparatively narrow, and to that northern people who, from the time of their first appearance in history, have been as much at home upon sea as upon land. For a thousand years past these hyperborean waters have been furrowed in many directions by stout Scandinavian keels, and if, in aiming at Greenland, the gallant mariners may now and then have hit upon Labrador or Newfoundland, and have made flying visits to coasts still farther southward, there is nothing in it all which need surprise us.[1]

Nothing can be clearer, however, from a survey of the whole subject, than that these pre-Columbian voyages were quite barren of results of historic importance. In point of colonization they produced the two ill-fated settlements on the Greenland coast, and nothing more. Otherwise they made no real addition to the stock of geographical knowledge, they wrought no effect whatever upon the European mind outside of Scandinavia, and even in Iceland itself the mention of coasts beyond Greenland awakened no definite ideas, and, except for a brief season, excited no interest. The Zeno narrative indicates that the Vinland voyages had practically lapsed from memory before the end of the four-

The pre-Columbian voyages made no real contributions to geographical knowledge ;

---

[1] The latest pre-Columbian voyage mentioned as having occurred in the northern seas was that of the Polish pilot John Szkolny, who, in the service of King Christian I. of Denmark, is said to have sailed to Greenland in 1476, and to have touched upon the coast of Labrador. See Gomara, *Historia de las Indias*, Saragossa, 1553, cap. xxxvii. ; Wytfliet, *Descriptionis Ptolemaicæ Augmentum*, Douay, 1603, p. 102 ; Pontanus, *Rerum Danicarum Historia*, Amsterdam, 1631, p. 763. The wise Humboldt mentions the report without expressing an opinion, *Examen critique*, tom. ii. p. 153.

teenth century.[1] Scholars familiar with saga literature of course knew the story ; it was just at this time that Jón Thórdharson wrote out the version of it which is preserved in the Flateyarbók. But by the general public it must have been forgotten, or else the Fisherman's tale of Estotiland and Drogio would surely have awakened reminiscences of Markland and Vinland, and some traces of this would have appeared in Antonio's narrative or upon his map. The principal naval officer of the Færoes, and personal friend of the sovereign, after dwelling several years among these Northmen, whose intercourse with their brethren in Iceland was frequent, apparently knew nothing of Leif or Thorfinn, or the mere names of the coasts which they had visited. Nothing had been accomplished by those voyages which could properly be called a contribution to geographical know- *and were in no true sense a Discovery of America* ledge. To speak of them as constituting, in any legitimate sense of the phrase, a Discovery of America is simply absurd. Except for Greenland, which was supposed to be a part of the European world, America remained as much undiscovered after the eleventh century as before. In the midsummer of 1492 it needed to be discovered as

[1] Practically, but not entirely, for we have seen Markland mentioned in the "Elder Skálholt Annals," about 1362. See above, p. 259.

much as if Leif Ericsson or the whole race of Northmen had never existed.

As these pre-Columbian voyages produced no effect in the eastern hemisphere, except to leave in Icelandic literature a scanty but interesting record, so in the western hemisphere they seem to have produced no effect beyond cutting down a few trees and killing a few Indians. In the outlying world of Greenland it is not improbable that the blood of the Eskimos may have received some slight Scandinavian infusion. But upon the aboriginal world of the red men, from Davis Strait to Cape Horn, it is not likely that any impression of any sort was ever made. It is in the highest degree probable that Leif Ericsson and his friends made a few voyages to *what we now know to have been* the coast of America; but it is an abuse of language to say that they " discovered " America. In no sense was any real contact established between the eastern and the western halves of our planet until the great voyage of Columbus in 1492.

III

EUROPE AND CATHAY

THE question has sometimes been asked, Why did the knowledge of the voyages to Vinland so long remain confined to the Scandinavian people or a portion of them, and then lapse into oblivion, insomuch that it did not become a matter of notoriety in Europe until after the publication of the celebrated book of Thormodus Torfæus in 1705? Why did not the news of the voyages of Leif and Thorfinn spread rapidly over Europe, like the news of the voyage of Columbus? and why was it not presently followed, like the latter, by a rush of conquerors and colonizers across the Atlantic?

Why the voyages of the Northmen were not followed up

Such questions arise from a failure to see historical events in their true perspective, and to make the proper allowances for the manifold differences in knowledge and in social and economic conditions which characterize different periods of history. In the present case, the answer is to be found, first, in the geographical ignorance which prevented the Northmen from realizing in the smallest degree what such voyages really signified or were going to signify to posterity ; and, secondly, in the political and commercial condition of Europe at the close of the tenth century.

In the first place the route which the Norse voyagers pursued, from Iceland to Greenland and thence to Vinland, was not such as to give them, in their ignorance of the shape of the earth, and with their imperfect knowledge of latitude and longitude, any adequate gauge wherewith Ignorance of to measure their achievement. The geography modern reader, who has in his mind a general picture of the shape of the northern Atlantic Ocean with its coasts, must carefully expel that picture before he can begin to realize how things must have seemed to the Northmen. None of the Icelandic references to Markland and Vinland betray a consciousness that these countries belong to a geographical world outside of Europe. There was not enough organized geographical knowledge for that. They were simply conceived as remote places beyond Greenland, inhabited by inferior but dangerous people. The accidental finding of such places served neither to solve any great commercial problem nor to gratify and provoke scientific curiosity. It was, therefore, not at all strange that it bore no fruit.

Secondly, even if it had been realized, and could have been duly proclaimed throughout

Europe, that across the broad Atlantic a new world lay open for colonization, Europe could not have taken advantage of the fact. Now and then a ship might make its way, or be blown, across the waste of waters without com- Lack of instruments for ocean navigation pass or astrolabe; but until these instruments were at hand anything like systematic ocean navigation was out of the question; and from a colonization which could only begin by creeping up into the Arctic seas and taking Greenland on the way, not much was to be expected, after all.

But even if the compass and other facilities for oceanic navigation had been at hand, the state of Europe in the days of Eric the Red was not such as to afford surplus energy for distant enterprise of this sort. Let us for a moment recall what was going on in Europe in the year of grace 1000, just enough to get a suggestive picture of the time. In England the Danish invader, fork-bearded Swend, father of the great Cnut, was wrestling the kingship from the feeble grasp of Ethelred the Redeless. Europe in the year 1000 In Gaul the little duchy of France, between the Somme and the Loire, had lately become the kingdom of France, and its sovereign, Hugh Capet, had succeeded to feudal rights of lordship over the great dukes and counts whose territories surrounded him on every side; and now Hugh's son, Robert the Debonair, better hymn-writer than warrior, was waging a doubtful struggle with these unruly vassals. It was not yet in any wise apparent what the kingdoms of England and France were going to be. In Germany the youthful Otto III., the "wonder of the world," had just made his weird visit to the tomb of his mighty predecessor at Aachen, before starting on that last journey to Rome which was so soon to cost him his life. Otto's teacher, Gerbert, most erudite of popes, — too learned not to have had dealings with the Devil, — was beginning to raise the papacy out of the abyss of infamy in which the preceding age had seen it sink, and so to prepare the way for the far-reaching reforms of Hildebrand. The boundaries of Christendom were as yet narrow and insecure. With the overthrow of Olaf Tryggvesson in this year 1000, and the temporary partition of Norway between Swedes and Danes, the work of Christianizing the North seemed, for the moment, to languish. Upon the eastern frontier the wild Hungarians had scarcely ceased to be a terror to Europe, and in this year Stephen, their first Christian king, began to reign. At the same time the power of heretical Bulgaria, which had threatened to overwhelm the Eastern Empire, was broken down by the sturdy blows of the Macedonian Emperor Basil. In this year the Christians of Spain met woeful defeat at the hands of Almansor, and there seemed no reason why the Mussulman rule over the greater part of that peninsula should not endure forever.

Thus, from end to end, Europe was a scene of direst confusion, and though, as we now look back upon it, the time seems by no means devoid of promise, there was no such cheering outlook then. Nowhere were the outlines of kingdoms or the ownership of crowns definitely settled. Private war was both incessant and universal; the Truce of God had not yet been proclaimed.[1] As for the common people, their hardships were well-nigh incredible. Amid all this anarchy and misery, at the close of the thousandth year from the birth of Christ, the belief was quite common throughout Europe that the Day of Judgment was at hand for a world grown old in wickedness and ripe for its doom.

It hardly need be argued that a period like this, in which all the vital energy in Europe was consumed in the adjustment of affairs at home, was not fitted for colonial enterprises. Before a

---

[1] The "Truce of God" (*Treuga Dei*) was introduced by the clergy in Guienne about 1032 ; it was adopted in Spain before 1050, and in England by 1080. See Datt, *De pace imperii publica*, lib. i. cap. ii. A cessation of all violent quarrels was enjoined, under ecclesiastical penalties, during church festivals, and from every Wednesday evening until the following Monday morning. This left only about eighty days in the year available for shooting and stabbing one's neighbours. The truce seems to have accomplished much good, though it was very imperfectly observed.

people can send forth colonies it must have solved the problem of political life so far as to insure stability of trade. It is the mercantile spirit that has supported modern colonization, aided by the spirit of intellectual curiosity and the thirst for romantic adventure. In the eleventh century there was no intellectual curiosity outside the monastery walls, nor had such a feeling become enlisted in the service of commerce. Of trade there was indeed, even in western Europe, a considerable amount, but the commercial marine was in its infancy, and on land the trader suffered sorely at the hands of the robber baron. In those days the fashionable method of compounding with your creditors was, not to offer them fifty cents on the dollar, but to inveigle them into your castle and broil them over a slow fire.

The condition of things was not such as to favour colonial enterprise

In so far as the attention of people in Europe was called to any quarter of the globe outside of the seething turbulence in which they dwelt, it was directed toward Asia. Until after 1492, Europe stood with her back toward the Atlantic. What there might be out beyond that " Sea of Darkness " (*Mare Tenebrosum*), as it used commonly to be called, was a question of little interest and seems to have excited no speculation. In the view of mediæval Europe the inhabited world was cut off on the west by this

300

mysterious ocean, and on the south by the burning sands of Sahara ; but eastward it stretched out no one knew how far, and in that direction dwelt tribes and nations which Europe, from time immemorial, had reason to fear. The outlook of Europe was toward Asia As early as the time of Herodotus, the secular antagonism between Europe and Asia had become a topic of reflection among the Greeks, and was wrought with dramatic effect by that great writer into the structure of his history, culminating in the grand and stirring scenes of the Persian war. A century and a half later the conquests of Alexander the Great added a still more impressive climax to the story. The struggle was afterward long maintained between Roman and Parthian, but from the fifth century after Christ onward through the Middle Ages, it seemed as if the Oriental world would never rest until it had inflicted the extremities of retaliation upon Europe. Whether it was the heathen of the steppes who were in question, from Attila in the fifth century to Batu Khan in the thirteenth, or the followers of the Prophet, who tore away from Christendom the southern shores of the Mediterranean, and held Spain in their iron grasp, while from age to age they exhausted their strength in vain against the Eastern Empire, the threatening danger was always coming with the morning sun ; whatever might be the shock that took the attention of Europe away from herself, it directed it upon Asia. This is a fact of cardinal importance for us, inasmuch as it was directly through the interest, more and more absorbing, which Europe felt in Asia that the discovery of the western hemisphere was at last effected.

It was not only in war, but in commerce, that the fortunes of Europe were dependent upon her relations with Asia. Since prehistoric times Routes of there has always been some commer- trade between cial intercourse between the eastern Europe and Asia shores of the Mediterranean and the peninsula of Hindustan. Tyre and Sidon carried on such trade by way of the Red Sea.[1] After Alexander had led his army to Samarcand and to the river Hyphasis, the acquaintance of the Greeks with Asia was very considerably increased, and important routes of trade were established. One was practically the old Phœnician route, with its western terminus moved from Tyre to Alexandria. Another was by way of the Caspian Sea, up the river Oxus, and thence with camels to the banks of the Indus.[2] An intermediate route was through Syria and by way of the Euphrates and the Persian Gulf; the route which at one time made the greatness of Palmyra. After the extension of Roman sway to the Nile, the Euphrates, and the Euxine, these same routes continued to be used. The

[1] Diodorus Siculus, i. 70.   [2] Strabo, xi. 7, § 3.

European commodities carried to India were light woollen cloths, linens, coral, black lead, various kinds of glass vessels, and wine. In exchange for these the traders brought back to Europe divers aromatic spices, black pepper, ivory, cotton fabrics, diamonds, sapphires, and pearls, silk thread and silk stuffs.[1] Detailed accounts of these commercial transactions, and of the wealth of personal experiences that must have been connected with them, are excessively scant. Of the Europeans who, during all the centuries between Alexander and Justinian, made their way to Hindustan or beyond, we know very few by name. The amount of geographical information that was gathered during the first half of this period is shown in the map representing Claudius Ptolemy's Claudius knowledge of the earth, about the Ptolemy middle of the second century after Christ. Except for the Scandinavian world, and some very important additions made to the knowledge of Asia by Marco Polo, this map fairly represents the maximum of acquaintance with the earth's surface possessed by Europeans previous to

[1] Robertson, *Historical Disquisition concerning the Knowledge which the Ancients had of India*, Dublin, 1791, p. 55. I never have occasion to consult Dr. Robertson without being impressed anew with his scientific habit of thought and the solidity of his scholarship ; and in none of his works are these qualities better illustrated than in this noble essay.

the great voyages of the fifteenth century. It shows a dim knowledge of the mouths of the Ganges, of the island of Ceylon, and of what we sometimes call Farther India. A very dim knowledge, indeed; for the huge peninsula of Hindustan is shrunk into insignificance, while Taprobane, or Ceylon, unduly magnified, usurps the place belonging to the Deccan. At the same time we see that some hearsay knowledge of China had made its way into the Roman world before the days of Ptolemy. The two names by which China was first known to Europeans were "Seres" or "Serica," and "Sinæ" or "Thin." These two differing names are the records of two different methods of approach to different parts of a vast country, very much as the Northmen called their part of eastern North America "Vinland," while the Spaniards called their part "Florida." The name "Seres" was given to northwestern China by traders who approached it through the highlands of central Asia from Samarcand, while "Sinæ" was the name given to southeastern China by traders who approached it by way of the Indian Ocean, and heard of it in India, but never reached it. Apparently no European ships ever reached China before the Portuguese, in 1517.[1] The name "Sinæ" or "Thin" seems to mean the

Early mention of China

---

[1] The Polos sailed back from China to the Persian Gulf in 1292–94; see below, p. 326.

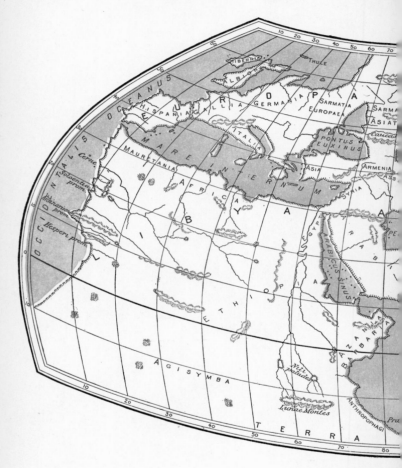

CLAUDIUS PTOLEM

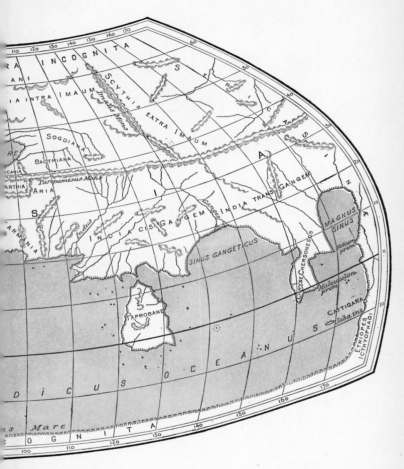

country of the "Tchin" dynasty, which ruled over the whole of China in the second century before Christ, and over a portion of it for a much longer time. The name "Seres," on the other hand, was always associated with the trade in silks, and was known to the Romans in the time of the Emperor Claudius,[1] and somewhat earlier. The Romans in Virgil's time set a high value upon silk, and every scrap of it they had came from China. They knew nothing about the silk-worm, and supposed that the fibres or threads of this beautiful stuff grew upon trees. Of actual intercourse between the Roman and Chinese empires there was no more than is implied in this current of trade, passing through many hands. But that each knew, in a vague way, of the existence of the other, there is no doubt.[2]

In the course of the reign of Justinian, we get references at first hand to India, and coupled withal to a general theory of cosmography.

[1] The name " Seres " appears on the map of Pomponius Mela (cir. A. D. 50), while " Sinæ " does not. See below, p. 350.

> Jam Tartessiaco quos solverat æquore Titan
> In noctem diffusus equos, jungebat Eoïs
> Littoribus, primique novo Phaethonte retecti
> Seres lanigeris repetebant vellera lucis.
> > Silius Italicus, lib. vi. *ad init.*

[2] For this whole subject see Colonel Sir Henry Yule's *Cathay and the Way Thither*, London, 1866, 2 vols., — a work of profound learning and more delightful than a novel.

This curious information we have in the book
of the monk Cosmas Indicopleustes, written
Cosmas Indi- somewhere between A. D. 530 and
copleustes 550. A pleasant book it is, after its
kind. In his younger days Cosmas had been a
merchant, and in divers voyages had become
familiar with the coasts of Ethiopia and the
Persian Gulf, and had visited India and Ceylon.
After becoming a monk at Alexandria, Cosmas
wrote his book of Christian geography,[1] main-

---

[1] Its title is Χριστιανῶν βίβλος, ἑρμηνεία εἰς τὴν 'Οκτάτευ-
χον, i. e. against Ptolemy's Geography in eight books. The
name Cosmas Indicopleustes seems merely to mean " the cos-
mographer who has sailed to India." He begins his book in
a tone of extreme and somewhat unsavoury humility : 'Ανοίγω
τὰ μογιλάλα καὶ βραδύγλωσσα χείλη ὁ ἁμαρτωλὸς καὶ τάλας
ἐγώ — " I, the sinner and wretch, open my stammering,
stuttering lips," etc. — The book has been the occasion of
some injudicious excitement within the last half century.
Cosmas gave a description of some comparatively recent inscriptions on the peninsula of Sinai, and because he could not
find anybody able to read them, he inferred that they must be
records of the Israelites on their passage through the desert.
(Compare the Dighton rock, above, p. 247.) Whether in
the sixth century of grace or in the nineteenth, your unre-
generate and unchastened antiquary snaps at conclusions as
a drowsy dog does at flies. Some years ago an English clergy-
man, Charles Forster, started up the nonsense again, and
argued that these inscriptions might afford a clue to man's
primeval speech ! Cf. Bunsen, *Christianity and Mankind*,
vol. iii. p. 231; Müller and Donaldson, *History of Greek Literature*, vol. iii. p. 353 ; Bury, *History of the Later Roman
Empire from Arcadius to Irene*, vol. ii. p. 177.

taining, in opposition to Ptolemy, that the earth is not a sphere, but a rectangular plane forming the floor of the universe ; the heavens rise on all four sides about this rectangle, like the four walls of a room, and, at an indefinite height above the floor, these blue walls support a vaulted roof or firmament, in which God dwells *Shape of the* with the angels. In the centre of the *earth, according* floor are the inhabited lands of the *mas* earth, surrounded on all sides by a great ocean, beyond which, somewhere out in a corner, is the Paradise from which Adam and Eve were expelled. In its general shape, therefore, the universe somewhat resembles the Tabernacle in the Wilderness, or a modern " Saratoga trunk." On the northern part of the floor, under the firmament, is a lofty conical mountain, around which the sun, moon, and planets perform their daily revolutions. In the summer the sun takes a turn around the apex of the cone, and is, therefore, hidden only for a short night ; but in the winter he travels around the base, which takes longer, and, accordingly, the nights are long. Such is the doctrine drawn from Holy Scripture, says Cosmas, and as for the vain blasphemers who pretend that the earth is a round ball, the Lord hath stultified them for their sins until they impudently prate of Antipodes, where trees grow downward and rain falls upward. As for such nonsense, the worthy Cosmas cannot abide it.

I cite these views of Cosmas because there can be no doubt that they represent beliefs current among the general public until after the time of Columbus,[1] in spite of the deference

[1] Such views have their advocates even now. There still lives, I believe, in England, a certain John Hampden, who with dauntless breast maintains that the earth is a circular plane with centre at the north pole and a circumference of nearly 30,000 miles where poor misguided astronomers suppose the south pole to be. The sun moves across the sky at a distance of about 800 miles. From the boundless abyss beyond the southern circumference, with its barrier of icy mountains, came the waters which drowned the antediluvian world ; for, as this author quite reasonably observes, "on a globular earth such a deluge would have been physically impossible." Hampden's title is somewhat like that of Cosmas, — *The New Manual of Biblical Cosmography*, London, 1877 ; and he began in 1876 to publish a periodical called *The Truth-Seeker's Oracle and Scriptural Science Review*. Similar views have been set forth by one Samuel Rowbotham, under the pseudonym of "Parallax," *Zetetic Astronomy. Earth not a Globe. An experimental inquiry into the true figure of the earth, proving it a plane without orbital or axial motion*, etc., London, 1873 ; and by a William Carpenter, *One Hundred Proofs that the Earth is not a Globe*, Baltimore, 1885. There is a very considerable quantity of such literature afloat, the product of a kind of mental aberration that thrives upon paradox. When I was superintendent of the catalogue of Harvard University Library, I made the class "Eccentric Literature" under which to group such books, — the lucubrations of circle-squarers, angle-trisectors, inventors of perpetual motion, devisers of recipes for living forever without dying,

paid to Ptolemy's views by the learned. Along with these cosmographical speculations, Cosmas shows a wider geographical knowledge of Asia than any earlier writer. He gives a good deal of interesting information about India and Ceylon, and has a fairly correct idea of the position of China, which he calls Tzinista or Chinistan. This land of silk is the remotest of all the Indies, and beyond it "there is neither navigation nor inhabited country. . . . And the Indian philosophers, called Brachmans, tell you that if you were to stretch a straight cord from Tzinista through Persia to the Roman territory, you would just divide the world in halves. And mayhap they are right." [1]

In the fourth and following centuries, Nestorian missionaries were very active in Asia, and not only made multitudes of converts The and established metropolitan sees in Nestorians such places as Kashgar and Herat, but even found their way into China. Their work forms

crazy interpreters of Daniel and the Apocalypse, upsetters of the undulatory theory of light, the Bacon-Shakespeare lunatics, etc. ; a dismal procession of long-eared bipeds, with very raucous bray. The late Professor De Morgan devoted a bulky and instructive volume to an account of such people and their crotchets. See his *Budget of Paradoxes*, London, 1872.

[1] Cosmas, ii. 138. Further mention of China was made early in the seventh century by Theophylactus Samocatta, vii. 7. See Yule's *Cathay*, vol. i. pp. xlix, clxviii.

an interesting though melancholy chapter in history, but it does not seem to have done much toward making Asia better known to Europe. As declared heretics, the Nestorians were themselves almost entirely cut off from intercourse with European Christians.

The immediate effect of the sudden rise of the vast Saracen empire, in the seventh and eighth centuries, was to interpose a barrier to the extension of intercourse between Europe and the far East. Trade between the eastern and western extremities of Asia went on more briskly than ever, but it was for a long time exclusively in Mussulman hands. The mediæval Arabs were bold sailors, and not only visited Sumatra and Java, but made their way to Canton. Upon the southern and middle routes the Arab cities of Cairo and Bagdad became thriving centres of trade; but as Spain and the whole of northern Africa were now Arab countries, most of the trade between east and west was conducted within Mussulman boundaries. Saracen cruisers prowled in the Mediterranean and sorely harassed the Christian coasts. During the eighth, ninth, and tenth centuries, Europe was more shut in upon herself than ever before or since. In many respects these were especially the dark ages of Europe, — the period of least comfort and least enlightenment since the days of pre-

Effects of the Saracen conquests

310

Roman barbarism. But from this general statement Constantinople should be in great measure excepted. The current of mediæval trade through the noble highway of the Dardanelles and the Bosphorus was subject to fluctuations, but it was always great. The city of the Byzantine emperors was before all things a commercial city, like Venice in later days. Until the time of the Crusades Constantinople was the centre of the Levant trade. The great northern route from Asia remained available for commercial intercourse in this direction. Persian and Armenian merchants sent their goods to Batoum, whence they were shipped to Constantinople; and silk was brought from northwestern China by caravan to the Oxus, and forwarded thence by the Caspian Sea, the rivers Cyrus and Phasis, and the Euxine Sea.[1] When it was visited by Benjamin of Tudela in the twelfth century, Constantinople was undoubtedly the richest and most magnificent city, and the seat of the highest civilization, to be found anywhere upon the globe.

Constantinople in the twelfth century

In the days of its strength the Eastern Empire was the staunch bulwark of Christendom against the dangerous assaults of Persian, Saracen, and Turk; alike in prosperity and in calamity, it proved to be the teacher and civilizer of

[1] See Robertson, *Historical Disquisition*, p. 93 ; Pears, *The Fall of Constantinople*, p. 177, — a book of great merit.

the western world. The events which, at the close of the eleventh century, brought thousands upon thousands of adventurous, keen-witted people from western Europe into this home of wealth and refinement, were the occasion of the most remarkable intellectual awakening that the world had ever witnessed up to that time. The Crusades, in their beginning, were a symptom of the growing energy of western Europe under the ecclesiastical reformation effected by the mighty Hildebrand. They were the military response of Europe to the most threatening, and, as time has proved, the most deadly of all the blows that have ever been aimed at her from Asia. Down to this time the Mahometanism with which Christendom had so long been in conflict was a Mahometanism of civilized peoples. The Arabs and Moors were industrious merchants, agriculturists, and craftsmen; in their society one might meet with learned scholars, refined poets, and profound philosophers. But at the end of the tenth century, Islam happened to make converts of the Turks, a nomad race in the upper status of barbarism, with flocks and herds and patriarchal families. Inspired with the sudden zeal for conquest which has always characterized new converts to Islam, the Turks began to pour down from the plains of central Asia like a deluge upon the Eastern Empire. In 1016 they over-

The Crusades

312

whelmed Armenia, and presently advanced into Asia Minor. Their mode of conquest was peculiarly baleful, for at first they deliberately annihilated the works of civilization in order to prepare the country for their nomadic life; they pulled down cities to put up tents. Though they long ago ceased to be nomads, they have to this day never learned to comprehend civilized life, and they have been simply a blight upon every part of the earth's surface which they have touched. At the beginning of the eleventh century, Asia Minor was one of the most prosperous and highly civilized parts of the world;[1] and the tale of its devastation by the terrible Alp Arslan and the robber chiefs that came after him is one of the most mournful chapters in history. At the end of that century, when the Turks were holding Nicæa and actually had their outposts on the Marmora, it was high time for Christendom to rise *en masse* in self-defence. The idea was worthy of the greatest of popes. Imperfectly and spasmodically as it was carried out, it un-

Barbarizing character of Turkish conquest

---

[1] "It is difficult for the modern traveller who ventures into the heart of Asia Minor, and finds nothing but rude Kurds and Turkish peasants living among mountains and wild pastures, not connected even by ordinary roads, to imagine the splendour and rich cultivation of this vast country, with its brilliant cities and its teeming population." Mahaffy, *The Greek World under Roman Sway*, London, 1890, p. 229.

313

doubtedly did more than anything that had ever gone before toward strengthening the wholesome sentiment of a common Christendom among the peoples of western Europe. The Crusades increased the power of the church, which was equivalent to putting a curb upon the propensities of the robber baron and making labour and traffic more secure. In another way they aided this good work by carrying off the robber baron in large numbers to Egypt and Syria, and killing him there. In this way they did much toward ridding European society of its most turbulent elements ; while at the same time they gave fresh development to the spirit of romantic adventure, and connected it with something better than vagrant freebooting.[1] By renewing the long-suspended intercourse between the minds of western Europe and the Greek culture of Constantinople, they served as a mighty stimulus to intellectual curiosity, and had a large share in bringing about that great thirteenth century renaissance which is forever associated with the names of Giotto and Dante and Roger Bacon.

General effects of the Crusades

There can be no doubt that in these ways the Crusades were for our forefathers in Europe the

---

[1] The general effects of the Crusades are discussed, with much learning and sagacity, by Choiseul-Daillecourt, *De l'Influence des Croisades sur l'état des peuples de l'Europe*, Paris, 1809.

most bracing and stimulating events that occurred
in the whole millennium between the complicated disorders of the fifth century and the out-
burst of maritime discovery in the fifteenth.
How far they justified themselves from the
military point of view, it is not so easy to say.
On the one hand, they had much to do with re-
tarding the progress of the enemy for two hundred years; they overwhelmed the Seljukian
Turks so effectually that their successors, the
Ottomans, did not become formidable until
about 1300, after the last crusading wave had
spent its force. On the other hand, the Fourth
Crusade, with better opportunities The Fourth
than any of the others for striking a Crusade
crushing blow at the Moslem, played false to
Christendom, and in 1204 captured and de-
spoiled Constantinople in order to gratify Venice's hatred of her commercial rival and superior. It was a sorry piece of business, and one
cannot look with unmixed pleasure at the four
superb horses that now adorn the front of the
church of St. Mark as a trophy of this unhal-
lowed exploit.[1] One cannot help feeling that

---

[1] They were taken from Chios in the fourth century by the
Emperor Theodosius, and placed in the hippodrome at Constantinople, whence they were taken by the Venetians in
1204. The opinion that " the results of the Fourth Crusade
upon European civilization were altogether disastrous " is ably
set forth by Mr. Pears, *The Fall of Constantinople*, London,

but for this colossal treachery, the great city of Constantine, to which our own civilization owes more than can ever be adequately told, might, perhaps, have retained enough strength to withstand the barbarian in 1453, and thus have averted one of the most lamentable catastrophes in the history of mankind.

The general effect of the Crusades upon Oriental commerce was to increase the amount of traffic through Egypt and Syria. Of this lucrative trade Venice got the lion's share, and while she helped support the short-lived Latin dynasty upon the throne at Constantinople, she monopolized a great part of the business of the Black Sea also. But in 1261 Venice's rival, Genoa, allied herself with the Greek emperor, Michael Palæologus, at Nicæa, placed him upon the Byzantine throne, and again cut off Venice from the trade that came through the Bosphorus. From this time forth the mutual hatred between Venice and Genoa " waxed fiercer than ever ; no merchant fleet of either state could go to sea without con-

Rivalry between Venice and Genoa

1885, and would be difficult to refute. Voltaire might well say in this case, " Ainsi le seul fruit des chrétiens dans leurs barbares croisades fut d'exterminer d'autres chrétiens. Ces croisés, qui ruinaient l'empire auraient pu, bien plus aisément que tous leurs prédecesseurs, chasser les Turcs de l'Asie." *Essai sur les Mœurs*, tom. ii. p. 158. Voltaire's general view of the Crusades is, however, very superficial.

voy, and wherever their ships met they fought. It was something like the state of things between Spain and England in the days of Drake." [1] In the one case as in the other, it was a strife for the mastery of the sea and its commerce. Genoa obtained full control of the Euxine, took possession of the Crimea, and thus acquired a monopoly of the trade from central Asia along the northern route. With the fall of Acre in 1291, and the consequent expulsion of Christians from Syria, Venice lost her hold upon the middle route. But with the Pope's leave [2] she succeeded in making a series of advantageous commercial treaties with the new Mameluke sovereigns of Egypt, and the dealings between the Red Sea and the Adriatic soon came to be prodigious. The Venetians gained control of part of the Peloponnesus, with many islands of the Ægean and eastern Mediterranean. During the fourteenth and fifteenth centuries their city was the most splendid and luxurious in all Christendom.

Such a development of wealth in Venice and Genoa implies a large producing and consuming area behind them, able to take and pay for the costly products of India and China. Before the

[1] Yule's *Marco Polo*, vol. i. p. lxxi.

[2] A papal dispensation was necessary before a commercial treaty could be made with Mahometans. See Leibnitz, *Codex Jur. Gent. Diplomat.*, i. 489.

end of the thirteenth century the volume of European trade had swelled to great proportions.

Centres and routes of mediæval trade

How full of historic and literary interest are the very names of the centres and leading routes of this trade as it was established in those days, with its outlook upon the Mediterranean and the distant East! Far up in the North we see Wisby, on the little isle of Gothland in the Baltic, giving its name to new rules of international law ; and the merchants of the famous Hansa towns extending their operations as far as Novgorod in one direction, and in another to the Steelyard in London, where the pound of these honest " Easterlings " was adopted as the " sterling" unit of sound money. Fats and tallows, furs and wax from Russia, iron and copper from Sweden, strong hides and unrivalled wools from England, salt cod and herring (much needed on meagre church fast-days) from the North and Baltic seas, appropriately followed by generous casks of beer from Hamburg, were sent southward in exchange for fine cloths and tapestries, the products of the loom in Ghent and Bruges, in Ulm and Augsburg, with delicious vintages of the Rhine, supple chain armour from Milan, Austrian yew-wood for English long-bows, ivory and spices, pearls and silks from Italy and the Orient. Along the routes from Venice and Florence to Antwerp and Rotterdam we see the progress in wealth and refinement, in artistic and literary productiveness. We see the early schools of music and painting in Italy meet with prompt response in Flanders; in the many-gabled streets of Nuremberg we hear the voice of the Meistersinger, and under the low oaken roof of a Canterbury inn we listen to joyous if sometimes naughty tales erst told in pleasant groves outside of fever-stricken Florence.

With this increase of wealth and culture in central Europe there came a considerable extension of knowledge and a powerful stimulus to curiosity concerning the remote parts of Asia. The conquering career of Jenghis Khan (1206–1227) had shaken the world to its foundations. In the middle of that century, to adopt Colonel Yule's lively expression, "throughout Asia and eastern Europe, scarcely a dog might bark without Mongol leave, from the borders of Poland and the coast of Cilicia to the Amur and the Yellow Sea." About these portentous Mongols, who had thus in a twinkling overwhelmed China and Russia, and destroyed the Caliphate of Bagdad, there was a refreshing touch of open-minded heathenism. They were barbarians willing to learn. From end to end of Asia the barriers were thrown down. It was a time when Alan chiefs from the Volga served as police in Tunking, and Chinese physicians could be consulted at Tabriz. For

Effects of the Mongol conquests

about a hundred years China was more accessible than at any period before or since, — more even than to-day ; and that country now for the first time became really known to a few Europeans. In the northern provinces of China, shortly before the Mongol deluge, there had reigned a dynasty known as the *Khitai*, and hence China was (and still is) commonly spoken of in central Asia as the country of the Khitai. When this name reached European ears it became *Cathay*,

Cathay the name by which China was best known in Europe during the next four centuries.[1] In 1245, Friar John of Plano Carpini, a friend and disciple of St. Francis, was sent by Pope Innocent IV. on a missionary er-

Carpini and rand to the Great Khan, and visited
Rubruquis him in his camp at Karakorum in the very depths of Mongolia. In 1253 the king of France, St. Louis, sent another Franciscan monk, Willem de Rubruquis, to Karakorum, on a mission of which the purpose is now not clearly understood. Both these Franciscans were men of shrewd and cultivated minds, especially Rubruquis, whose narrative, " in its rich detail, its vivid pictures, its acuteness of observation and strong good sense . . . has few superiors in the whole library of travel." [2] Neither Ru-

[1] Yule's *Cathay*, vol. i. p. cxvi ; *Marco Polo*, vol. i. p. xlii.

[2] Yule's *Marco Polo*, vol. i. p. cxxx ; Humboldt, *Examen*

320

bruquis nor Friar John visited China, but they fell in with Chinese folk at Karakorum, and obtained information concerning the geography of eastern Asia far more definite than had ever before been possessed by Europeans. They both describe Cathay as bordering upon an eastern ocean, and this piece of information constituted the first important leap of geographical knowledge to the eastward since the days of Ptolemy, who supposed that beyond the " Seres and Sinæ " lay an unknown land of vast extent, " full of reedy and impenetrable swamps." [1] The information gathered by Rubruquis and Friar John indicated that there was an end to the continent of Asia ; that, not as a matter of vague speculation, but of positive knowledge, Asia was bounded on the east, just as Europe was bounded on the west, by an ocean.

First knowledge of an eastern ocean beyond Cathay

Here we arrive at a notable landmark in the history of the Discovery of America. Here

critique, tom. i. p. 71. The complete original texts of the reports of both monks, with learned notes, may be found in the *Recueil de Voyages et de Mémoires, publié par la Société de Geographie*, Paris, 1839, tom. iv., viz. : *Johannis de Plano Carpini Historia Mongolorum quos nos Tartaros appellamus*, ed. M. d'Avezac ; *Itinerarium Willelmi de Rubruk*, ed. F. Michel et T. Wright.

[1] Yule's *Cathay*, vol. i. p. xxxix ; Ptolemy, i. 17. Cf. Bunbury's *History of Ancient Geography*, London, 1883, vol. ii. p. 606.

from the camp of bustling heathen at Karakorum there is brought to Europe the first announcement of a geographical fact from which

The data were thus prepared for Columbus ; the poetic mind of Christopher Columbus will hereafter reap a wonderful harvest. This is one among many instances of the way in which, throughout all departments of human thought and action, the glorious thirteenth century was beginning to give shape to the problems of which the happy solution has since made the modern world so different from the ancient.[1] Since there is an ocean east of Cathay and an ocean west of Spain, how natural the inference — and albeit quite wrong, how amazingly fruitful — that these oceans are one and the same, so that by sailing westward from Spain one might go straight to Cathay ! The data for such an in-

but as yet nobody reasoned from these data to a practical conclusion ference were now all at hand, but it does not appear that any one as yet reasoned from the data to the conclusion, although we find Roger Bacon, in 1267, citing the opinions of Aristotle and other ancient writers to the effect that the distance by sea from the western shores of Spain to the eastern shores of Asia cannot be

[1] See my *Beginnings of New England*, chap. i. How richly suggestive to an American is the contemporaneity of Rubruquis and Earl Simon of Leicester !

so very great.[1] In those days it took a long
time for such ideas to get from the heads of
philosophers into the heads of men of action;
and in the thirteenth century, when Cathay was
more accessible by land than at any time before
or since, there was no practical necessity felt for
a water route thither. Europe still turned her
back upon the Atlantic and gazed more intently
than ever upon Asia. Stronger and more general grew the interest in Cathay.

In the middle of the thirteenth century, some
members of the Polo family, one of the aristocratic families of Venice, had a   The Polo
commercial house at Constantinople.   brothers
Thence, in 1260, the brothers Nicolò and
Maffeo Polo started on a trading journey to the
Crimea, whence one opportunity after another
for making money and gratifying their curiosity
with new sights led them northward and eastward to the Volga, thence into Bokhara, and so
on until they reached the court of the Great
Khan, in one of the northwestern provinces of
Cathay. The reigning sovereign was the famous
Kublai Khan, grandson of the all-conquering
Jenghis. Kublai was an able and benevolent
despot, earnest in the wish to improve the
condition of his Mongol kinsmen. He had

[1] Roger Bacon, *Opus Majus*, ed. Jebb, London, 1733,
p. 183.

never before met European gentlemen, and was charmed with the cultivated and polished Venetians. He seemed quite ready to enlist the Roman Church in aid of his civilizing schemes, and entrusted the Polos with a message to the Pope, asking him for a hundred missionary teachers. The brothers reached Venice in 1269, and found that Pope Clement IV. was dead and there was an interregnum. After two years Gregory X. was elected and received the Khan's message, but could furnish only a couple of Dominican friars, and these men were seized with the dread not uncommonly felt for " Tartareans," and at the last moment refused to go. Nicolò and his brother then set out in the autumn of 1271 to return to China, taking with them Nicolò's son Marco, a lad of seventeen years. From Acre they went by way of Bagdad to Hormuz, at the mouth of the Persian Gulf, apparently with the intention of proceeding thence by sea, but for some reason changed their course, and travelled through Kerman, Khorassan, and Balkh, to Kashgar, and thence by way of Yarkand and Khotan, and across the desert of Gobi into northwestern China, where they arrived in the summer of 1275, and found the Khan at Kaipingfu, not far from the northern end of the Great Wall.

It has been said that the failure of Kublai's

Kublai Khan's message to the Pope

mission to the Pope led him to apply to the
Grand Lama, at Thibet, who responded more
efficiently and successfully than Gregory X., so
that Buddhism seized the chance which Catholi-
cism failed to grasp. The Venetians, however,
lost nothing in the good Khan's es- Marco Polo
teem. Young Marco began to make and his travels
himself proficient in speaking and in Asia
writing several Asiatic languages, and was presently taken into the Khan's service. His name
is mentioned in the Chinese Annals of 1277 as
a newly appointed commissioner of the privy
council.[1] He remained in Kublai's service until
1292, while his father and uncle were gathering
wealth in various ways. Marco made many
official journeys up and down the Khan's vast
dominions, not only in civilized China, but in
regions of the heart of Asia seldom visited by
Europeans to this day, — "a vast ethnological
garden," says Colonel Yule, "of tribes of various race and in every stage of uncivilization."
In 1292 a royal bride for the Khan of Persia
was to be sent all the way from Peking to Tabriz, and as war that year made some parts of
the overland route very unsafe, it was decided
to send her by sea. The three Polos had for
some time been looking for an opportunity to
return to Venice, but Kublai was unwilling to
have them go. Now, however, as every Vene-

[1] Pauthier's *Marco Polo,* p. 361 ; Yule's *Marco Polo,* p. li.

tian of that day was deemed to be from his very
cradle a seasoned sea-dog, and as the kindly old
Mongol sovereign had an inveterate land-lub-
ber's misgivings about ocean voyages, he con-
sented to part with his dear friends, so that he
might entrust the precious princess to their care.

First recorded voyage of Europeans around the Indo-Chinese peninsula, 1292–94

They sailed from the port of Zaiton
(Chinchow) early in 1292, and after
long delays on the coasts of Sumatra
and Hindustan, in order to avoid
unfavourable monsoons, they reached
the Persian Gulf in 1294. They found that the
royal bridegroom, somewhat advanced in years,
had died before they started from China; so
the young princess became the bride of his son.
After tarrying awhile in Tabriz, the Polos re-

Return of the Polos to Venice

turned by way of Trebizond and the
Bosphorus to Venice, arriving in 1295.
When they got there, says Ramusio,
after their absence of four and twenty years,
"the same fate befell them as befell Ulysses,
who, when he returned to his native Ithaca, was
recognized by nobody." Their kinsfolk had long
since given them up for dead; and when the three
wayworn travellers arrived at the door of their
own palace, the middle-aged men now wrinkled
graybeards, the stripling now a portly man, all
three attired in rather shabby clothes of Tartar
cut, and "with a certain indescribable smack of
the Tartar about them, both in air and accent,"

some words of explanation were needed to prove their identity. After a few days they invited a party of old friends to dinner, and bringing forth three shabby coats, ripped open the seams and welts, and began pulling out and tumbling upon the table such treasures of diamonds and emeralds, rubies and sapphires, as could never have been imagined, "which had all been stitched up in those dresses in so artful a fashion that nobody could have suspected the fact." In such wise had they brought home from Cathay their ample earnings ; and when it became known about Venice that the three long-lost citizens had come back, "straightway the whole city, gentle and simple, flocked to the house to embrace them, and to make much of them, with every conceivable demonstration of affection and respect." [1]

Three years afterward, in 1298, Marco commanded a galley in the great naval battle with the Genoese near Curzola. The Venetians were totally defeated, and Marco was one of the 7000 prisoners taken to Genoa, where he was kept in durance for about a year. One of his companions in captivity was a certain Rusticiano, of Pisa, who was glad to listen to his descriptions of Asia, and to act as his amanuensis. French was then, at the close of the Crusades, a language as generally

Marco Polo's book written in prison at Genoa, 1299

[1] Ramusio *apud* Yule's *Marco Polo,* vol. i. p. xxxvii.

understood throughout Europe as later, in the age of Louis XIV. ; and Marco's narrative was duly taken down by the worthy Rusticiano in rather lame and shaky French. In the summer of 1299 Marco was set free and returned to Venice, where he seems to have led a quiet life until his death in 1324.

" The Book of Ser Marco Polo concerning the Kingdoms and Marvels of the East " is one of the most famous and important books of the Middle Ages. It contributed more new facts toward a knowledge of the earth's surface than any book that had ever been written before. Its author was " the first traveller to trace a route across the whole longitude of Asia ; " the first to describe China in its vastness, with its immense cities, its manufactures and wealth, and to tell, whether from personal experience or direct hearsay, of Thibet and Burmah, of Siam and Cochin China, of the Indian Archipelago, with its islands of Spices, of Java and Sumatra, and of the savages of Andaman. He knew of Japan and the woeful defeat of the Mongols there, when they tried to invade the island kingdom in 1281. He gave a description of Hindustan far more complete and characteristic than had ever before been published. From Arab sailors, accustomed to the Indian Ocean, he learned something about Zanzibar and Madagascar and the semi-Chris-

Its great contributions to geographical knowledge

tian kingdom of Abyssinia. To the northward from Persia he described the country of the Golden Horde, whose khans were then holding Russia in subjection ; and he had gathered some accurate information concerning Siberia as far as the country of the Samoyeds, with their dog-sledges and polar bears.[1]

Here was altogether too much geographical knowledge for European ignorance in those days to digest. While Marco's book attracted much attention, its influence upon the progress of geography was slighter than it would have been if addressed to a more enlightened public. Many of its sober statements of fact were received with incredulity. Many of the places described were indistinguishable, in European imagination, from the general multitude of fictitious countries mentioned in fairy-tales or in romances of chivalry. Perhaps no part of Marco's story was so likely to interest his readers as his references to Prester John. In the course of the twelfth century the notion had somehow gained possession of the European mind that somewhere out in the dim vastness of the Orient there dwelt a mighty Christian potentate, known as John the Presbyter or " Prester." [2] At different times he was identi-

Prester John

---

[1] Yule's *Marco Polo*, vol. i. p. cxxxi.

[2] " But for to speake of riches and of stones,
   And men and horse, I trow the large wones

fied with various known Asiatic sovereigns. Marco Polo identified him with one Togrul Wang, who was overcome and slain by the mighty Jenghis; but he would not stay dead, any more than the gruesome warlock in Russian nursery lore. The notion of Prester John and his wealthy kingdom could no more be expelled from the European mind in the fourteenth and fifteenth centuries than the kindred notion of El Dorado in the sixteenth. The position of this kingdom was shifted about here and there, as far as from Chinese Tartary to Abyssinia and back again, but somewhere or other in people's vague mental picture of the East it was sure to occur. Other remote regions in

> Of Prestir John, ne all his tresorie,
> Might not unneth have boght the tenth partie."
> Chaucer, *The Flower and the Leaf*, 200.

The fabulous kingdom of Prester John is ably treated in Yule's *Cathay*, vol. i. pp. 174–182 ; *Marco Polo*, vol. i. pp. 204–216. Colonel Yule suspects that its prototype may have been the semi-Christian kingdom of Abyssinia. This is very likely. As for its range, shifted hither and thither as it was, all the way from the upper Nile to the Thian-Shan Mountains, we can easily understand this if we remember how an ignorant mind conceives all points distant from its own position as near to one another ; *i. e.* if you are about to start from New York for Arizona, your housemaid will perhaps ask you to deliver a message to her brother in Manitoba. Nowhere more than in the history of geography do we need to keep before us, at every step, the limitations of the untutored mind and its feebleness in grasping the space-relations of remote regions.

Asia were peopled with elves and griffins and "one-eyed Arimaspians," [1] and we may be sure that to Marco's readers these beings were quite as real as the polished citizens of Cambaluc (Peking) or the cannibals of the Andaman Islands. From such a chaos of ideas sound geographical knowledge must needs be a slow evolution, and Marco Polo's acquisitions were altogether too far in advance of his age to be readily assimilated.

The " Arimaspians "

[1] These Arimaspians afford an interesting example of the uncritical statements of travellers at an early time, as well as of their tenacious vitality. The first mention of these mythical people seems to have been made by Greek travellers in Scythia as early as the seventh century before Christ ; and they furnished Aristeas of Proconnesus, somewhat later, with the theme of his poem " Arimaspeia," which has perished, all except six verses quoted by Longinus. See Mure's *Literature of Ancient Greece*, vol. iv. p. 68. Thence the notion of the Arimaspians seems to have passed to Herodotus (iii. 116 ; iv. 27) and to Æschylus : —

> ὀξυστόμους γὰρ Ζηνὸς ἀκραγεῖς κύνας
> γρῦπας φύλαξει, τόν τε μουνῶπα στρατὸν
> Ἀριμασπὸν ἱπποβάμον᾽, οἳ χρυσόρρυτον
> οἰκοῦσιν ἀμφὶ νᾶμα Πλούτωνος πόρου ·
> τούτοις σὺ μὴ πέλαζε.
>
> *Prometheus*, 802.

Thence it passed on to Pausanias i. 24 ; Pomponius Mela, ii. 1 ; Pliny, *Hist. Nat.*, vii. 2 ; Lucan, *Pharsalia*, iii. 280 ; and so on to Milton : —

> " As when a gryphon through the wilderness,
> With winged course o'er hill or moory dale,
> Pursues the Arimaspian who by stealth
> Had from his wakeful custody purloined
> The guarded gold."
>
> *Paradise Lost*, ii. 944.

Nevertheless, in the Catalan map, made in 1375, and now to be seen in the National Library at Paris, there is a thorough-going and
Other visits to China not unsuccessful attempt to embody the results of Polo's travels. In the interval of three quarters of a century since the publication of Marco's narrative, several adventurous travellers had found their way to Cathay. There was Friar Odoric, of Pordenone, who, during the years 1316–30 visited Hindustan, Sumatra, Java, Cochin China, the Chinese Empire, and Thibet.[1] It was from this worthy monk that the arrant old impostor, " Sir John Mandeville," stole his descriptions of India and Cathay, seasoning them with yarns from Pliny and Ktesias, and grotesque conceits of his own.[2]

[1] Odoric mentions Juggernaut processions and the burning of widows ; in Sumatra he observed cannibalism and community of wives ; he found the kingdom of Prester John in Chinese Tartary ; " but as regards him," says wise Odoric, " not one hundredth part is true of what is told of him as if it were undeniable." Yule's *Cathay*, vol. i. pp. 79, 85, 146.

[2] Colonel Yule gives a list of fourteen important passages taken bodily from Odoric by Mandeville. *Op. cit.* i. 28. It is very doubtful if that famous book, " Sir John Mandeville's Travels," was written by a Mandeville, or by a knight, or even by an Englishman. It seems to have been originally written in French by Jean de Bourgogne, a physician who lived for some years at Liège, and died there somewhere about 1370. He may possibly have been an Englishman named John Burgoyne, who was obliged some years before

TWO SHEETS OF

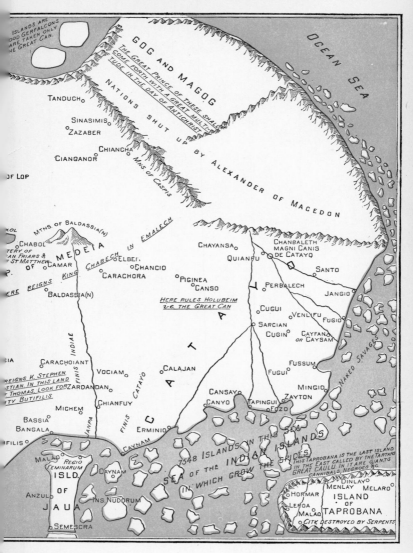

ISLANDS ARE
GOOD GERFALCONS
ARE TAKEN ONLY
THE GREAT CAN.

OCEAN SEA

GOG AND MAGOG

THE GREAT PRINCE OF THESE SHALL
COME FORTH WITH A GREAT MULTI-
TUDE IN THE DAY OF ANTICHRIST.

NATIONS SHUT UP BY ALEXANDER OF MACEDON

TANDUCHo

SINASIMISo
ZAZABER

CHIANCHAo

CIANGANORo

Mns of CASPIS

OF LOP

MTNS. OF BALDASSIA(N)

CHABECH IN EMALECH

CHAYANSAo

CHANBALETH
magni Canis
de CATAYo

QUIANFUo

SANTOo

CHABOLo
TERY OF
AN FRIARS &
ST MATTHEW
P. OF

MEDEIA

ERE REIGNS KING

ELBEIo
CHANCIOo
CARACHORA

CAMARo

PERBALECH

JANGIOo

BALDASSIA(N)

PIGINEAo
CANSO

HERE RULES HOLUBEIM
i.e. THE GREAT CAN

CUGUIo

VENLIFUo
FUGIOo

SARCIANo
CUGINo

CAYFANo
or CAYSAMo

SIA

CARACHOIANTo

VOCIAMo

CALAJANo

FUSSUMo

REIGNS K. STEPHEN
STIAN IN THIS LAND
T THOMAS, LOOK FORZARDANDANo
TY BUTIFILIS

FUGUIo

MINGIOo
ZAYTONo

MICHEMo

CHIANFUYo

CANSAYo
CANYOo

TAPINGUIo
oFOZO

BASSIAo
BANGALAo

ERMINIOo

IFILISo

MALAo
Regio
Feminarum
ISLD.
OF
JAUA

CAYNAMo

7548 ISLANDS IN THIS SEA
OF THE INDIAN ISLANDS
IN WHICH GROW THE SPICES

THIS TAPROBANA IS THE LAST ISLAND
IN THE EAST CALLED BY THE TARTARS
GREAT CAULII. IN IT ARE GIANTS
CANNIBALS, NEGROES &c

ANZULOo

INS. NUDORUM

DINLAYOo

MENLAY MELAROo

HORMARo

MALAo

LERoAo

ISLAND
OF
TAPROBANA

o SEMESCRA

o CITE DESTROYED BY SERPENTS

TALAN MAP, 1375

Several other missionary friars visited China between 1302 and 1330, and about ten years after
the latter date the Florentine merchant, Fran-
cesco Pegolotti, wrote a very useful handbook
for commercial travellers on the overland route
to that country.[1] Between 1338 and 1353 Gio-
vanni Marignolli spent some years at Peking,
as papal legate from Benedict XI. to the Great
Khan, and also travelled in Ceylon and Hindustan.[2] That seems to have been the last of these

that date to flee his country for homicide or for some political
offence. He had travelled as far as Egypt and Palestine, but
no farther. His book is almost entirely cribbed from others,
among which may be mentioned the works of Jacques de Vitry,
Plano Carpini, Hayton the Armenian, Boldensele's Itinerary,
Albert of Aix's chronicle of the first crusade, Brunetto Latini's *Trésor*, Petrus Comestor's *Historia scholastica*, the
Speculum of Vincent de Beauvais, etc., etc. It is one of the
most wholesale and successful instances of plagiarism and imposture on record. See *The Buke of John Mandevill, from
the unique copy (Egerton MS. 1982) in the British Museum.
Edited by G. F. Warner*, Westminster, 1889. (Roxburghe
Club.)

[1] One piece of Pegolotti's advice is still useful for travellers
in the nineteenth century who visit benighted heathen countries
afflicted with robber tariffs : " And don't forget that if you
treat the custom-house officers with respect, and make them
something of a present in goods or money, they will behave
with great civility and always be ready to appraise your wares
below their real value." *Op. cit.* ii. 307.

[2] The works of all the writers mentioned in this paragraph,
or copious extracts from them, may be found in Yule's *Cathay*,
which comprises also the book of the celebrated Ibn Batuta,

journeys to the far East. In 1368, the people of China rose against the Mongol dynasty and

Overthrow of the Mon-gol dynasty, and shutting up of China overthrew it. The first emperor of the native Ming dynasty was placed upon the throne, and the Chinese retorted upon their late conquerors by overrunning vast Mongolia and making it Chinese Tartary. The barriers thrown down by the liberal policy of the Mongol sovereigns were now put up again, and no more foreigners were allowed to set foot upon the sacred soil of the Flowery Kingdom.

Thus, for just a century, — from Carpini and Rubruquis to Marignolli, — while China was open to strangers as never before or since, a few Europeans had availed themselves of the opportunity in such wise as to mark the beginning of a new era in the history of geographical knowledge. Though the discoveries of Marco Polo were as yet but imperfectly appreciated, one point, and that the most significant of all, was thoroughly established. It was shown that the continent of Asia did not extend indefinitely eastward, nor was it bounded and barricaded on that side, as Ptolemy had imagined, by vast im-

of Tangier, whose travels, between 1325 and 1355, covered pretty much the whole of Asia except Siberia, besides a journey across Sahara to the river Niger. His book does not seem to have attracted attention in Europe until early in the present century.

penetrable swamps. On the contrary, its eastern shores were perfectly accessible through an open sea, and half a dozen Europeans in Chinese ships had now actually made the voyage between the coast of China and the Persian Gulf. Moreover, some hearsay knowledge — enough to provoke curiosity and greed — had been gained of the existence of numerous islands in that far-off eastern ocean, rich in the spices which *First rumours* from time immemorial had formed *of the Mo-* *lucca Islands* such an important element in Med- *and Japan* iterranean commerce. News, also, had been brought to Europe of the wonderful island kingdom of Japan (Cipango or Zipangu) lying out in that ocean some hundreds of miles beyond the coast of Cathay. These were rich countries, abounding in objects of lucrative traffic. Under the liberal Mongol rule the Oriental trade had increased enough for Europe to feel in many ways its beneficial effects. Now this trade began to be suddenly and severely checked, and while access to the interior of Asia was cut off, European merchants might begin to reflect upon the value of what they were losing, and to consider if there were any feasible method of recovering it.

It was not merely the shutting up of China by the first Ming emperor, in 1368, that checked the intercourse between Europe and Asia. A still more baleful obstacle to all such intercourse had lately come upon the scene. In Asia Minor the beastly Turk, whose career had been for two centuries arrested by the Crusades, now reared his head again. The Seljukian had been only scotched, not killed ; and now he sprang to life as the Ottoman, with sharper fangs than before. In 1365 the Turks established themselves in the Balkan peninsula, with Adrianople as their capital, and began tightening their coils about the doomed city of Constantine. Each point that they gained meant the strangling of just so much Oriental trade ; for, as we have seen, the alliance of Constantinople with Genoa since 1261 had secured to the latter city, and to western Europe, the advantages of the overland routes from Asia, whether through the Volga country or across Armenia. When at length, in 1453, the Turks took Constantinople, the splendid commercial career of Genoa was cut with the shears of Atropos. At the same time, as their power was rapidly extending over Syria and down toward Egypt, threatening the overthrow of the liberal Mameluke dynasty there, the commercial prosperity of Venice also was seriously imperilled. Moreover, as Turkish corsairs began to swarm in the eastern waters of the Mediterranean, the voyage became more and more unsafe for Christian vessels. It was

The accustomed routes of Oriental trade cut off by the Ottoman Turks

thus, while the volume of trade with Asia was, in the natural course of things, swelling year by year, that its accustomed routes were being ruthlessly cut off. It was fast becoming necessary to consider whether there might not be other practicable routes to " the Indies " than those which had from time immemorial been followed. Could there be such a thing as an " outside route " to that land of promise? A more startling question has seldom been propounded; for it involved a radical departure from the grooves in which the human mind had been running ever since the days of Solomon. Two generations of men lived and died while this question was taking shape, and all that time Cathay and India and the islands of Spices were objects of increasing desire, clothed by eager fancy with all manner of charms and riches. The more effectually the eastern Mediterranean was closed, the stronger grew the impulse to venture upon unknown paths in order to realize the vague but glorious hopes that began to cluster about those remote countries. Such an era of romantic enterprise as was thus ushered in, the world has never seen before or since. It was equally remarkable as an era of discipline in scientific thinking. In the maritime ventures of unparalleled boldness now to be described, the human mind was grop-

Necessity for finding an " outside route to the Indies "

ing toward the era of enormous extensions of knowledge in space and time represented by the names of Newton and Darwin. It was learning the right way of putting its trust in the Unseen.

THE SEARCH FOR THE INDIES

EASTWARD OR PORTUGUESE ROUTE

A S it dawned upon men's minds that to find some oceanic route from Europe to the remote shores of Asia was eminently desirable, the first attempt would naturally be to see what could be done by sailing down the western coast of Africa, and ascertaining whether that continent could be circumnavigated. It was also quite in the natural order of things that this first attempt should be made by the Portuguese.

Question as to whether Asia could be reached by sailing around Africa

In the general history of the Middle Ages the Spanish peninsula had been to some extent cut off from the main currents of thought and feeling which actuated the rest of Europe. Its people had never joined the other Christian nations in the Crusades, for the good reason that they always had quite enough to occupy them in their own domestic struggle with the Moors. From the throes of this prolonged warfare Portugal emerged somewhat sooner than the Spanish kingdoms, and thus had somewhat earlier a surplus of energy released for work of another sort. It was not strange that the Portuguese should be the first people since the old Northmen to engage in distant maritime adventure upon a grand scale. Nor was it strange that Portuguese seamanship should at first have thriven upon naval warfare with Mussulmans. It was in attempting to suppress the intolerable nuisance of Moorish piracy that Portuguese ships became accustomed to sail a little way down the west coast of Africa ; and such voyages, begun for military purposes, were kept up in the interests of commerce, and presently served as a mighty stimulus to geographical curiosity. We have now to consider at some length how grave was the problem that came up for immediate solution.

With regard to the circumnavigability of Africa two opposite opinions were maintained by the ancient Greek and Latin writers whose authority the men of the Middle Ages were wont to quote as decisive of every vexed question. The old Homeric notion of an ocean encompassing the terrestrial world, although mentioned with doubt by Herodotus,[1] continued to

---

[1] Τὸν δὲ Ὠκεανὸν λόγῳ μὲν λέγουσι ἀπ' ἡλίου ἀνατολέων ἀρξάμενον γῆν περὶ πᾶσαν ῥέειν, ἔργῳ δέ οὐκ ἀποδεικνῦσι. Herodotus, iv. 8.

survive after the globular form of the earth had come to be generally maintained by ancient geographers. The greatest of these geographers, Eratosthenes, correctly assumed that the Indian Ocean was continuous with the Atlantic,[1] and that Africa could be circumnavigated, just as he incorrectly assumed that the Caspian Sea was a huge gulf communicating with a northern ocean, by which it would be possible to sail around the continent of Asia as he imagined it.[2] A similar opinion as to Africa was held by Posidonius and by Strabo.[3] It was called in question, however, by Polybius,[4] and was flatly denied by the great astronomer Hipparchus, who thought that certain observations on the tides, recorded by Seleucus of Babylon, proved that there could be no connection between the Atlantic and Indian oceans.[5] Claudius Ptolemy, writing in the second century after Christ, followed the opinion of

Views of Eratosthenes, B. C. 276– 196

[1] Καὶ γὰρ κατ' αὐτὸν Ἐρατοσθένη τὴν ἐκτὸς θάλατταν ἅπασαν σύρρουν εἶναι, ὥστε καὶ τὴν Ἑσπέριον καὶ τὴν Ἐρυθρὰν θάλατταν μίαν εἶναι. Strabo, i. 3, § 13.

[2] Bunbury, *History of Ancient Geography*, vol. i. p. 644.

[3] Strabo, ii. 3, § 4 ; xvii. 3, § 1.

[4] Καθάπερ δὲ καὶ τῆς Ἀσίας καὶ τῆς Λιβύης, καθὸ συνάπτουσιν ἀλλήλαις περὶ τὴν Αἰθιοπίαν, οὐδεὶς ἔχει λέγειν ἀτρεκῶς ἕως τῶν καθ' ἡμᾶς καιρῶν, πότερον ἤπειρός ἐστι κατὰ τὸ συνεχὲς τὰ πρὸς τὴν μεσημβρίαν, ἢ θαλάττῃ περιέχεται. Polybius, iii. 38.

[5] Bunbury, *op. cit.* vol. ii. p. 15.

Hipparchus, and carried to an extreme the re-action against Eratosthenes. By Ptolemy's time

Opposing
theory of
Ptolemy, cir.
A. D. 150

the Caspian had been proved to be an inland sea, and it was evident that Asia extended much farther to the north and east than had once been supposed. This seems to have discredited in his mind the whole conception of outside oceans, and he not only gave an indefinite northward and eastward extension to Asia and an indefinite southern extension to Africa, but brought these two continents together far to the southeast, thus making the Indian Ocean a land-locked sea.[1]

These views of Hipparchus and Ptolemy took no heed of the story told to Herodotus of the circumnavigation of Africa by a Phœni-

Story of the
Phœnician
voyage, in
the time of
Necho

cian squadron at some time during the reign of Necho in Egypt (610–595 B. C.).[2] The Phœnician ships were said to have sailed from the Red Sea and to have returned through the Mediterranean in the third year after starting. In each of the two autumn seasons they stopped and

---

[1] See the map of Ptolemy's world, above, p. 304.

[2] Ptolemy expressly declares that the equatorial regions had never been visited by people from the northern hemisphere : Τίνες δέ εἰσιν αἱ οἰκήσεις οὐκ ἂν ἔχοιμεν πεπεισμένως εἰπεῖν. Ἄτριπτοι γάρ εἰσι μέχρι τοῦ δεῦρο τοῖς ἀπὸ τῆς καθ' ἡμᾶς οἰκουμένης, καὶ εἰκασίαν μᾶλλον ἄν τις ἢ ἱστορίαν ἡγήσαιτο τὰ λεγόμενα περὶ αὐτῶν. Syntaxis, ii. 6.

sowed grain and waited for it to ripen, which in southern Africa would require ten or twelve weeks.[1] On their return to Egypt they declared (" I for my part do not believe them," says Herodotus, " but perhaps others may ") that in thus sailing from east to west around Africa they had the sun upon their right hand. About this alleged voyage there has been a good deal of controversy.[2] No other expedition in any wise comparable to it for length and difficulty can be cited from ancient history, and a critical scholar is inclined to look with suspicion upon

[1] Rawlinson's *Herodotus*, vol. iii. p. 29, note 8.

[2] The story is discredited by Mannert, *Geographie der Griechen und Römer*, bd. i. pp. 19–26 ; Gossellin, *Recherches sur la géographie des Anciens*, tom. i. p. 149 ; Lewis, *Astronomy of the Ancients*, pp. 508–515 ; Vincent, *Commerce and Navigation of the Ancients in the Indian Ocean*, vol. i. pp. 303–311, vol. ii. pp. 13–15 ; Leake, *Disputed Questions of Ancient Geography*, pp. 1–8. It is defended by Heeren, *Ideen über die Politik, den Verkehr*, etc., 3e aufl., Göttingen, 1815, bd. i. abth. ii. pp. 87–93 ; Rennell, *Geography of Herodotus*, pp. 672–714 ; Grote, *History of Greece*, vol. iii. pp. 377–385. The case is ably presented in Bunbury's *History of Ancient Geography*, vol. i. pp. 289–296, where it is concluded that the story " cannot be disproved or pronounced to be absolutely impossible ; but the difficulties and improbabilities attending it are so great that they cannot reasonably be set aside without better evidence than the mere statement of Herodotus, upon the authority of unknown informants." Mr. Bunbury (vol. i. p. 317) says that he has reasons for believing that Mr. Grote afterwards changed his opinion and came to agree with Sir George Lewis.

all such accounts of unique and isolated events. As we have not the details of the story, it is impossible to give it a satisfactory critical examination. The circumstance most likely to convince us of its truth is precisely that which dear old Herodotus deemed incredible. The position of the sun, to the north of the mariners, is something that could hardly have been imagined by people familiar only with the northern hemisphere. It is therefore almost certain that Necho's expedition sailed beyond the equator.[1] But that is as far as inference can properly carry us ; for our experience of the uncritical temper of ancient narrators is enough to suggest that such an achievement might easily be magnified by rumour into the story told,

[1] In reading the learned works of Sir George Cornewall Lewis, one is often reminded of what Sainte-Beuve somewhere says of the great scholar Letronne, when he had spent the hour of his lecture in demolishing some pretty or popular belief: " Il se frotta les mains et s'en alla bien content." When it came to ancient history, Sir George was undeniably fond of " the everlasting No." In the present case his scepticism seems on the whole well judged, but some of his arguments savour of undue haste toward a negative conclusion. He thus strangely forgets that what we call autumn is springtime in the southern hemisphere (*Astronomy of the Ancients*, p. 511). His argument that the time alleged was insufficient for the voyage is fully met by Major Rennell, who has shown that the time was amply sufficient, and that the direction of winds and ocean currents would make the voyage around southern Africa from east to west much easier than from west to east.

more than a century after the event, to Herodotus. The data are too slight to justify us in any dogmatic opinion. One thing, however, is clear. Even if the circumnavigation was effected, — which, on the whole, seems improbable, — it remained quite barren of results. It produced no abiding impression upon men's minds [1] and added nothing to geographical knowledge. The veil of mystery was not lifted from southern Africa. The story was doubted by Strabo and Posidonius, and passed unheeded, as we have seen, by Hipparchus and Ptolemy.

Of Phœnician and other voyages along the Atlantic coast of Africa we have much more detailed and trustworthy information. As early as the twelfth century before Christ traders from Tyre had founded Cadiz (Gades),[2] and at a later date the same hardy people seem to have made the beginnings of Lisbon (Olisipo). From such advanced stations Tyrian and Carthaginian ships sometimes found their way northward as far as Cornwall, and in the opposite direction fishing voyages were made along the African coast.

---

[1] "No trace of it could be found in the Alexandrian Library, either by Eratosthenes in the third, or by Marinus of Tyre in the second, century before Christ, although both of them were diligent examiners of ancient records." Major, *Prince Henry the Navigator*, p. 90.

[2] Rawlinson's *History of Phœnicia*, pp. 105, 418 ; Pseudo-Aristotle, *Mirab. Auscult.*, 146 ; Velleius Paterculus, i. 2, § 6.

The most remarkable undertaking in this quarter was the famous voyage of the Carthaginian commander Hanno, whose own brief but interesting account of it has been preserved.[1] This expedition consisted of sixty penteconters (fifty-oared ships), and its chief purpose was colonization. Upon the Mauritanian coast seven small trading stations were founded, one of which — Kerne, at the mouth of the Rio d'Ouro [2] — existed for a long time. From this point Hanno made two voyages of exploration, the second of which carried him as far as Sierra Leone and the neighbouring Sherboro Island, where he found " wild men and women covered with hair," called by the interpreters " gorillas." [3] At that point the ships turned back, apparently for want of provisions.

Voyage of Hanno

[1] Hanno, *Periplus*, in Müller, *Geographi Græci Minores,* tom. i. pp. 1–14. Of two or three commanders named Hanno it is uncertain which was the one who led this expedition, and thus its date has been variously assigned from 570 to 470 B. C.

[2] For the determination of these localities see Bunbury, *op. cit.* vol. i. pp. 318–335. There is an interesting Spanish description of Hanno's expedition in Mariana, *Historia de España,* Madrid, 1783, tom. i. pp. 89–93.

[3] The sailors pursued them, but did not capture any of the males, who scrambled up the cliffs out of their reach. They captured three females, who bit and scratched so fiercely that it was useless to try to take them away. So they killed them and took their skins home to Carthage. *Periplus,* xviii. According to Pliny (*Hist. Nat.,* vi. 36) these skins were hung

No other expedition in ancient times is known to have proceeded so far south as Sierra Leone. Two other voyages upon this Atlantic coast are mentioned, but without definite details. The one was that of Sataspes (about 470 B. C.), narrated by Herodotus, who merely tells us that a coast was reached where undersized men, clad in palm-leaf garments, fled to the hills at sight of the strange visitors.[1] The other was that of Eudoxus (about 85 B. C.), related by Posidonius, the friend and teacher of Cicero. The story is that this Eudoxus, in a voyage upon the east coast of Africa, having a philological turn of mind, wrote down the words of some of the natives whom he met here and there along the shore. He also picked up a ship's prow in the form of a horse's head, and upon his return to Alexandria some merchants professed to recognize it as belonging to a ship of Cadiz. Eudoxus thereupon concluded that Africa was circumnavigable, and presently sailed through the Mediterranean and out upon the Atlantic. Somewhere upon the coast of Mauritania he found natives who used some

Voyages of Sataspes and Eudoxus

up as a votive offering in the temple of Juno (*i. e.* Astarte or Ashtoreth : see Apuleius, *Metamorph.*, xi. 257 ; Gesenius, *Monumenta Phœnic.*, p. 168), where they might have been seen at any time before the Romans destroyed the city.

[1] Herodotus, iv. 43.

words of similar sound to those which he had written down when visiting the eastern coast, whence he concluded that they were people of the same race. At this point he turned back, and the sequel of the story was unknown to Posidonius.[1]

It is worthy of note that both Pliny and Pomponius Mela, quoting Cornelius Nepos as their authority, speak of Eudoxus as having circumnavigated Africa from the Red Sea to Cadiz ; and Pliny, moreover, tells us that Hanno sailed around that continent as far as Arabia,[2] — a statement which is clearly false. These examples show how stories grow when carelessly and uncritically repeated, and they strongly tend to Wild exaggerations confirm the doubt with which one is inclined to regard the tale of Necho's sailors above mentioned. In truth, the island of Gorillas, discovered by Hanno, was doubtless the most southerly point on that coast reached by navigators in ancient times. Of the islands in the western ocean the Carthaginians certainly knew the Canaries (where they have left undoubted inscriptions), probably also the Madeiras, and possibly the Cape Verde group.[3]

---

[1] The story is preserved by Strabo, ii. 3, §§ 4, 5, who rejects it with a vehemence for which no adequate reason is assigned.

[2] Pliny, *Hist. Nat.*, ii. 67 ; Mela, *De Situ Orbis*, iii. 9.

[3] After the civil war of Sertorius (B. C. 80–72), the Ro-

The extent of the knowledge which the ancients thus had of western Africa is well illustrated in the map representing the geographical theories of Pomponius Mela, whose book was written about A. D. 50. Of the eastern coast and the interior Mela knew less than Views of Pomponius Mela, cir. A. D. 50 Ptolemy a century later, but of the Atlantic coast he knew more than Ptolemy. The fact that the former geographer was a native of Spain and the latter a native of Egypt no doubt had something to do with this. Mela had profited by the Carthaginian discov-

mans became acquainted with the Canaries, which, because of their luxuriant vegetation and soft climate, were identified with the Elysium described by Homer, and were commonly known as the Fortunate Islands. "Contra Fortunatæ Insulæ abundant sua sponte genitis, et subindè aliis super aliis innascentibus nihil sollicitos alunt, beatius quam aliæ urbes excultæ." Mela, iii. 10.

> Ἀλλά σ' ἐς Ἠλύσιον πεδίον καὶ πείρατα γαίης
> ἀθάνατοι πέμψουσιν, ὅθι ξανθὸς Ῥαδάμανθυς,
> τῇπερ ῥηΐστη βιοτὴ πέλει ἀνθρώποισιν·
> οὐ νιφετὸς, οὔτ' ἄρ χειμὼν πολὺς οὔτε ποτ' ὄμβρος,
> ἀλλ' αἰεὶ Ζεφύροιο λιγὺ πνείοντας ἀήτας
> Ὠκεανὸς ἀνίησιν ἀναψύχειν ἀνθρώπους.
>
> *Odyssey*, iv. 563.

Since Horace's time (*Epod.*, vi. 41–66) the Canary Islands have been a favourite theme for poets. It was here that Tasso placed the loves of Rinaldo and Armida, in the delicious garden where

> Vezzosi augelli infra le verde fronde
> Temprano a prova lascivette note.
> Marmora l' aura, e fa le foglie e l' onde
> Garrir, che variamente ella percote.
>
> *Gerusalemme Liberata*, xvi. 12.

eries. His general conception of the earth was substantially that of Eratosthenes. It was what has been styled the "oceanic" theory, in contrast with the "continental" theory of Ptolemy. In the unvisited regions on all sides of the known world Eratosthenes imagined vast oceans, Ptolemy imagined vast deserts or impenetrable swamps. The former doctrine was of course much more favourable to maritime enterprise than the latter. The works of Ptolemy exercised over the mediæval mind an almost despotic sway, which, in spite of their many merits, was in some respects a hindrance to progress; so that, inasmuch as the splendid work of Strabo, the most eminent follower of Eratosthenes, was unknown to mediæval Europe until about 1450, it was fortunate that the Latin treatise of Mela was generally read and highly esteemed. People in those days were such uncritical readers that very likely the antagonism between Ptolemy and Mela may have failed to excite comment,[1] especially in view of the lack of suitable maps such as emphasize that antagonism to our modern minds. But in

---

[1] Just as our grandfathers used to read the Bible without noticing such points as the divergences between the books of Kings and Chronicles, the contradictions between the genealogies of Jesus in Matthew and Luke, the radically different theories of Christ's personality and career in the Fourth Gospel as compared with the three Synoptics, etc.

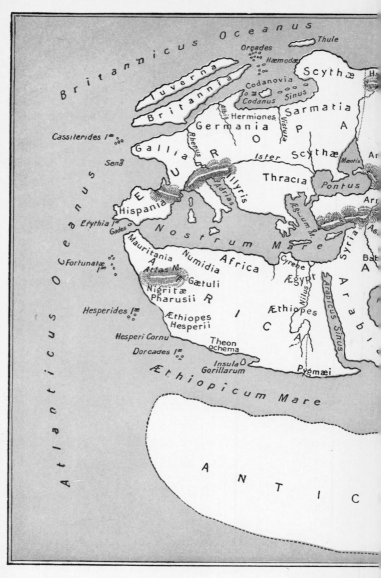

POMPONIUS MEI

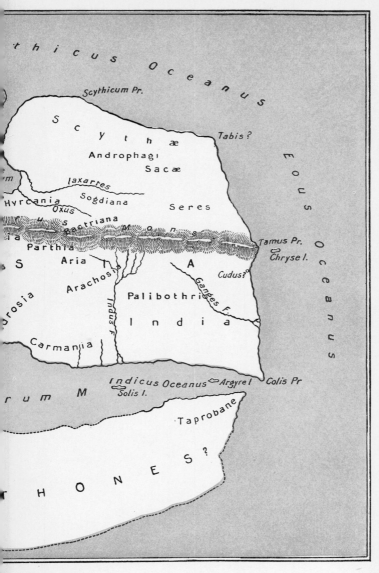

Scythicus Oceanus

Scythicum Pr.

Scythæ

Tabis?

Androphagi

Sacæ

Iaxartes

Hyrcania   Sogdiana

Oxus

Seres

Bactriana   Mons

Parthia

Aria

Tamus Pr.

Chryse I.

Arachosia

Cudus?

A

Palibothri

Ganges F.

Indus F.

India

Carmania

urosia

Indicus Oceanus   Argyre I   Colis Pr

rum M   Solis I.

Taprobane

H O N E S ?

Eous Oceanus

the fifteenth century, when men were getting their first inklings of critical scholarship, and when the practical question of an ocean voyage to Asia was pressing for solution, such a point could no longer fail to attract attention ; and it happened fortunately that the wet theory, no less than the dry theory, had a popular advocate among those classical authors to whose authority so much deference was paid.

If the Portuguese mariners of the generation before Columbus had acquiesced in Ptolomy's views as final, they surely would not have devoted their energies to the task of circumnavigating Africa. But there were yet other theoretical or fanciful obstacles in the way. When you look at a modern map of the world, the " five zones " may seem like a mere graphic device for marking conveniently the relations of different regions to the solar source of heat ; but before the great Portuguese voyages and the epoch-making third voyage of Vespucius, to be described hereafter, a discouraging doctrine was entertained with regard to these zones. Ancient travellers in Scythia and voyagers to " Thule " — which in Ptolemy's scheme perhaps meant the Shetland Isles[1] — had learned something of

Ancient theory of the five zones

[1] Bunbury, *op. cit.* vol. ii. pp. 492, 527. The name is used in different geographical senses by various ancient writers,

Arctic phenomena. The long winter nights,[1] the snow and ice, and the bitter winds, made a deep impression upon visitors from the Mediterranean;[2] and when such facts were con-

as is well shown in Lewis's *Astronomy of the Ancients,* pp. 467–481.

[1] The Romans, at least by the first century A. D., knew also of the shortness of northern nights in summer.

> Arma quidem ultra
> Littora Invernæ promovimus, et modo captas
> Orcadas, ac minima contentos nocte Britannos.
>
> Juvenal, ii. 159.

See also Pliny, *Hist. Nat.,* iv. 30 ; Martianus Capella, vi. 595 ; Achilles Tatius, xxxv.

[2] The reader will remember Virgil's magnificent description of a Scythian winter (*Georg.,* iii. 352) : —

> Illic clausa tenent stabulis armenta ; neque ullæ
> Aut herbæ campo apparent, aut arbore frondes :
> Sed jacet aggeribus niveis informis, et alto
> Terra gelu late, septemque assurgit in ulnas ;
> Semper hiems, semper spirantes frigora Cauri.
> Tum Sol pallentes haud unquam discutit umbras ;
> Nec cum invectus equis altum petit æthera, nec cum
> Præcipitem Oceani rubro lavit æquore currum.
> Concrescunt subitæ currenti in flumine crustæ ;
> Undaque jam tergo ferratos sustinet orbes,
> Puppibus illa prius patulis, nunc hospita plaustris,
> Æraque dissiliunt vulgo, vestesque rigescunt
> Indutæ, cæduntque securibus humida vina
> Et totæ solidam in glaciem vertêre lacunæ,
> Stiriaque impexis induruit horrida barbis.
> Interea toto non secius aëre ningit ;
> Intereunt pecudes ; stant circumfusa pruinis
> Corpora magna boum ; confertoque agmine cervi
> Torpent mole nova, et summis vix cornibus exstant.
>
> . . . .
>
> Ipsi in defossis specubus, secura sub alta
> Otia agunt terra, congestaque robora, totasque

352

trasted with the scorching blasts that came from Sahara, the resulting theory was undeniably plausible. In the extreme north the ocean must be frozen and the country uninhabitable by reason of the cold ; contrariwise, in the far south the ocean must be boiling hot and the country inhabitable only by gnomes and salamanders. Applying these ideas to the conception of the earth as a sphere, Pomponius Mela tells us that the surface of the sphere is divided into five zones, of which only two are fit to support human life. About each pole stretches a dead and frozen zone ; the southern and northern hemispheres have each a temperate zone, with the same changes of seasons, but not occurring at the same (but opposite) times ; the north temperate zone is the seat of the Œcumene (οἰκουμένη), or Inhabited World ; the south temperate zone is also inhabited by the Antichthones or Antipodes, but about these people we know nothing, because between us and them there intervenes

The Inhabited World and the Antipodes

> Advolvere focis ulmos, ignique dedere.
> Hic noctem ludo ducunt, et pocula læti
> Fermento atque acidis imitantur vitea sorbis.
> Talis Hyperboreo Septem subjecta trioni
> Gens effræna virûm Rhipæo tunditur Euro,
> Et pecudum fulvis velantur corpora sætis.

The Roman conception of the situation of these " Hyperboreans " and of the Rhipæan mountains may be seen in the map of Mela's world.

the burning zone, which it is impossible to cross.[1]

This notion of an antipodal world in the southern hemisphere will have especial interest for us when we come to deal with the voyages of Vespucius. The idea seems to have originated in a guess of Hipparchus that Taprobane — the island of Ceylon, about which the most absurd reports were brought to Europe — might be the beginning of another world. This is very probable, says Mela, with delightful *naïveté*, because Taprobane is inhabited, and still we do not know of anybody who has ever made the tour of it.[2] Mela's contemporary, the elder

[1] "Huic medio terra sublimis cingitur undique mari : eodemque in duo latera, quæ hemisphæria nominantur, ab oriente divisa ad occasum, zonis quinque distinguitur. Mediam æstus infestat, frigus ultimas : reliquæ habitabiles paria agunt anni tempora, verum non pariter. Antichthones alteram, nos alteram incolimus. Illius situ ab ardorem intercedentis plagæ incognito, hujus dicendus est," etc. *De Situ Orbis*, i. 1. A similar theory is set forth by Ovid (*Metamorph.*, i. 45), and by Virgil (*Georg.*, i. 233) : —

> Quinque tenent cœlum zonæ ; quarum una corusco
> Semper Sole rubens, et torrida semper ab igni ;
> Quam circum extremæ dextra lævaque trahuntur,
> Cærulea glacie concretæ atque imbribus atris.
> Has inter mediamque, duæ mortalibus ægris
> Munere concessæ Divûm ; et via secta per ambas,
> Obliquus qua se signorum verteret ordo.

[2] "Taprobane aut grandis admodum insula aut prima pars orbis alterius Hipparcho dicitur ; sed quia habitata, nec quisquam circummeasse traditur, prope verum est." *De Situ Orbis*, iii. 7.

Pliny, declares that Taprobane " has long been regarded" as part of another world, the name of which is Antichthon, or Opposite-Earth; [1] at the same time Pliny vouchsafes three closely printed pages of information about this mysterious country. Throughout the Middle Ages the conception of some sort of an antipodal inhabited world was vaguely entertained by writers here and there, but many of the clergy condemned it as implying the existence of people cut off from the knowledge of the gospel and not included in the plan of salvation.

Curious notions about Ceylon

As to the possibility of crossing the torrid zone, opinion was not unanimous. Greek explorers from Alexandria (cir. B. C. 100) seem to have gone far up the Nile toward the equator, and the astronomer Geminus quotes their testimony in proof of his opinion that the torrid zone is inhabitable.[2] Panætius, the friend of the younger Scipio Africanus, had already expressed a similar opinion. But the flaming theory prevailed. Macrobius, writing about six hundred years later, maintained that the southernmost limit of the habitable earth was 850 miles south of Syene, which lies just under the

[1] "Taprobanen alterum orbem terrarum esse, diu existimatum est, Antichthonum appellatione." *Hist. Nat.*, vi. 24.

[2] Geminus, *Isagoge*, cap. 13.

tropic of Cancer.[1] Beyond this point no man could go without danger from the fiery atmosphere. Beyond some such latitude on the *The fiery zone* ocean no ship could venture without risk of being engulfed in some steaming whirlpool.[2] Such was the common belief before the great voyages of the Portuguese.

Besides this dread of the burning zone, another fanciful obstacle beset the mariner who proposed to undertake a long voyage upon the outer ocean. It had been observed that a ship which disappears in the offing seems to be going downhill; and many people feared that if they should happen thus to descend too far away *Going down-hill* from the land they could never get back again. Men accustomed to inland sea travel did not feel this dread within the

[1] Macrobius, *Somnium Scipionis*, ii. 8. Strabo (ii. 5, §§ 7, 8) sets the southern boundary of the Inhabited World eight hundred miles south of Syene, and the northern boundary at the north of Ireland.

[2] Another notion, less easily explicable and less commonly entertained, but interesting for its literary associations, was the notion of a mountain of loadstone in the Indian Ocean, which prevented access to the torrid zone by drawing the nails from ships and thus wrecking them. This imaginary mountain, with some variations in the description, is made to carry a serious geographical argument by the astrologer Pietro d' Abano, in his book *Conciliator Differentiarum*, written about 1312. (See Major, *Prince Henry the Navigator*, p. 100.) It plays an important part in one of the finest tales in the *Arabian Nights*, — the story of the " Third Royal Mendicant."

regions of which they had experience, but it assailed them whenever they thought of braving the mighty waters outside.[1] Thus the master mariner, in the Middle Ages, might contemplate the possible chance of being drawn by force of gravity into the fiery gulf, should he rashly approach too near; and in such misgivings he would be confirmed by Virgil, who was as much read then as he is to-day and esteemed an authority, withal, on scientific questions; for ac-

[1] Ferdinand Columbus tells us that this objection was urged against the Portuguese captains and afterwards against his father: "E altri di ciò quasi così disputavano, come già i Portoghesi intorno al navigare in Guinea; dicendo che, se si allargasse alcuno a far cammino diritto al occidente, come l' Ammiraglio diceva, non potrebbe poi tornare in Ispagna per la rotondità della sfera; tenendo per certissime, che qualunque uscisse del emisperio conosciuto da Tolomeo, anderebbe in giù, e poi gli sarebbe impossibile dar la volta; e affermando che ciò sarebbe quasi uno ascendere all' insù di un monte. Il che non potrebbono fare i navigli con grandissimo vento." *Vita dell' Ammiraglio*, Venice, 1571, cap. xii. The same thing is told, in almost the same words, by Las Casas, since both writers followed the same original documents: "Añidian mas, que quien navegase por vía derecha la vuelta del poniente, como el Cristóbal Colon proferia, no podria despues volver, suponiendo que el mundo era redondo y yendo hácia el occidente iban cuesta abajo, y saliendo del hemisferio que Ptolomeo escribiò, á la vuelta érales necesario subir cuesta arriba, lo que los navíos era imposible hacer." The gentle but keen sarcasm that follows is very characteristic of Las Casas: "Esta era gentil y profunda razon, y señal de haber bien el negocio entendido!" *Historia de las Indias*, tom. i. p. 230.

cording to Virgil the Inhabited World descends toward the equator and has its apex in the extreme north.[1]

To such notions as these, which were supposed to have some sort of scientific basis, we must add the wild superstitious fancies that clustered about all remote and unvisited corners of the world. In maps made in the fifteenth and sixteenth centuries, in such places as we should label " Unexplored Region," there were commonly depicted uncouth shapes of " Gorgons and Hydras and Chimæras dire," furnishing eloquent testimony to the feelings with which the unknown was regarded. The barren

Superstitious fancies

wastes of the Sea of Darkness awakened a shuddering dread like that with which children shrink from the gloom of a cellar. When we remember all these things, and consider how the intelligent purpose which urged the commanders onward was scarcely within the comprehension of their ignorant and refractory crews, we can begin to form some idea of the difficulties that confronted the brave mariners

---

[1] Mundus, ut ad Scythiam Rhipæasque arduus arces
Consurgit, premitur Libyæ devexus in austros.
Hic vertex nobis semper sublimis ; at illum
Sub pedibus Styx atra videt Manesque profundi.

Georg., i. 240.

For an account of the deference paid to Virgil in the Middle Ages, as well as the grotesque fancies about him, see Tunison's *Master Virgil*, 2d ed., Cincinnati, 1890.

who first sought an ocean route to the far-off shores of Cathay.

Less formidable than these obstacles based on fallacious reasoning or superstitious whim were those that were furnished by the clumsiness of the ships and the crudeness of the appliances for navigation. As already observed, the Spanish and Portuguese caravels of the fifteenth century were less swift and manageable craft Clumsiness of than the Norwegian "dragons" of the caravels the tenth. Mere yachts in size we should call them, but far from yacht-like in shape or nimbleness. With their length seldom more than thrice their width of beam, with narrow tower-like poops, with broad-shouldered bows and bowsprit weighed down with spritsail yards, and with no canvas higher than a topsail, these clumsy caravels could make but little progress against headwinds, and the amount of tacking and beating to and fro was sometimes enough to quadruple the length of the voyage. For want of metallic sheathing below the water-line the ship was liable to be sunk by the terrible worm which, in Hakluyt's phrase, "many times pearceth and eateth through the strongest oake." For want of vegetable food in the larder, or anything save the driest of bread and beef stiffened with brine, the sailors were sure to be attacked by scurvy, and in a very long voyage the crew was deemed fortunate that did not lose half its number from that foul disease. Often in traversing unknown seas the sturdy men who Famine and scurvy survived all other perils were brought face to face with starvation when they had ventured too far without turning back.[1] We need not wonder that the first steps in oceanic discovery were slow and painful.

First among the instruments without which systematic ocean navigation would have been impossible, the magnetic compass had been introduced into southern Europe and was The mariner's compass used by Biscayan and Catalan sailors before the end of the twelfth century.[2] Parties of Crusaders had learned the virtues of the suspended needle from the Arabs, who are said to have got their knowledge indirectly from China in the course of their eastern voyages.[3] It seems

---

[1] Or simply because a wrong course happened to be taken, through ignorance of atmospheric conditions, as in the second homeward and third outward voyages of Columbus. See below, vol. ii. pp. 177, 182.

[2] Navarrete, *Discurso historico sobre los progresos del arte de navegar en España*, p. 28 ; see also Raymond Lully's treatise, *Libro felix, ó Maravillas del mundo* (A. D. 1286).

[3] See Humboldt's *Kosmos*, bd. i. p. 294 ; Klaproth, *Lettre à M. de Humboldt sur l'invention de la boussole*, pp. 41, 45, 50, 66, 79, 90. But some of Klaproth's conclusions have been doubted : "Pour la boussole, rien ne prouve que les Chinois l'aient employée pour la navigation, tandis que nous la trouvons dès le xie siècle chez les Arabes qui s'en servent non seulement dans leurs traversées maritimes, mais dans les

CARAVEL OF THE TIME OF COLUMBUS

to have been at Amalfi that the needle was first enclosed in a box and connected with a graduated compass-card. Apparently it had not come into general use in the middle of the thirteenth century, for in 1258 the famous Brunetto Latini, afterwards tutor of Dante, made a visit to Roger Bacon, of which he gives a description in a letter to his friend the poet Guido Cavalcanti: "The Parliament being summoned to assemble at Oxford, I did not fail to see Friar Bacon as soon as I arrived, and (among other things) he showed me a black ugly stone called a magnet, which has the surprising property of drawing iron to it; and upon which, if a needle be rubbed, and afterwards fastened to a straw so that it shall swim upon water, the needle will instantly turn toward the Pole-star: therefore, be the night ever so dark, so that neither moon nor star be visible, yet shall the mariner be able, by the help of this needle, to steer his vessel aright. This discovery, which appears useful in so great a degree to all who travel by sea, must remain concealed until other times; because no master mariner dares to use it lest he should fall under the imputation of being a magician; nor would the sailors venture themselves out to sea under his command, if he took with him an instrument which carries so great an appearance of being

voyages de caravanes au milieu des déserts," etc. Sédillot, *Histoire des Arabes*, tom. ii. p. 130.

constructed under the influence of some infernal spirit.[1] A time may arrive when these prejudices, which are of such great hindrance to researches into the secrets of nature, will be overcome; and it will be then that mankind shall reap the benefit of the labours of such learned men as Friar Bacon, and do justice to that industry and intelligence for which he and they now meet with no other return than obloquy and reproach." [2]

That time was after all not so long in arriving, for by the end of the thirteenth century the compass had come to be quite generally used,[3] and the direction of a ship's course could be watched continuously in foul and fair weather alike. For taking the sun's altitude rude astrolabes and jackstaffs were in use, very crazy affairs as com-

Latitude and longitude

pared with the modern quadrant, but sufficiently accurate to enable a well-trained observer, in calculating his latitude, to

[1] Is it not a curious instance of human perversity that while customary usage from time immemorial has characterized as "acts of God" such horrible events as famines, pestilences, and earthquakes, on the other hand when some purely beneficent invention has appeared, such as the mariner's compass or the printing press, it has commonly been accredited to the Devil ? The case of Dr. Faustus is the most familiar example.

[2] This version is cited from Major's *Prince Henry the Navigator*, p. 58.

[3] Hüllmann, *Städtewesen des Mittelalters*, bd. i. pp. 125–137.

get somewhere within two or three degrees of the truth. In calculating longitude the error was apt to be much greater, for in the absence of chronometers there were no accurate means for marking differences in time. It was necessary to depend upon the dead-reckoning, and the custom was first to sail due north or south to the parallel of the place of destination and then to turn at right angles and sail due east or west. Errors of eight or even ten degrees were not uncommon. Thus at the end of a long outward voyage the ship might find itself a hundred miles or more to the north or south, and six or seven hundred miles to the east or west, of the point at which it had been aimed. Under all these difficulties, the approximations made to correct sailing by the most skilful mariners were sometimes wonderful. Doubtless this very poverty of resources served to sharpen their watchful sagacity.[1] To sail the seas was in those days a task requiring high mental equipment; it was no work for your commonplace skipper. Human faculty was taxed to its utmost, and human courage has never been more grandly displayed than by the glorious sailors of the fifteenth and sixteenth centuries.

[1] Compare the remarks of Mr. Clark Russell on the mariners of the seventeenth century, in his *William Dampier*, p. 12.

We are now prepared to appreciate the character of the work that was done in the course of the first attempts to find an oceanic route from Prince Henry the Navigator, 1394–1463 Europe to Asia. Then, as in other great epochs of history, men of genius arose to meet the occasion. In 1394 was born Prince Henry of Portugal, since known as Henry the Navigator.[1] He was fourth son of King John I., the valiant and prudent king under whom began the golden age of Portugal, which lasted until the conquest of that country in 1580 by Philip II. of Spain. Henry's mother was Philippa, daughter of John of Gaunt. He was therefore cousin to our own Henry V. of England, whom he quite equalled in genius, while the laurels that he won were more glorious than those of Agincourt. In 1415, being then in his twenty-first year, Prince Henry played a distinguished part in the expedition

---

[1] My chief authorities for the achievements of Prince Henry and his successors are the Portuguese historians, Barros and Azurara. The best edition of the former is a modern one, Barros y Couto, *Decadas da Asia, nova edicão con Indice geral,* Lisbon, 1778–88, 24 vols. 12mo. I also refer sometimes to the Lisbon, 1752, edition of the *Decada primeira,* in folio. The priceless contemporary work of Azurara, written in 1453 under Prince Henry's direction, was not printed until the present century : Azurara, *Chronica do Descobrimento e Conquista de Guiné,* Paris, 1841, a superb edition in royal quarto, edited by the Viscount da Carreira, with introduction and notes by the Viscount de Santarem.

which captured Ceuta from the Moors. While in Morocco he gathered such information as he could concerning the interior of the continent; he learned something about the oases of Sahara, the distant river Gambia, and the caravan trade between Tunis and Timbuctoo, whereby gold was carried from the Guinea coast to Mussulman ports on the Mediterranean. If this coast could be reached by sea, its gold might be brought to Lisbon as well. To divert such treasure from the infidel and secure it for a Christian nation was an enterprise fitted to kindle a prince's enthusiasm. While Henry felt the full force of these considerations, his thoughts took a wider range. The views of Pomponius Mela had always been held in high esteem by scholars of the Spanish peninsula,[1] and down past that Gold Coast Prince Henry saw the ocean route to the Indies, the road whereby a vast empire might be won for Portugal and millions of wandering heathen souls might be gathered into the fold of Christ. To doubt the sincerity of the latter mo-

His idea of an ocean route to the Indies, and what it might bring

---

[1] Partly, perhaps, because Mela was himself a Spaniard, and partly because his opinions had been shared and supported by St. Isidore, of Seville (A. D. 570–636), whose learned works exercised immense authority throughout the Middle Ages. It is in one of St. Isidore's books (*Etymologiarum*, xiii. 16, apud Migne, *Patrologia*, tom. lxxxii. col. 484) that we first find the word " Mediterranean " used as a proper name for that great land-locked sea.

tive, or to belittle its influence, would be to do injustice to Prince Henry, — such cynical injustice as our hard-headed age is only too apt to mete out to that romantic time and the fresh enthusiasm which inspired its heroic performances. Prince Henry was earnest, conscientious, large-minded, and in the best sense devout; and there can be no question that in his mind, as in that of Columbus, and (with somewhat more alloy) in the minds of Cortes and others, the desire of converting the heathen and strengthening the church served as a most powerful incentive to the actions which in the course of little more than a century quite changed the face of the world.

Filled with such lofty and generous thoughts, Prince Henry, on his return from Morocco, in 1418, chose for himself a secluded place of abode where he could devote himself to his purposes undisturbed by the court life at Lisbon or by political solicitations of whatever sort. In the Morocco campaign he had won such military renown that he was now invited by Pope Martin V. to take chief command of the papal army; and presently he received similar flattering offers from his own cousin, Henry V. of England, from John II. of Castile, and from the Emperor Sigismund, who, for shamefully violating his imperial word and permitting the burning of John Huss, was now sorely pressed

366

by the enraged and rebellious Bohemians. Such invitations had no charm for Henry. Refusing them one and all, he retired to the promontory of Sagres, in the southernmost province The Sacred of Portugal, the ancient kingdom of Promontory Algarve, of which his father now appointed him governor. That lonely and barren rock, protruding into the ocean, had long ago impressed the imagination of Greek and Roman writers ; they called it the Sacred Promontory, and supposed it to be the westernmost limit of the habitable earth.[1] There the young prince proceeded to build an astronomical observatory, the first that his country had ever seen, and to gather about him a school of men competent to teach and men eager to learn the mysteries of map-making and the art of navigation. There he spent the greater part of his life ; thence he sent forth his captains to plough the southern seas ; and as year after year the weather-beaten ships returned from their venturesome pilgrimage, the first glimpse of home that greeted them was likely to be the beacon-light in the tower where the master sat poring over problems of Archimedes or watching the stars. For

---

[1] Ὁμοίως δὲ καὶ περὶ τῆς ἔξω στηλῶν λέγεται · δυσμικώτατον μὲν γὰρ σημεῖον τῆς οἰκουμένης, τὸ τῶν Ἰβήρων ἀκρωτήριον, ὃ καλοῦσιν Ἱερόν. Strabo, ii. 5, § 14; cf. Dionysius Periegetes, v. 161. In reality it lies not quite so far west as the country around Lisbon.

Henry, whose motto was "Talent de bien faire," or (in the old French usage) "Desire [1] to do well," was wont to throw himself whole-hearted into whatever he undertook, and the study of astronomy and mathematics he pursued so zealously as to reach a foremost place among the experts of his time. With such tastes and such ambition, he was singularly fortunate in wielding ample pecuniary resources ; if such a combination could be more often realized, the welfare of mankind would be notably enhanced. Prince Henry was Grand Master of the Order of Christ, an organization half military, half religious, and out of its abundant revenues he made the appropriations needful for the worthy purpose of advancing the interests of science, converting the heathen, and winning a commercial empire for Portugal. At first he had to encounter the usual opposition to lavish expenditure for a distant object without hope of immediate returns ; but after a while his dogged perseverance began to be rewarded with such successes as to silence all adverse comment.

The first work in hand was the rediscovery of coasts and islands that had ceased to be visited

---

[1] See Littré, *Dictionnaire*, s. v. "Talent ; " Du Cange, *Glossarium*, "talentum, animi decretum, voluntas, desiderium, cupiditas," etc. ; cf. Raynouard, *Glossaire Provençale*, tom. v. p. 296. French was then fashionable at court, in Lisbon as well as in London.

even before the breaking up of the Roman Empire. For more than a thousand years the Madeiras and Canaries had been well-nigh forgotten, and upon the coast of the African continent no ship ventured beyond Cape Non, the headland so named because it said " No ! " to the wistful mariner.[1] There had been some re-awakening of maritime activity in the course of the fourteenth century, chiefly due, no doubt, to the use of the compass. Between 1317 and 1351 certain Portuguese ships, with Genoese pilots, had visited not only the Madeiras and Canaries, but even the Azores, a thousand miles out in the Atlantic; and these groups of islands are duly laid down upon the so-called Medici map of 1351, preserved in the Laurentian Library at Florence.[2] The voyage to the Azores was probably the

The Madeira and Canary islands

[1] The Portuguese proverb was " Quem passar o Cabo de Não ou voltará ou *não,*" *i. e.* " Whoever passes Cape *Non* will return or *not.*" See Las Casas, *Hist. de las Indias,* tom. i. p. 173; Mariana, *Hist. de España,* tom. i. p. 91; Barros, tom. i. p. 36.

[2] An engraved copy of this map may be found in Major's *Prince Henry the Navigator,* London, 1868, facing p. 107. I need hardly say that in all that relates to the Portuguese voyages I am under great obligation to Mr. Major's profoundly learned and critical researches. He has fairly conquered this subject and made it his own, and whoever touches it after him, however lightly, must always owe him a tribute of acknowledgment.

greatest feat of ocean navigation that had been performed down to that time, but it was not followed by colonization. Again, somewhere about 1377 Madeira seems to have been visited by Robert Machin, an Englishman, whose adventures make a most romantic story; and in 1402 the Norman knight, Jean de Béthencourt, had begun to found a colony in the Canaries, for which, in return for aid and supplies, he did homage to the king of Castile.[1] As for the African coast, Cape Non had also been passed at some time during the fourteenth century, for Cape Bojador is laid down on the Catalan map of 1375; but beyond that point no one had dared take the risks of the unknown sea.

The first achievement under Prince Henry's guidance was the final rediscovery and colonization of Porto Santo and Madeira in 1418–25 by Gonsalvez Zarco, Tristam Vaz, and Bartholomew Perestrelo.[2] This work occupied the

[1] See Bontier and Le Verrier, *The Canarian, or, Book of the Conquest and Conversion of the Canaries,* translated and edited by R. H. Major, London, 1872 (Hakluyt Soc.). In 1414, Béthencourt's nephew, left in charge of these islands, sold them to Prince Henry, but Castile persisted in claiming them, and at length in 1479 her claim was recognized by treaty with Portugal. Of all the African islands, therefore, the Canaries alone came to belong, and still belong, to Spain.

[2] Perestrelo had with him a female rabbit which littered on the voyage, and being landed, with her young, at Porto Santo,

prince's attention for some years, and then came up the problem of Cape Bojador. The difficulty was twofold : the waves about that headland were apt to be boisterous, and wild sailor's fancies were apt to enkindle a mutinous spirit in the crews. It was not until 1433–35 that Gil Eannes, a commander of unusually clear head and steady nerves, made three attempts and fairly passed

Gil Eannes passes Cape Bojador

forthwith illustrated the fearful rate of multiplication of which organisms are capable in the absence of enemies or other adverse circumstances to check it. (Darwin, *Origin of Species*, chap. iii.) These rabbits swarmed all over the island and devoured every green and succulent thing, insomuch that they came near converting it into a desert. Prince Henry's enemies, who were vexed at the expenditure of money in such colonizing enterprises, were thus furnished with a wonderful argument. They maintained that God had evidently created those islands for beasts alone, not for men! "En este tiempo habia en todo Portugal grandísimas murmuraciones del Infante, viéndole tan cudicioso y poner tanta diligencia en el descubrir de la tierra y costa de África, diciendo que destruia el reino en los gastos que hacia, y consumia los vecinos dél en poner en tanto peligro y daño la gente portoguesa, donde muchos morian, enviándolos en demanda de tierras que nunca los reyes de España pasados se atrevieron á emprender, donde habia de hacer muchas viudas y huérfanos con esta su porfia. Tomaban por argumento, que Dios no habia criado aquellas tierras sino para bestias, pues en tan poco tiempo en aquella isla tantos conejos habia multiplicado, que no dejaban cosa que para sustentacion de los hombres fuese menester." Las Casas, *Hist. de las Indias*, tom. i. p. 180. See also Azurara, *Chronica do descobrimento e conquista de Guine*, cap. lxxxiii.

the dreaded spot. In the first attempt he failed, as his predecessors had done, to double the cape; in the second attempt he doubled it; in the third he sailed nearly two hundred miles beyond.

This achievement of Gil Eannes (*anglicè*, plain Giles Jones) marks an era. It was the beginning of great things. When we think of the hesitation with which this step was taken, and the vociferous applause that greeted the successful captain, it is strange to reflect that babes were already born in 1435 who were to live to hear of the prodigious voyages of Columbus and Gama, Vespucius and Magellan. After seven years a further step was taken in advance; in 1442 Antonio Gonçalves brought gold and negro slaves from the Rio d' Ouro, or Rio del Oro, four hundred miles beyond Cape Bojador. Of this beginning of the modern slave-trade I shall treat in a future chapter.[1] Let it suffice here to observe that Prince Henry did not discourage but sanctioned it. The first aspect which this baleful traffic assumed in his mind was that of a means for converting the heathen, by bringing black men and women to Portugal to be taught the true faith and the ways of civilized people, that they might in due season be sent back to their native land to instruct their heathen brethren. The kings of Portugal should have a Christian

Beginning of the modern slave-trade, 1442

[1] See below, vol. iii. pp. 249–252.

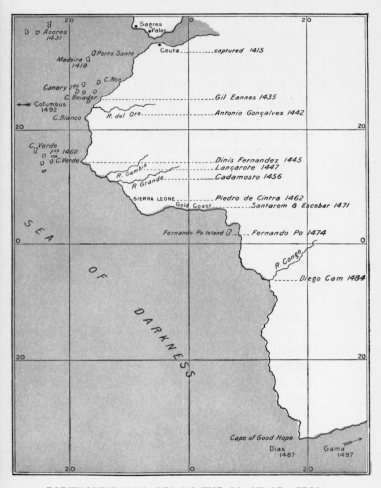

PORTUGUESE VOYAGES ON THE COAST OF AFRICA

empire in Africa, and in course of time the good work might be extended to the Indies. Accordingly a special message was sent to Pope Eugenius IV., informing him of the discovery of the country of these barbarous people beyond the limits of the Mussulman world, and asking for a grant in perpetuity to Portugal of all heathen lands that might be discovered in further voyages beyond Cape Bojador, even so far as to include the Indies.[1] The request found favour

Papal grant of heathen countries to the Portuguese Crown

---

[1] "En el año de 1442, viendo el Infante que se habia pasado el cabo del Boxador y que la tierra iba muy adelante, y que todos los navíos que inviaba traian muchos esclavos moros, con que pagaba los gastos que hacia y que cada dia crecia más el provecho y se prosperaba su amada negociacion, determinó de inviar á suplicar al Papa Martino V., . . . que hiciese gracia á la Corona real de Portugal de los reinos y señoríos que habia y hobiese desde el cabo del Boxador adelante, hácia el Oriente y la India inclusive ; y ansí se las concedió, . . . con todas las tierras, puertos, islas, tratos, rescates, pesquerías y cosas á esto pertenecientes, poniendo censuras y penas á todos los reyes cristianos, príncipes, y señores y comunidades que á esto le perturbasen ; despues, dicen, que los sumos pontífices, sucesores de Martino, como Eugenio IV. y Nicolas V. y Calixto IV. lo confirmaron." Las Casas, *Hist. de las Indias*, tom. i. p. 185. The name of Martin V. is a slip of the memory on the part of Las Casas. That Pope had died of apoplexy eleven years before. It was Eugenius IV. who made this memorable grant to the Crown of Portugal. The error is repeated in Irving's *Columbus*, vol. i. p. 339.

in the eyes of Eugenius, and the grant was solemnly confirmed by succeeding popes. To these proceedings we shall again have occasion to refer. We have here to observe that the discovery of gold and the profits of the slave-trade — though it was as yet conducted upon a very small scale — served to increase the interest of the Portuguese people in Prince Henry's work and to diminish the obstacles in his way. A succession of gallant captains, whose names make a glorious roll of honour, carried on the work of exploration, reaching the farthest point that had been attained by the ancients. In 1445 Dinis Fernandez passed Cape Verde, and two years later Lançarote found the mouth of the Gambia. In 1456 Luigi Cadamosto — a Venetian captain in the service of Portugal — went as far as the Rio Grande ; in 1460 Diego Gomez discovered the Cape Verde Islands; and in 1462 Piedro de Cintra reached Sierra Leone.[1] At the same time, in various expeditions between 1431 and 1466, the Azores (*i. e.* " Hawk " Islands) were rediscovered and colonized, and voyages out into the Sea of

Advance to Sierra Leone

[1] The first published account of the voyages of Cadamosto and Cintra was in the *Paesi nouamente retrouati*, Vicenza, 1507, a small quarto which can now sometimes be bought for from twelve to fifteen hundred dollars. See also Grynæus, *Novvs Orbis*, Basel, 1532.

Darkness began to lose something of their manifold terrors.

Prince Henry did not live to see Africa circumnavigated. At the time of his death, in 1463, his ships had not gone farther than the spot where Hanno found his gorillas two thousand years before. But the work of this excellent prince did not end with his death. His adventurous spirit lived on in the school of accomplished navigators he had trained. Many voyages were made after 1462, of which we need mention only those that marked new stages of discovery. In 1471 two knights of the royal household, João de Santarem and Pedro de Escobar, sailed down the Gold Coast and crossed the equator; three years later the line was again crossed by Fernando Po, discoverer of the island that bears his name. In 1484 Diego Cam went on as far as the mouth of the Congo, and entered into very friendly relations with the negroes there. In a second voyage in 1485 this enterprising captain pushed on a thousand miles farther, and set up a cross in 22° south latitude on the coast of the Hottentot country. Brisk trading went on along the Gold Coast, and missionaries were sent to the Congo.[1]

Advance to the Hottentot coast

[1] It was in the course of these voyages upon the African coast that civilized Europeans first became familiar with people below the upper status of barbarism. Savagery and barbarism

These voyages into the southern hemisphere
dealt a damaging blow to the theory of an im-

of the lower types were practically unknown in the Middle
Ages, and almost, though probably not quite unknown, to the
civilized peoples of the Mediterranean in ancient times. The
history of the two words is interesting. The Greek word
βάρβαρος, whence Eng. *barbarian* (= Sanskrit *barbara*,
Latin *balbus*), means " a stammerer," or one who talks gib-
berish, *i. e.* in a language we do not understand. Aristophanes
(*Aves*, 199) very prettily applies the epithet to the inarticu-
late singing of birds. The names *Welsh, Walloon, Wallachian*,
and *Belooch*, given to these peoples by their neighbours, have
precisely the same meaning (Kuhn's *Zeitschrift*, ii. 252) ;
and in like manner the Russians call the Germans *Nyemetch*
or people who cannot talk (Schafarik, *Slawische Alterthumer*,
i. 443 ; Pott, *Etym. Forsch.*, ii. 521). The Greeks called all
men but themselves barbarians, including such civilized people
as the Persians. The Romans applied the name to all tribes
and nations outside the limits of the Empire, and the Italians
of the later Middle Ages bestowed it upon all nations outside
of Italy. Upon its lax use in recent times I have already com-
mented (above, pp. 30–42). The tendency to apply the
epithet to savages is modern. The word *savage*, on the other
hand, which came to us as the Old French *sauvage* or *sal-
vage* (Ital. *selvaggio, salvatico*), is the Latin *silvaticus, sylvaticus, salvaticus*, that which pertains to a forest and is sylvan
or wild. In its earliest usage it had reference to plants and
beasts rather than to men. Wild apples, pears, or laurels are
characterized by the epithet *sylvaticus* in Varro, *De re rustica*,
i. 40 ; and either this adjective, or its equivalent *silvestris*,
was used of wild animals as contrasted with domesticated
beasts, as wild sheep and wild fowl, in Columella, vii. 2; viii.
12, or wolves, in Propertius, iii. 7, or mice, in Pliny, xxx.
22. (Occasionally it is used of men, as in Pliny, viii. 79.)

passable fiery zone; but as to the circumnavigability of the African continent, the long stretch

The meaning was the same in mediæval Latin (Du Cange, *Glossarium*, Niort, 1886, tom. vii. p. 686) and in Old French, as " La douce voiz du loussignol sauvage " (Michel, *Chansons de chatelain de Coucy*, xix.). In the romance of *Robert le Diable*, in the verses

> Sire, se vos fustes Sauvages
> Viers moi, je n'i pris mie garde, etc.,

the reference is plainly to degenerate civilized men frequenting the forests, such as bandits or outlaws, not to what we call savages.

Mediæval writers certainly had some idea of savages, but it was not based upon any actual acquaintance with such people, but upon imperfectly apprehended statements of ancient writers. At the famous ball at the Hôtel de Saint Pol in Paris, in 1393, King Charles VI. and five noblemen were dressed in close-fitting suits of linen, thickly covered from head to foot with tow or flax, the colour of hair, so as to look like " savages." In this attire nobody recognized them, and the Duke of Orleans, in his eagerness to make out who they were, brought a torch too near, so that the flax took fire, and four of the noblemen were burned to death. See Froissart's *Chronicles*, tr. Johnes, London, 1806, vol. xi. pp. 69–76. The point of the story is that savages were supposed to be men covered with hair, like beasts, and Froissart, in relating it, evidently knew no better. Whence came this notion of hairy men ? Probably from Hanno's gorillas (see above, p. 346), through Pliny, whose huge farrago of facts and fancies was a sort of household Peter Parley in mediæval monasteries. Pliny speaks repeatedly of men covered with hair from head to foot, and scatters them about according to his fancy, in Carmania and other distant places (*Hist. Nat.*, vi. 28, 36 ; vii. 2).

Greek and Roman writers seem to have had some slight

of coast beyond the equator seemed more in
harmony with Ptolemy's views than
with those of Mela. The eastward
trend of the Guinea coast was at first
in favour of the latter geographer, but
when Santarem and Escobar found it turning
knowledge of savagery and the lower status of barbarism as pre-
vailing in remote places (" Ptolomée dit que es extremités de
la terre habitable sont gens sauvages," Oresme, *Les Éthiques
d'Aristote*, Paris, 1488), but their remarks are usually vague.
Seldom do we get such a clean-cut statement as that of
Tacitus about the Finns, that they have neither horses nor
houses, sleep on the ground, are clothed in skins, live by the
chase, and for want of iron use bone-tipped arrows (*Germania*, cap. 46). More often we have unconscionable yarns
about men without noses, or with only one eye, tailed men,
solid-hoofed men, Amazons, and parthenogenesis. The Trog-
lodytes, or Cave-dwellers, on the Nubian coast of the Red
Sea seem to have been in the middle status of barbarism (Diodorus, iii. 32 ; Agatharchides, 61–63), and the Ichthyophagi,
or Fish-eaters, whom Nearchus found on the shores of Ge-
drosia (Arrian, *Indica*, cap. 29), were probably in a lower
stage, perhaps true savages. It is exceedingly curious that
Mela puts a race of pygmies at the headwaters of the Nile (see
map above, p. 350). Is this only an echo from *Iliad*, iii. 6,
or can any ancient traveller have penetrated far enough inland
toward the equator to have heard reports of the dwarfish race
lately visited by Stanley (*In Darkest Africa*, vol. ii. pp. 100–
104, 164) ? Strabo had no real knowledge of savagery in
Africa (cf. Bunbury, *Hist. Ancient Geog.*, ii. 331). Sataspes
may have seen barbarians of low type, possibly on one of the
Canary Isles (see description of Canarians in Major's *Prince
Henry*, p. 212). Ptolemy had heard of an island of cannibals in the Indian Ocean, perhaps one of the Andaman group,

southward to the equator, the facts began to refute him. According to Mela they should have
found it possible at once to sail eastward to the
Gulf of Aden. What if it should turn out after
all that there was no connection between the
Atlantic and Indian oceans? Every added
league of voyaging toward the tropic of Capricorn must have been fraught with added dis-
couragement, for it went to prove that, even if
Ptolemy's theory was wrong, at any rate the
ocean route to Asia was indefinitely longer than
had been supposed. But was it possible to
imagine any other route that should be more
direct? To a trained mariner of original and
imaginative mind, sojourning in Portugal and
keenly watching the progress of African discovery, the years just following the voyage of
Santarem and Escobar would be a period emi-

---

visited A. D. 1293 by Marco Polo. The people of these
islands rank among the lowest savages on the earth, and Marco
was disgusted and horrified ; their beastly faces, with huge
prognathous jaws and projecting canine teeth, he tried to describe by calling them a dog-headed people. Sir Henry Yule
suggests that the mention of Cynocephali, or Dog-heads, in
ancient writers may have had an analogous origin (*Marco
Polo*, vol. ii. p. 252). This visit of the Venetian traveller
to Andaman was one of very few real glimpses of savagery
vouchsafed to Europeans before the fifteenth century ; and a
general review of the subject brings out in a strong light the
truthfulness and authenticity of the description of American
Indians in Eric the Red's Saga, as shown above, pp. 213–221.

nently fit for suggesting such a question. Let us not forget this date of 1471 while we follow Prince Henry's work to its first grand climax.

About the time that Diego Cam was visiting the tribes on the Congo, the negro king of Benin, a country by the mouth of the Niger, sent an embassy to John II. of Portugal (Prince Henry's nephew), with a request that missionary priests might be sent to Benin. It has been thought that the woolly-haired chieftain was really courting an alliance with the Portuguese, or perhaps he thought their "medicine men" might have the knack of confounding his foes. The negro envoy told King John that a thousand miles or so east of Benin there was an august sovereign who ruled over many subject peoples, and at whose court there was an order of chivalry whose badge or emblem was a brazen cross. Such, at least, was the king's interpretation of the negro's words, and forthwith he News of jumped to the conclusion that this Prester John African potentate must be Prester John, whose name was redolent of all the marvels of the mysterious East. To find Prester John would be a long step toward golden Cathay and the isles of Spice. So the king of Portugal rose to the occasion, and attacked the problem on both flanks at once. He sent Pedro de Covilham by way of Egypt to Aden, and he sent Bartholomew Dias, with three fifty-ton caravels, to make one more attempt to find an end to the Atlantic coast of Africa.

Covilham's journey was full of interesting experiences. He sailed from Aden to Hindustan, and on his return visited Abyssinia, where the semi-Christian king took such a liking to him that he would never let him go. So Covilham spent the rest of his life, more than thirty years, in Abyssinia, whence he was able now and then to send to Portugal items of information concerning eastern Africa that were afterwards quite serviceable in voyages upon the Indian Ocean.[1]

Covilham's journey

The daring captain, Bartholomew Dias, started in August, 1486, and after passing nearly four hundred miles beyond the tropic of Capricorn, was driven due south before heavy winds for thirteen days without seeing land. At the end of this stress of weather he turned his prows eastward, expecting soon to reach the coast. But as he had passed the southernmost point of Africa, and no land appeared before him, after a while he steered northward and landed near the mouth of Gauritz River, more than two hundred miles east of the Cape of Good Hope. Thence he pushed on about four hundred miles farther eastward as far as the Great

Bartholomew Dias passes the Cape of Good Hope and enters the Indian Ocean

[1] See Major's *India in the Fifteenth Century*, pp. lxxxv-xc.

Fish River (about 33° 30′ S., 27° 10′ E.), where the coast begins to have a steady trend to the northeast. Dias was now fairly in the Indian Ocean, and could look out with wistful triumph upon that waste of waters, but his worn-out crews refused to go any farther and he was compelled reluctantly to turn back. On the way homeward the ships passed in full sight of the famous headland which Dias called the Stormy Cape; but after arriving at Lisbon, in December, 1487, when the report of this noble voyage was laid before King John II., his Majesty said, Nay, let it rather be called the Cape of Good Hope, since there was now much reason to believe that they had found the long-sought ocean route to the Indies.[1] Though this opinion turned out to be correct, it is well for us to remember that the proof was not yet com-

---

[1] The greatest of Portuguese poets represents the Genius of the Cape as appearing to the storm-tossed mariners in cloud-like shape, like the Jinni that the fisherman of the Arabian tale released from a casket. He expresses indignation at their audacity in discovering his secret, hitherto hidden from mankind : —

> Eu sou aquelle occulto e grande Cabo,
> A quem chamais vós outros Tormentorio,
> Que nunca á Ptolomeo, Pomponio, Estrabo,
> Plinio, e quantos passaram, fui notorio :
> Aqui toda a Africana costa acabo
> Neste meu nunca vista promontorio,
> Que para o polo Antarctico se estende,
> A quem vossa ousadia tanto offende.

Camoens, *Os Lusiadas*, v. 50.

plete. No one could yet say with certainty that the African coast, if followed a few miles east of Great Fish River, would not again trend southward and run all the way to the pole. The completed proof was not obtained until Vasco da Gama crossed the Indian Ocean ten years later.

This voyage of Bartholomew Dias was longer and in many respects more remarkable than any that is known to have been made before that time. From Lisbon back to Lisbon, reckoning the sinuosities of the coast, but making no allowance for tacking, the distance run by those tiny craft was not less than thirteen thousand miles. This voyage completed the overthrow of the fiery-zone doctrine, so far as Africa was concerned; it penetrated far into the southern temperate zone where Mela had placed his antipodal world; it dealt a staggering blow to the continental theory of Ptolemy; and its success made men's minds readier for yet more daring enterprises. Among the shipmates of Dias on this ever memorable voyage was a well-trained and enthusiastic Italian mariner, none other than Bartholomew, the younger brother of Christopher Columbus. There was true dramatic propriety in the presence of that man at just this time; for not only did all these later African voyages stand in a direct causal relation to the discovery of America, but as an immediate con-

Some effects of the discovery

Bartholomew Columbus

sequence of the doubling of the Cape of Good Hope we shall presently find Bartholomew Columbus in the very next year on his way to England, to enlist the aid of King Henry VII. in behalf of a scheme of unprecedented boldness for which his elder brother had for some years been seeking to obtain the needful funds. Not long after that disappointing voyage of Santarem and Escobar in 1471, this original and imaginative sailor, Christopher Columbus, had conceived (or adopted and made his own) a new method of solving the problem of an ocean route to Cathay. We have now to sketch the early career of this epoch-making man, and to see how he came to be brought into close relations with the work of the Portuguese explorers.

END OF VOLUME I

The Riverside Press
Electrotyped and printed by H. O. Houghton & Co.
Cambridge, Mass., U. S. A.

VIGILANTE DEATH

Spur looked at the man again. "Upton, why are you bellowing?"

"Broke my right leg. Run and get Doc Gaylord quick."

Spur chuckled. "Not a chance. You just tried to kill me and Iona Ewing and now you want me to do you a favor? Hell, I should put a bullet right between your murdering eyes."

Upton's eyes widened and he began to shake. "No, no. Don't do that. I really didn't want to do this vigilante stuff. They made me come."

"Sure, Upton. Now, let's see who the other vigilante over ___ who right now is sitting on a hot bed of hickory coals ___ evil's furnace room."

___ed the flour sack hood off the man, but didn't ___ your dead friend here, Upton?"

___ ho is he?"